Cases in International Organizational Behavior

Cases in International Organizational Behavior

Edited by

Gary Oddou and Mark Mendenhall

Copyright © Blackwell Publishers Ltd 1998

First published 1998

2 4 6 8 10 9 7 5 3 1

Blackwell Publishers Inc.
350 Main Street
Malden, Massachusetts 02148
USA

Blackwell Publishers Ltd
108 Cowley Road
Oxford OX4 1JF
UK

Library of Congress Cataloging-in-Publication Data

Cases in international organizational behavior / edited by Gary Oddou
 and Mark Mendenhall.
        p.   cm.
    ISBN 13: 978-0-631-21127-3
    1. International business enterprises—Management—Case studies.
 2. International business enterprises—Personnel management.—Case
 studies.   3. Organizational behavior—Case Studies.   I. Oddou,
 Gary R.   II. Mendenhall, Mark A.
 HD62.4.C368   1998
 658'.049—DC21   98-6189
                                                          CIP

British Library Cataloguing in Publication Data

A CIP catalogue record for this book is available from the British Library.

Contents

List of Exhibits

List of Contributors

David T. Beaty is Professor and Head, Department of Management at the University of South Africa's Graduate school of Business Leadership. His research interests are in international management and the influence of race and gender on leader behavior.

Thomas Begley is Associate Professor of Human Resources Management in the College of Business Administration at Northeastern University. He recently held a Visiting Senior Fellow position at Nanyang Technological University in Singapore. He has published articles on cross-cultural management, entrepreneurship, and employee response to stress.

Allan Bird is Professor of Management and International Business at California Polytechnic State University, San Luis Obispo. Previously he taught at New York University, and has visited at Columbia University, Nihon University and Monterey Institute of International Studies. He has published in the area of international human resource management and Japanese management, particularly that of Japanese multinational corporations. He has published three books, most recently an edited volume with Schon Beechler, *Japanese Multinationals Abroad: Individual and Organizational Learning* (Oxford University Press, 1998).

J. Stewart Black is Managing Director of Global Leadership Institute and a former Associate Professor at The Amos Tuck School of Business Administration, Dartmouth College. He has published widely in the areas of global leadership and international assignments.

Dianne J. Cyr is Adjunct Professor in International Business and

HRM at Simon Fraser University in Vancouver. She is the author of *The Human Resource Challenge of International Ventures* (Quorum Books, 1995), *Scaling the Ivory Tower: Stories from Women in Business School Faculties* (Praeger, 1996), and numerous journal articles on the topic of HRM in international joint ventures.

Gail Ellement is a management consultant working with one of the world's leading consulting firms, A. T. Kearney. She has worked in several industries, providing a wide variety of consulting services for clients located in North America, Asia and the Middle East. She recently completed another international management business case titled "Ellen Moore: Living and Working in Korea."

Hal B. Gregersen is Associate Professor of International Strategy and Leadership in the Marriott School of Management at Brigham Young University. He is the co-author of *Global Assignments: Successfully Expatriating and Repatriating International Managers* (Jossey-Bass, 1992). His research interests include international human resource management, global leadership, and corporate cartography.

Paul Grol lives in Belgium where he conducts research and writes on intercultural management. He worked extensively as senior staff member of Credit Lyonnais international divisions, and was director of that bank's Center for International Leadership Development. He lectures at Erasmus University, at Paris University's Leonardo da Vinci Center and at the CPA (Centre de Perfectionnement des Affaires) run by the Paris Chamber of Commerce. He also conducts management seminars and consults for multinationals in Europe and the US.

Nina Hatvany was formerly a faculty member of the Graduate School of Business, Columbia University. She is now in the real estate business in San Francisco, California.

Martin Hilb is Professor of Business Administration and Director of the Institute for Leadership and Human Resource Management at the University of St. Gallen (Switzerland) and Adjunct Professor of International Human Resource Management at the University of Dallas, Texas.

Henry W. Lane is Professor of Organizational Behavior and International Business at the Richard Ivey School of Business at the University of Western Ontario. He has published widely in international management and his most recent book is *International Management*

Behavior, 3rd edn (with Joseph Distefano and Martha Maznevski: Blackwell, 1997). He is responsible for the Ivey Business School's activities in Latin America and his primary areas of interest are cross-cultural management and organizational learning.

Martha Maznevski is an Assistant Professor at the McIntire School of Commerce, University of Virginia. Her research interests are in the area of international and cross-cultural management, especially the effectiveness of multicultural teams, and she has authored several articles on these subjects. She is also a co-author of the textbook *International Management Behavior* (with Joseph Distefano and Henry Lane: Blackwell, 1997).

Mark Mendenhall holds the J. Burton Frierson Chair of Excellence in Business Leadership at the University of Tennessee, Chattanooga. He has published widely in the area of international human resource management. He is the co-author of *Global Management* (Blackwell, 1995), *Readings and Cases in International Human Resource Management* (Southwestern, 1995), and *Global Assignments: Successfully Expatriating and Repatriating International Managers* (Jossey-Bass, 1992).

Asbjorn Osland studied at Case Western Reserve University and is Assistant Professor of Business at George Fox University in Newberg, Oregon. He has published on stress, TQM, and numerous cases based on his previous career in international management. In addition to case writing, his research interest is currently focused on the dynamic tension between leadership and participation in organizational systems where shared governance is assumed. He prefers the role of participant observer, where possible, in his organizational research.

Joyce S. Osland, formerly Professor of Organizational Behavior at INCAE (Central American Institute of Business Administration), currently teaches at the University of Portland. She is the author of *The Adventure of Working Abroad* (Jossey-Bass, 1995), two textbooks on *Organizational Behavior* (Prentice-Hall, 1995), and various articles on Latin American management.

Vladimir Pucik is Professor at the International Institute of Management Development (IMD), Lausanne, Switzerland. His research interests are global strategy and organization, international human resource management and strategic alliances. His latest works include "Globalizing Management: Creating and Leading the Competitive Organization."

Sheila M. Puffer is Professor of International Business and Human Resources Management at Northeastern University, Boston, and Associate at the Davis Center for Russian Studies at Harvard University. She has published widely on topics in Russian management, including the books *Behind the Factory Walls* (Harvard Business School Press, 1990), *The Russian Management Revolution* (M. E. Sharpe, 1992), and *Business and Management in Russia* (Elgar, 1996). Her co-authored book, *Russian Enterprises in the New Capitalism*, is forthcoming from Edward Elgar Publishers.

Lynne H. Rosansky, PhD is President of LHR International, Inc., a consulting firm specializing in international management education. She serves as an adjunct faculty member at the Graduate School of International Economics and Finance at Brandeis University and the Arthur D. Little School of Management. Her interests include international business strategy, cross-cultural management and international training.

Christopher Schoch is based in Paris and teaches in the MIB (Management of International Business) program of l'Ecole Nationale des Ponts et Chaussées, and the CPA (Centre de Perfectionnement des Affaires). Formerly director of international training and development for the Accor Group, he consults with European multinationals and has written articles for journals both in Europe and the USA. Christopher is presently adjunct faculty member of the University of Antioch Seattle's Graduate Management Program.

Susan C. Schneider is Chaired Professor of HRM at HEC (Hautes études de Commerce) University of Geneva in Switzerland. She was an Associate Professor at INSEAD from 1985 to 1997 (where she continues as visiting faculty). Professor Schneider has a PhD in Clinical Psychology and worked for several years in mental health care in New York City. She has recently published a book *Managing Across Cultures* (with J. L. Barsoux: Prentice Hall, 1997). Her research interests are in organizational cognition and cross-cultural management.

Stanislav V. Shekshnia is Manager of the St. Petersburg region of Otis Elevator International, and has held managerial positions in other US multinationals in Russia. He holds an MBA from Northeastern University and a PhD from Moscow State University. He has published a number of articles on Russian management as well as a book on human resources for Russian managers.

Manab Thakur was a Professor of Management at California State University, Fresno until his death in December 1997. He published widely in professional journals and was author of two books published in recent years: *International Management: Concepts and Cases* (Tata McGraw-Hill) and *Management: Practices and Problems* (Tata McGraw-Hill). He also conducted numerous management development seminars in India, Taipei and Germany, among other countries.

Preface

Doing business with a foreign firm or in a foreign culture is not the same as doing business domestically. Businesses involved in global partnerships and markets face unique and complex challenges. Success is dependent on much more than simply determining the product characteristics that will sell in foreign cultures. Businesses must also meet the challenge of managing human relationships:

- Understanding how to influence and lead those from a different culture
- Knowing what kind of organizational structure is best in view of the firm's business needs and foreign culture's traditions
- Being aware that what is considered ethical in one country might not be so in another
- Knowing how to deal with misperceptions between two cultural groups and why the misperceptions developed
- Understanding the power structure in the host national culture where business is done.

Cases in International Organizational Behavior is designed to help students understand the complexities of international business, while specifically focusing on the management of human relationships in a cross-cultural context. This focus is supported by integrative coverage, and a user-friendly approach that we hope will complement the teaching and learning process.

Selection Criteria

The cases were selected based on their overall quality, focus on organizational behavior topics, geographical and cultural representation, and interest from a reader perspective. Most cases are short to medium in length. As such, the cases move quickly and appropriately to the key organizational behavior topics. Background information required to adequately understand the context is provided as necessary. The cases are based on actual situations to encourage lively in-class discussion, and emphasize the real world application of the concepts.

The cases are appropriate for undergraduate and graduate students. The book is intended for use in traditional organizational behavior (OB) courses that include an international perspective. *Cases in International Organizational Behavior* will also work well as a supplement to standard texts in international OB courses.

Our decision to focus on a case format rather than on a combination of cases and readings is based on several factors. We wanted a book that was fairly short, affordable for students, and offered the most flexibility for the instructor. In our opinion, a clearly focused casebook could meet these requirements more fully than a collection of cases and readings.

Focus on Management of Human Relationships in a Cross-Cultural Context

To help students better understand the complexities of international business, the cases focus on the topics central to organizational behavior in a cross-cultural context. Key topics covered are:

● Ethics
● Perception
● Communication
● Culturally based values
● Motivation
● Power and influence
● Organizational design and culture
● Group and intergroup dynamics
● Organizational change

Readers explore these topics in cases covering such diverse countries and cultures as: Russia, Japan, French-speaking Africa, the Czech Republic, the People's Republic of China, Central America, France, India, Bahrain, Sweden, South Africa, Mexico, Italy, Germany, and the United States.

Integrative Coverage

Most cases are integrative. That is, they address two to four topical areas. These multi-focused cases allow instructors to integrate topics and/or to focus on the one or two topics that they feel are most important. To permit a more in-depth exploration, several cases are included that have one distinct focus.

In addition to the multifocused approach taken in the individual cases, the casebook offers at least three cases per topical area. This gives instructors the opportunity to select the case they feel most appropriate. Alternatively, instructors can assign multiple cases on the same topic representing different cultures. This approach should help students make connections between the concepts as applied in different cultures

Instructor's Manual

Case notes for all the cases are included in the Instructor's Manual. The Instructor's Manual details the topical areas for each case and suggests various ways to approach a discussion on those topics. It also includes a grid which cross-lists the different cases and OB topics. This helps the instructor to see quickly which cases cover the various topics.

If you have any feedback for us – suggestions to improve the casebook or the teaching notes, or if you have any questions – please e-mail either one of us at the following addresses:

Gary Oddou, oddou-g@cob.sjsu.edu or oddou@cc.usu.edu
Mark Mendenhall, mark-Mendenhall@utc.edu

Thanks for choosing our casebook!

Acknowledgments

First, we thank the authors of the cases and the institutions supporting our use of the material. We think they've done a wonderful job in writing the cases and responding to our requests for timely submission of material. Second, we would like to thank Mary Beckwith, our developmental editor, for her regular interaction, cooperation and reminders of what needed to be done. She managed the team very well. We would also like to thank Paul Stringer, our production editor, for his consistent follow-up, flexibility, and great sense of humor. Finally, we'd like to express gratitude for living in such a diverse world that brings change, challenge, and fascination to all our lives. Aren't we lucky we're not all the same!

1

Rough Times at Nomura

Allan Bird

The Problem

George Rosebush sat at his desk pondering the magnitude of the decision that lay before him. He still couldn't quite believe the events that had transpired over the past year. It was July of 1988, he had been with Nomura Securities International (NSI), the American subsidiary of the Japanese giant, Nomura Securities Company Ltd, since July of 1986. During that time, George had acquired the skills necessary to be a successful stock trader, but he now felt prevented from utilizing his skills to the fullest extent.

The management at NSI, all Japanese personnel on assignment from the home office in Tokyo, had refused to give Americans, such as George, the latitude to aggressively pursue business. Like his predecessors, George was experiencing great frustration at having to cope with Japanese culture and business norms. In particular, the Japanese were very slow to make either decisions or changes – primarily because of their consensus method of decision making.

Nomura was a monolithic machine where decisions emerged from the system with little need for creativity. This was a significant impediment to achieving success in the trading business, where the ability of a trader to respond quickly to customer needs was vital to success. As a pure service industry, the ability to develop strong client

This case was prepared by Ron Dalbello, Richard Madigan, Jim Noble and Prema Venkat under the supervision of Assistant Professor Allan Bird as a basis for class discussion rather than to illustrate either effective or ineffective handling of an administrative situation.

relationships was imperative. Here again, Nomura insisted upon doing things the Japanese way. Among the factors that frequently noted as holding Nomura back were: adherence to Japanese tradition; inflexibility in negotiations; lack of imagination; little expertise in critical investment banking sectors; and weak relationships with US and European institutional investors. To make matters worse, the business environment in the securities industry was suffering a major recession following the stock market crash of October 1987. Despite this, since the late 1970s, NSI's staff had grown to 750, a tenfold increase.

In the post-crash era, NSI was experiencing a larger fall in revenues and profits than other firms in the industry. This slump was particularly acute in George's department, Japanese equities, which entailed marketing Japanese stocks to US institutional clients.

Despite the market's downturn, changing Japanese trading habits had accounted for much of the problem. Industry analysts noted that in actuality the Japanese had ". . . severely misjudged the difficulty of mounting major expansion drives overseas." In numerous meetings George had made recommendations to improve business, but management remained unwilling to take the steps necessary to reverse the drop in market share and profits that the department was experiencing.

Business had slowed down so much that George and his colleagues soon found themselves doing crossword puzzles to pass the time. This was occurring in the fast-paced world of global trading.

Each day dragged slowly, and George found himself faced with a decision: he could stay at NSI and continue to develop new plans to improve business at the company, or he could leave the firm. He decided to conduct preliminary discussions about employment opportunities with some of the other firms on the Street. Meanwhile, some of his friends had even suggested that he quit NSI and enroll in a leading business school, such as Stern at NYU, in order to pursue an MBA.

Background

Nomura Securities, the world's largest stockbroker, continued to suffer from both host and home country regulatory pressures and related political risks associated with its globalization strategy. The Japanese securities industry, like that of the United States, had undergone extensive liberalization, in terms of deregulation, over the five year period from 1986 to 1991. Within this ever-changing environment,

Nomura had continued with its global expansion policy – aggressively expanding into both the London and New York markets.

The premise governing Nomura's growth was based on its commitment to opening-up international financial markets to Japanese clients and to bringing foreign investors to the Japanese market place. Being the beneficiaries of a society geared towards an unusually high savings rate, Japanese brokerage houses had allowed Japanese investors to seek out higher yielding foreign investments. This approach was not unique to Nomura, but was pursued by a number of Japanese securities firms. The chairman of European operations for Daiwa Securities, the number two securities firm globally, stated, "we started off providing two-way information to US and European clients interested in the Japanese markets and to Japanese clients. We knew that Japan would prove to be an economic force, and we foresaw that brokerage would be profitable."

By the mid-1980s, Japan had become the world's largest creditor nation. Capitalizing on this development, Nomura's expansion was predicated upon its desire to allow borrowers, internationally, to tap into Japan's vast pool of potential investors. Additionally, Nomura was concerned with enhancing its domestic image as a true global market player. Increasing its presence abroad not only boosted its name recognition internationally, but enhanced Nomura's reputation domestically. It generated goodwill and demonstrated the firm's commitment to international markets. In turn, such actions gave evidence of its desire to continue to strengthen its position in the growing Japanese domestic market. In short, Nomura Securities was positioning itself as the pre-eminent Japanese brokerage firm, able to service the large amounts of Japanese capital targeted for future US investment.

Nomura expanded aggressively into the New York market throughout the early and mid-1980s. The result was an office that underwent rapid growth in terms of staffing, profits, and overall market presence.

Nomura's Growth Phase

Nomura was founded in 1878. Over the years its focus remained on high-quality research and the development of a worldwide financial network. It was the first Japanese securities firm to open an office in the United States (1927), as well as the first to become a member of the New York Stock Exchange. Its American operation suffered a major interruption as a result of World War II. Nomura did not reestablish an American presence until the 1950s. With the improvement of relations between the US and Japan, and growth of trade between the two countries that occurred in the late 1960s and 1970s, Nomura sought to increase its activities in the US securities markets. Nomura's expansion plans led to the formation of a wholly owned subsidiary in the 1970s: Nomura Securities International.

NSI's expansionary plans required the hiring of a large number of Americans – the intent was to rely upon talented local professionals to further market expansion. Nomura could not afford to rely on non-management personnel from the parent company who were in New York for, at best, two to three year rotations.

Because Nomura now planned to serve American clients and compete directly with US firms, it needed Americans who could build the strong client relationships necessary to achieve success in a service industry, particularly in the American securities market. Yoshihisa Tabuchi, president and chief executive of Nomura Securities Company Ltd stated: "[t]he style and structure Nomura uses to sell securities in Japan cannot work well in the US. Nomura's traditional culture is as a Japanese brokerage firm, but, as it expands, it must become multicultural." It is important to develop good working relationships with other firms in the industry. Americans were hired to be on the "front lines" and, more importantly, to lend credibility to the firm within the US market.

As a critical success factor, the internal working relationships at NSI are as important, if not more so, than its external relationships with clients – the firm cannot hope to properly service its client base without being able to benefit from the synergies created from internal employee "harmony." Unfortunately, cultural barriers and differences still existed within the firm. All managers were Japanese, with little experience or knowledge about either the American market or, more importantly, American cultural and business values. This created a paradox. The "front line" American workers knew how to serve their home market but were not allowed to make the significant and timely decisions needed for success in the American securities market place. These decisions were made by Japanese personnel who did not have the working knowledge necessary to properly analyze the situation. Decisions regarding risk-taking and the scope of the firm's operations usually required the consent and approval of Japanese management. However, these managers were often not qualified to make such critical decisions (being unaware of many of the nuances associated with the American market's operation and function). In particular, management was unwilling to delegate to traders the authority to commit the firm's capital. This was a major impediment to "getting a deal done." Traders could not give a quick response to client inquiries. Instead management wanted to discuss the trade under consideration. Only after much deliberation and when a consensus had been reached would the firm be willing to commit capital to a large trade. This slow response time remained unacceptable to customers in the American securities markets. Due to potential rapid changes in prices and investor perceptions, clients expected and demanded quick responses to their inquiries. NSI's failure to make quick decisions severely hampered its ability to effectively compete in the American securities markets. Furthermore, this lack of trust on behalf of Japanese management had a devastating effect upon the morale of the American workforce.

Setting the Scene

Nomura's drive to build a full service securities firm in the US began in the 1970s. Its ultimate goal was to compete on "even terms" with US securities firms. Following the start of the bull market in 1982, the firm hired several recent American college graduates to work as traders. These new employees had no prior work experience in the securities industry. Nomura planned to let them learn "on the job" – gradually assuming increased responsibilities. NSI frequently utilized such a hiring strategy, as did the remaining "Big Four" Japanese securities firms (Daiwa, Nikko, and Yamaichi).

By hiring inexperienced workers, the Japanese firms were able to keep down their labor costs. This approach did require new traders to undergo an extended learning phase. However, generally it takes but a few months to learn the fundamental techniques behind stock trading. For the most part, Nomura's selection process chose talented people to fill these important trading positions. This success was accomplished by recruiting candidates from top B-schools, and by including experienced on-line American traders as part of the candidate screening and selection process.

Mark Blanchard and Steve Montana were two traders who were hired directly out of college in 1982 to trade Japanese stocks. Neither had prior work experience in the industry. Before they were assigned to the trading desk, both Mark and Steve spent six months in Tokyo as part of Nomura's in-house training program. While in Tokyo, they gained exposure to the Japanese stock market, as well as an awareness of some of the local customs and cultural norms. Their training was consistent with Chairman Tabuchi's new internationalization policies. Indeed, Tabuchi believed that reinforcement of the in-house training system for employees was his best move as President.

In January 1983, Mark and Steve returned to New York and joined the trading desk. Their timing could not have been better. The primary international stock markets (including New York, London and Tokyo), were beginning to come out of the prolonged bear market of the 1970s. The Japanese stock market was particularly strong, led by booming Japanese exports.

The strength of the Japanese stock market, combined with its partial deregulation, attracted many American money managers to invest funds in Japan. As the undisputed market leader of the Japanese securities industry, fund managers flocked to Nomura for investment advice. The Japanese equities department was thriving. Clients wanted fast replies to inquiries and requests for bids and offers on block trades. Although Nomura could not deliver the level of timeliness expected by American clients, it nevertheless remained the best game in town, as American brokerage houses were not yet equipped to handle large transactions in Japanese stocks.

Both Mark and Steve played a central role in the firm's success. They were the ones dealing directly with clients. Furthermore, they were an important information source to people who traded American stocks. As the Japanese stock market continued to grow in size and importance, investors in all markets began to show increased interest in Japanese financial news. Mark and Steve kept the traders of American stocks up to date on any special developments in Japan. The American stock traders were then able to pass this information along to their clients. In this fashion, the Japanese equities department helped attract business to the burgeoning American equities department.

As time passed, American and European firms began to trade and sell Japanese stocks in the US. The deregulation of the securities markets in Japan helped to expedite this process. And, as competition increased, NSI gradually lost market share in providing Japanese brokerage services to American clients. NSI faced strong competition from houses such as Salomon Brothers, Merrill Lynch, and S.G. Warburg. These firms were able to provide superior execution of orders. They established more normal working relationships by being more responsive to customer needs.

NSI still had the best research and, therefore, most investors continued to direct a portion of their business to NSI. However, NSI was on the decline. They needed to drastically improve the quality of their client relationships – to a level at least on par with their American and European counterparts. It was no longer enough to merely retain Americans to interact with customers on the front lines. As long as the major decisions impacting client relationships continued to be made by Japanese managers, the American traders would continue to function as little more than pawns, something their clients were unwilling to tolerate. Changes had to be made to reverse the recent decline in NSI's position within the industry. However, Japanese firms had thus far been unable to convince American clients to trust them as their chief advisers. Nomura in particular faced two key issues: (1) they were either operating in markets they should not be in; or (2) they had proven unable, to date, to effectively run a foreign business.

NSI, however, retained two major competitive advantages over its rivals. First, its parent company remained the major driving force behind the Japanese stock market. Being the market leader, Nomura dominated the already oligopolistic Japanese securities market. When it made a strong buy recommendation in Japan, the market usually responded accordingly. NSI's knowledge of which Japanese stocks were likely to be pushed (or, in industry jargon, "rammed") was a tremendous client draw. Second, with the market capitalization of Nomura at approximately $70 billion, its financial resources far exceeded those of its competitors. Potentially, NSI could tap into to this vast source of funds as needed to attract business. Nomura should additionally have been able to shift toward more sophisticated approaches to building a lasting market presence.

The ability to take the other side of a client trade remains one of the most important services that large institutional clients seek. NSI could easily have been a market leader in this capacity. However, up until this point, it had lagged far behind its lower-capitalized competition. This was primarily due to Nomura's high risk aversion, as well as slow client response time.

NSI's other New York departments were experiencing mixed results. The firm's effort to become a major player in the US equity market was proceeding slowly. Despite expanding its New York staff, NSI was nevertheless having difficulty making any serious gains in market share. As a departure from past practices, NSI hired several high-priced traders with the hope of boosting departmental performance.

By contrast to other departments, the fixed income department flourished. This was primarily due to the tremendous placing power Nomura had in its home market, as Japanese investors maintained an almost insatiable appetite for US government securities. Nomura continued to increase its US trading staff in order to ultimately position itself as the primary Japanese dealer in US government securities.

By 1985, Mark and Steve had become seasoned professionals. They had helped the business grow and had established strong client relationships. However, they realized that NSI's performance was rapidly deteriorating. They made frequent recommendations to management on how this trend might be reversed. However, their suggestions were ignored.

The traders in the US equities department were experiencing similar problems with management. Traders from both departments were becoming increasingly frustrated with policies that continued to hinder their ability to perform. Their dissatisfaction with management's policies became so great that on one occasion, all of the traders went on a wildcat strike – each called in sick. Such an action by traders was unprecedented within the industry. It was a drastic measure by the traders to demonstrate to management that their current policies were out of line. Additionally, it was an effective way to show management the strength and solidarity behind their convictions. That day NSI's trading operations in both Japanese and US equities came to a halt. Not only were revenues forsaken but, more importantly, the firm's reputation was tarnished. The traders, nonetheless, were able to maintain their personal relationships with clients by telling customers the changes sought would benefit both the traders and their accounts, by improving the level of service provided.

Mark and Steve were also grossly underpaid by U.S. securities firms standards. Though they now were experienced traders, their salaries were not much higher than when they had originally joined NSI back in 1982. Their counterparts at competing firms were receiving two or three times as much in compensation – further depressing their already low morale. They felt that employees could be expected, in certain instances, to cope with poor working conditions or low compensation, but to accept both low pay and poor working conditions, over an extended period of time, was intolerable.

At the end of 1985, Mark and Steve were seriously considering leaving the firm. That year, both had received specific promises regarding their bonuses, promises which were subsequently broken. At the start of 1986, they initiated discussions with several competing firm's regarding available employment opportunities. They waited until April, when annual salary raises at NSI were given out. Once again, both Mark and Steve had been promised significant increases. Once again, they were disappointed. This time they protested vehemently. The Japanese manager who had promised Mark a large salary increase responded, "we can't pay someone your age so much money. Wait until December, we will make it up to you at bonus time." Mark felt he could wait no longer. He left NSI in May to work for a European firm's New York subsidiary starting up a Japanese equity trading department. A few weeks later Mark hired away Steve.

George's Tale

In June of 1986, George was looking to gain entrance into the securities business. He had just quit his job at an employee benefits consulting firm to seek work in the area of global finance. George had previous work experience selling Individual Retirement Accounts and tax sheltered annuities in the New England area. Much of that work involved cold calling and building a client base. While his previous jobs had helped him develop strong interpersonal skills, as well as given him some familiarity with the stock market, George did not have any direct experience trading financial securities. He found it very difficult to gain entrance into the trading business without that experience. Most of the opportunities he found were for lower level operations positions.

George had two brothers who worked in the securities industry. Both knew people who worked, or had worked, at NSI. One of their acquaintances was Mark Blanchard, who, as it turned out, George would later succeed at Nomura. George learned that Nomura needed to hire traders to replace Mark Blanchard and Steve Montana, as well as some traders from the American equities department who had also resigned. George was able to arrange an interview with Nomura to discuss trading opportunities at the firm. Before going on the interview George spoke with Mark Blanchard to get the inside story as to what life at Nomura was actually like.

Prior to the fourth of July holiday in 1986, George had his first interview at NSI. From the interview's onset, many of the cultural differences George had been forewarned about became readily apparent. George was greeted by the head of the sales department, Mr Yoshida, and, after a few common pleasantries were exchanged, was whisked into a small conference room. The two were then joined by another Japanese manager, and Mike, the head of the Japanese equity trading department. Mike was also a Japanese national, but, rather than go by his last name, as was the custom in Japan, he had adopted the American nickname "Mike."

George would later call the interview intense. He was bombarded by questions from each of those present. While George found many of the questions seemingly unrelated to the job at hand (e.g. questions regarding his family, as well as his personal views of the work ethic and company allegiance), he nevertheless answered them.

Occasionally there were interruptions to the flow of questions when the interviewers stopped to carry on a conversation among themselves in Japanese. George found these interruptions both rude and unprofessional, but was reluctant to say anything that might ruin his prospects for the job.

After a time, other Japanese men were ushered into the room and took their turn interviewing George. Finally, several American traders from the American equities department were brought in. At this point the interview became more conventional. Specific job duties and the requisite skills were discussed. Finally, the director of personnel, another American, finished the interview. The next day George received a job offer. He started working for NSI on July 14, 1986.

George maintained no illusions of either climbing NSI's ladder of success or of making a life-long career with Nomura. Furthermore, George held some personal reservations about working for a foreign firm, especially one from such a different culture. He viewed the position as an opportunity to learn the business. If after a few years things were not working out, he knew that he would be able to parlay his newly acquired skills to land a job elsewhere. After trading Japanese stocks for the top Japanese brokerage house, he would be very marketable to the many firms who were seeking to enter this area of the securities business. For George, the simple fact remained that there were few westerners with experience trading Japanese securities. Should things really go sour, George had a fall-back position of returning to school for his MBA.

At the time George started at NSI, the Japanese equity department was in a state of disarray. Mark and Steve had been gone for two months and there were no Americans left in the department. Client relationships had deteriorated rapidly, and new traders were desperately needed. George was not the only trader to start work in the Japanese equity department on July 14. He was joined by Francois Beaudreau. While growing up, Francois had lived in both France and the US and had gone to college at Columbia University in New York. He had spent a month working as a retail broker before coming to NSI, but was, for all intents and purposes, fresh out of college.

Neither George nor Francois had the experience necessary to step in and immediately start trading with clients or other firms. To make matters worse, Mike, their boss, was the only other trader in the department. George and Francois had no western colleagues or mentors. Mike was trying to do as much as he could to keep the business going, which meant that he had little time available to train either George or Francois. Moreover, Mike was introverted and did not enjoy interacting with clients. The result was that neither the clients, nor George and Francois, received much attention.

Mike had been working in the United States for five years. He had been in the New York office for the past three years, and prior to that had spent two year's in Nomura's Honolulu branch. Mike was much more westernized than his Japanese colleagues. If they had to have a Japanese boss, both George and Francois felt fortunate to be working for Mike. Mike was viewed by Japanese management as a renegade of sorts – willing to test the limits of the Japanese business rules and hierarchy. He had an excellent understanding of the underlying forces driving the US securities industry. He, however, did not have the authority to make important policy decisions, which continued to be made by more senior Japanese managers. Senior managers were typically far removed from the daily operations of the firm. Some were even based in Tokyo, 7,000 miles away.

In Japanese corporations, new hires often spend their first year or two on the job in low level positions which expose them to the fundamental operations of the company's business. In manufacturing firms, this typically involves working on the production line. For financial organizations, the initial period usually involves door-to-door sales solicitations. While NSI could not realistically expect American professionals to go through such a process, at the same time, they were unwilling to let Americans do too much too soon.

Both Francois and George were initially instructed to sit with the traders in the American equities department. There they were supposed to watch and listen in order to learn the fundamentals of stock trading. At first this was a worthwhile activity. However, after a few weeks, they both felt they had learned as much as they were going to. Francois and George were anxious to start trading on their own, and wanted to start assuming more responsibilities. Their superiors, however, did not feel they were ready to get directly involved in the daily trading operations. George thought this particularly odd considering how short-handed the Japanese equity department was.

For six months George and Francois watched the traders from the US equities department and did little else. Most of their days were spent answering the telephones and relaying information to the trading desk. George was growing restless and started asking for additional responsibilities. To appease him, Mike allowed him to start trading Japanese ADRs on NASDAQ, the over-the-counter market. ADRs, American Depository Receipts, represent Japanese stock which are held by a custodian bank in Japan. Investors cannot actually take delivery of Japanese stock outside Japan, but can take delivery of ADRs. ADRs are denominated in dollars which further simplifies their purchase, as investors do not have to make foreign exchange arrangements.

NSI used to trade a few hundred thousand ADRs each day, but that number had recently fallen to just a few thousand. As a market-maker in ADRs and other issues, NSI used its own capital to make trades with other market-makers and clients. Market-makers risk their own capital in the hope of making money on the bid/ask spread. To be successful at doing this, volume is important for two reasons. First, if the spread earned is small, sizable profits can only be made through large volume. More importantly, active market-makers attract more client orders because of their ability to provide more liquidity as well as their increased market presence.

Before George could rebuild the client side of the ADR business, he first had to stimulate the firm's trading activity with other market-makers on the Street. George gradually built good working relationships with the other major market-makers of Japanese ADRs. Within a few months, he was making a modest but steady profit for the firm. He often did this by taking advantage of arbitrage opportunities between the ADRs and the underlying Japanese common stock. However, the upside potential of these activities was limited, as the size of position that George could take and the amount of time that he could hold them was restricted. Being a prominent market-maker, George was able to attract additional business to NSI. He was, however, capturing a larger share of a shrinking market.

After George had been with NSI for one year, he began to take on the responsibilities of a sales trader for Japanese common stocks – the position for which he had originally been hired. He also continued to function as a market-maker for ADRs. Sales traders are responsible for facilitating client activity. This involves providing daily market information and late breaking news, sending orders for execution on stock exchanges or in a third market, and negotiating prices on trades.

The job of sales trader differs from that of salesman, in that a salesman concentrates on developing investment strategies, while the sales trader is more concerned with the execution of these strategies. The sales trader is the intermediary between the position trader and the client for trades in which the firm takes the other side of the transaction. It is the trader's responsibility to negotiate the best price possible without losing the trade. The sales trader is also responsible for instructing floor brokers on the strategy to employ when executing discretionary orders.

To be a successful sales trader one must develop a good relationship with clients and be able to provide them the services they value on a timely basis. These include company research, market information and analysis, and superior trading execution. While Nomura was one of the leaders in research on Japanese companies, its advantage over other firms in the industry was narrowing as competition continued to intensify. Moreover, Nomura's analysts were stationed solely in Japan and thus not readily accessible to salesmen, traders, and clients in New York. Other non-Japanese firms made their analysts directly available to parties in New York via telephone and periodic visits. This gave their New York employees and clients the opportunity to go directly to the source with any questions they might have. While Nomura's research still led the industry, NSI was unable to deliver it to clients in the timely fashion they demanded.

George also found it difficult to provide clients with top-quality daily Japanese market information. This information was available in New York, but only to those who spoke Japanese. Each morning there was a conference call with the Tokyo headquarters where the most important news of the day was discussed, as well as expected future market developments (i.e. which stocks were going to be rammed). The meetings were attended in New York by the salesmen (all of whom were Japanese), George's boss Mike, and a few other managers. George and Francois had asked several times if the meeting could be held in English. This seemed like a reasonable request to them, especially since all of the participants, both in New York, and Tokyo, spoke English. However, each request was refused.

To further complicate the situation, communication between the salesmen and the traders was poor. Important information discussed during the morning meetings would inevitably not be relayed. This lack of communication between Japanese and American employees hindered the traders' ability to effectively serve their clients. Salesmen would routinely fail to tell traders which stocks clients were interested in. This precluded the sales trader from informing customers of any late breaking information related to the recommended stock or from matching clients' buy and sell orders. Usually, a trader from the buy side would telephone orders to be executed overnight in Tokyo to a sales trader. However, on occasion, the portfolio manager might also call in the same order. If the salesman then failed to notify the trading desk, duplicate orders were sometimes passed on to the Tokyo office.

Since Nomura's information pipeline was not functioning efficiently, NSI's best chance for success in the New York market lay in the firm being able to commit its capital – taking the other side of its customers' trades. The only ingredients necessary were money and a good position trader. George's boss, Mike, who did the position trading for Japanese common stocks, possessed the trading talent. In terms of available capital, Nomura had the ability to raise billions of dollars. However, management in Tokyo refused to supply NSI with any additional capital. This forced the already limited available capital to be rationed among the different departments, and prevented many deals from being closed. The actual amount of money available to position

trades varied from day to day, depending on the positions held by
other departments. The combination of limited capital and management's aversion to risk taking made it extremely difficult to effectively
position trades for clients.

George and Francois did their best to cope with the many internal
problems at NSI. However, the decline of client interest in Japanese
stocks made the situation more difficult, and encouraged them to seek
new ways to stimulate business. Every time they came up with a
proposal which they felt would stimulate client interest they were
turned down.

Following the stock market crash of October 1987, the business
climate slowed drastically. The deterioration of NSI's profitability
accelerated, and management decided to implement new austerity
measures to help reduce costs. Cuts were made across the board,
without regard for either the level of profits or expenses of individual
departments. The Japanese equities department did not suffer any
losses associated with the crash. In fact, late October was one of the
most profitable periods for the department due to the temporary surge
in trading volume. The department also had the lowest overhead of
any of the trading areas. Despite its low-cost structure and the fact
that it was operating profitably while other departments were operating in the red, the department was not spared from cost-cutting measures. Management canceled the departments' subscriptions to the _Wall
Street Journal_ and the _Financial Times_. The papers had been shared
within the department and provided information vital to running a
trading operation. George and Francois found it very difficult to com-
prehend the logic behind the cost-cutting decision.

In February of 1988, Mike was transferred back to Tokyo. George
and Francois had mixed feelings about his departure. On the one
hand, as the head of their department, they blamed Mike for some of
the poor decisions and operating policies that had subsequently hurt
business. However, they realized that he had confronted his superiors
in order to enact changes and that his efforts were a risky venture
within a conservative Japanese firm such as Nomura.

Before his departure, Mike did manage to obtain greater authority
for both George and Francois to commit the firm's capital in trading
transactions. While they welcomed this change, George and Francois
were now concerned with who would replace him.

Mike's replacement was Mr Yamaguchi, a bond trader who had
been working in Nomura's Hong Kong office for the past seven years.
The Hong Kong bond market had been a profitable one for Nomura
over the past couple of years and, consequently, Yamaguchi had been
riding on the crest of success.

Due to delays in obtaining a work permit, Yamaguchi was not expected to arrive until April. This gave George and Francois a two month window with no boss. During this time, George was able to expand the firm's ADR market-making activities. Francois was allowed to assume some of the position trading responsibilities vacated by Mike, although major decisions still required approval from either Nomura's London or Tokyo office. Francois was also permitted to start making markets in Japanese stock warrants, and was soon earning sizable profits for the firm in this capacity. George and Francois were able to stimulate substantial new business. This boosted their morale and for the first time in a long while they were consistently busy and enjoying their work.

All of this came to a dramatic halt soon after Yamaguchi's arrival in New York. Mr Yamaguchi had no previous experience trading stocks. Equally important, he had no familiarity with either American business or accepted cultural practices and norms. Nevertheless, he had been placed in a position where he was supposed to manage American employees who were working in a field in which he had no related expertise.

Mr Yamaguchi sat quietly and observed during his first few weeks on the job. Quite unexpectedly, however, he began to initiate widespread changes. First, in their role as market-makers for ADRs and warrants respectively, George and Francois were no longer allowed to take any positions unless specifically to fill a client's order. This eliminated almost all trading with other brokers, which effectively ended NSI's role as a market-maker for these instruments.

Even more damaging to the department was Yamaguchi's assumption of position trading responsibilities for common stock. Because he had little experience in this capacity, he rapidly began to accumulate sizable trading losses – at one point totaling several hundred thousand dollars per week. Two months later, his supervisor withdrew Yamaguchi's authority to make investment decisions on his own. Instead, he was required to seek approval from the head of the sales department. In just three months, Yamaguchi had destroyed the trading operation of the Japanese equities department.

Because the department was unable to offer trading related services to its clients, George and Francois found it very difficult to attract any business. There was little cooperation between the sales and trading departments, the result of which was to keep both the sales and trading departments in the dark as to important information regarding individual client needs and activities. Additionally, NSI was unable to effectively make bids and offers to clients upon request. The deep-rooted mistrust between Americans and Japanese growing out of these events hurt NSI's ability to build solid relationships. If NSI did not have something special to offer an American client, it remained unlikely that they would attract business.

As business activity in the Japanese equities department slowed to a virtual standstill, George and Francois once again became quite proficient at crossword puzzles. Once again, their morale was extremely low. To make matters worse, George and Francois found it nearly impossible to maintain a reasonable working relationship with their new boss. Yamaguchi liked to call frequent departmental meetings which George and Francois were expected to attend. However, he would announce the location of the meetings only in Japanese. Not able to understand Japanese, George and Francois often missed meetings. When they failed to show up, Yamaguchi would become angry and demand an explanation.

Yamaguchi also wanted to change how they interacted with clients and other employees at the company. One incident in particular led to a heated confrontation between George and Yamaguchi. George had been made responsible for covering NSI's other branch offices in the US (Honolulu, Los Angeles, Chicago, and San Francisco). These offices were small operations consisting primarily of retail brokers, support staff, and a few institutional salesmen. In addition to executing their orders, George provided each office with a daily market analysis. Mr Yamaguchi informed George that he must give this information directly to Mr Honda, the sales manager of the Honolulu branch. In the past George had spoken with whichever salesman was available, who, in turn, would pass along the information to the rest of the office. George's attempts to talk with Mr Honda became a disaster. Honda's English was poor and he spoke with a heavy accent. Honda eventually suggested that it might be easier if George were to talk to the salesmen as before. George could not have agreed more, however, Mr Yamaguchi continued to insist that George speak directly with Honda.

Late one Friday afternoon, Yamagachi brought up the subject again during a meeting with George and a Japanese salesman. Once again, George tried to explain the problem. Yamaguchi replied, "you must spend more time in Chinatown so you can learn how to understand people who speak English with an Asian accent." At first, George thought this remark a joke, but soon realized Yamaguchi was serious. Yamaguchi then went on to explain to George that if he ever expected to amount to any form of true businessman, he must overcome his inability to understand people who speak with a foreign accent.

George could not believe what he was hearing. Moreover, he was exasperated by Mr Yamaguchi's obvious failure to recognize the need for foreign nationals to respect the language and customs of their host country. George was fed up with Yamaguchi and the current state of affairs. It was time to teach Yamaguchi that business is conducted differently outside of Japan. Much to Yamaguchi's surprise, George mounted a vociferous attack on his unprofessional behavior and lack of cultural respect. Yamaguchi was stunned that a subordinate would dare raise his voice, let alone scold him, especially in front of another person.

George returned to his desk to consider what real options he had before him. He had some important and timely decisions to make . . .

2
Chiba International, Inc.

Vladimir Pucik and Nina Hatvany

Ken Morikawa, the general manager for administration of a Japanese manufacturing plant under construction in rural Georgia, was troubled. Earlier that morning, his American personnel manager, John Sinclair, had walked eagerly across the temporary, open-plan office and announced, "I've found a professor of Japanese at Georgia State University who is willing to help translate our corporate philosophy. I'd like to hire him for the job." He felt pressured. In his mind, Sinclair, like many Americans, was expecting too much of Japanese companies. The company philosophy that he, Ken, had learned to live by in Tokyo would continue to guide him, but he did not feel that Americans would welcome or even understand a Japanese company philosophy.

Ken had a very large task in supervising the building of a plant that might one day provide jobs for up to 2,000 employees, in a region where very few workers had any industrial experience. He wanted to show them that his company cared about the welfare of its workers and their job security, and could be trusted to treat them fairly and not to lay them off. He believed that such a philosophy, if it could be properly explained to workers and carefully implemented, would help build a high morale among the employees. And that would improve productivity.

Ken also wanted to ensure that high morale be maintained while the workforce expanded to full capacity. Aside from issues of ease of transportation and distribution, the characteristics of the local workforce – mainly their "Japanese" work ethic – had been one of the primary reasons for establishing the plant here. He believed that the training costs involved in transforming very "green" workers were well worth it. With training, you could avoid people who had picked up "bad habits" or had had their morale lowered in prior industrial jobs. In Japan, Ken knew, teaching company philosophy was an important part of the company's introductory training program. But would it work in rural Georgia?

Ken wondered if his new administrative duties were lowering his concern for personnel matters. Ever since he'd read Alfred Sloan's *My Years with General Motors* during the company training program and had written a review that focused on human resource issues, he had held positions in HR. Even though he had majored in mathematical economics in college, his first assignment had been in the personnel "design center," which controlled training and salary administration for white-collar employees. After two years, he was sent to a district office as a salesman. He returned after 13 months to the employee welfare section of the personnel department at the head office, administering such programs as house loans and recreational activities. Eight years with the company had passed by the time he was sent to an American college to study personnel related subjects and improve his English.

After receiving his MBA, he returned to the head office. His most recent assignment before coming to Georgia was in personnel development research, planning new wages systems. In this new job in Georgia, it was expected that he would eventually hand the reins over to an American general manager and remain only in an advisory capacity. However, at this vital stage he felt that the corporation depended on his human relations expertise to set the scene for future success. Was he neglecting an area in which he had been trained to be sensitive?

He brought the subject up at lunch with John Sinclair. "Let me tell you something, John. I have a hunch why the Japanese are more successful in achieving high quality and productivity than Americans have been recently. It has to do with application, rather than ideas. Many great ideas have come from the United States, but the Japanese concentrate on applying them very carefully. Americans emphasize creating something new and then moving on. The Japanese meticulously analyze a problem from all angles and see how a solution might be implemented. However, John, as they say, Rome wasn't built in a day. I'm not sure our American workers will understand what it really means to have a company philosophy. Let's take it slowly and see what kind of people we hire and then see what best meets their needs."

John, who had worked at a rather traditional US company for 11 years and had become increasingly interested in how Japanese companies managed their US employees, had been eager to join a Japanese company. He wanted to see in action such "Japanese" strategies as long-term employment, the expression of a company philosophy, and careful attention to integrating the employees into the company. He answered comfortingly, "Ken, I know you hate conflict. But you also think it's important to gather information. One of our purchasing agents, Billy, told me about a Japanese company he recently visited, Chiba International. Apparently, they have already fully implemented their company philosophy and I understand that they're doing very well with it. Why don't we go out to California and talk with their management and try and understand how and why they concentrated on communicating their philosophy to their American workforce."

"And soak up some sun, too," beamed Ken. "You're on!"

The Company

Chiba International, Inc. in San Jose, California makes high-precision, sophisticated electronics parts used in the final assembly of customized and semicustomized integrated circuits, particularly the expensive memory chips used in computers and military hardware. In such products, reliability is everything (price is a lesser consideration). The similar, but cheaper, parts that manufacturers use once a product reaches high volume are left for others to make.

Chiba International is a subsidiary of Chiba Electronics Company. *Nihon Keizai Shimbun*, Japan's preeminent business paper, recently ranked Chiba Electronics as one of the foremost companies in Japan on the basis of its management earnings stability and performance, ahead of such better-known giants as Sony, Matsushita Electric and Toyota Motor. Chiba Electronics has 70 percent of the $350 million-a-year world market for its products. Chiba International likewise has a 70 percent share of the $250 million-a-year US market.

Chiba International started with a small sales office in the US 12 years ago. A manufacturing plant that had been losing $100,000 to $200,000 a month was acquired from an American competitor. The American management was replaced by a team of Japanese headed by a Canadian-born Japan-reared executive. They succeeded in turning it around in two years.

Today, 14 out of the 24 top executives and 65 out of 70 salesman at Chiba are Americans. All the employees in other categories are also American.

Chiba's Philosophy

As the sun rises brilliantly in the sky,
Revealing the size of the mountain, the market,
Oh this is our goal.
With the highest decree of mission in our heart we serve our industry
Meeting the strictest decree of customer requirement.
We are the leader in this industry and our future path
Is ever so bright and satisfying.

"That's a translation of our company song," said a high-ranking Japanese executive, one of the group of Japanese and American managers who had agreed to meet with Ken and John. "But we haven't introduced it to our employees yet. That's typical of the way we brought the company philosophy to our employees – slowly and carefully. Every line worker gets a leaflet explaining our company philosophy when he or she starts work. We don't have a specific training session on it and we don't force them to swallow it. It's up to them to digest and understand it."

"What about when you acquire a company, as you have done over the past few years?" asked John.

"The same thing: it's very gradual. If we force it, it causes nothing but indigestion. Here it has been easy: the work is very labor intensive, repetitive, tedious assembly. In other places, the soil is different. At one, for example, almost all the employees are salaried. They understand the philosophy, but won't necessarily go by it. Engineers and technical people also seem to be less receptive than people in sales, personnel and administration. In other sites, though, where the technology is more similar to this one, we have had no problems at all."

One of the other managers present in the group, an American, interrupted to show Ken and John a copy of the leaflet. It was quite rhetorical in tone and a few paragraphs struck them as particularly interesting.

The Leaflet

Management philosophy: Our goal is to strive toward both the material and spiritual fulfillment of all employees in the Company, and through this successful fulfillment, serve mankind in its progress and prosperity.

Management policy: Our purpose is to fully satisfy the needs of our customers and in return gain a just profit for ourselves. We are a family united in common bonds and singular goals. One of these bonds is the respect and support we feel for our fellow family co-workers.

Other exhortations: When there is a need, we all rally to meet it and consider no task too menial or demeaning; all that matters is that it should be done! We are all ready to sweep floors, sort parts, take inventory, clean machines, inspect parts, load trucks, carry boxes, wash windows, file papers, run furnaces, and do just about anything that has to be done.

Meetings

"Daily meetings at the beginning of each shift are held in the courtyard," explained a manager. "All the workers stand in lines (indicated by metal dots in the asphalt). Each day, a different member of management speaks for about five minutes. On Mondays, executives speak; on Tuesday, personnel and administration are represented; Wednesdays are about safety concerns; and on Thursdays and Fridays, members of production and sales speak. They are all free to say whatever they like. The shift workers tend to develop favorites, especially among the more extroverted sales managers.

"Then a personnel coordinator delivers news about sports events and so on, and perhaps a motivational message, and goes on to lead the group in exercises for one minute. These calisthenics are voluntary, but most of the employees join in. After that, the large group breaks up for brief departmental meetings.

"Again, in the departmental meetings, a speaker is chosen for the day and speaks for about five minutes. Even people at the lowest exempt ('salaried') level speak. Then the department manager discusses yesterday's performance, today's schedule and any other messages such as that housekeeping is inadequate or that certain raw materials are in short supply.

"Once a month, there is an announcement of total company performance versus plans. This is important, as all company employees share at the same rate in the annual company bonus, which is based on profitability and usually equals about one month's salary or wages."

Another Japanese manager continued: "Years ago, there were complaints about having so many meetings, but I haven't heard any for a long time now. The employees like to hear important announcements and even less important ones, such as who is selling theater tickets, bowling league reports, and tennis match dates."

The American personnel manager chimed in. "I was the one who came up with the idea of exercises. I saw it on my visit to Japan. They are just a part of the rituals and symbols that you need in order to get better mutual understanding. The atmosphere was right and the timing was good. Even so, because they weren't mandatory, it took about one-and-a-half years until everyone joined in. Now most people understand the meaning behind it. If we were to stop it now, we'd get complaints.

"Besides the morning meeting, we have several other meetings. On Mondays, we have a very large liaison meeting for information sharing. All the executives attend: sales managers and staff managers, the plant manager and the assistant plant manager. On Tuesdays, we have a production meeting attended by the production managers and any staff involved with their problems. On Monday at four o'clock every second week we have a supervisors' meeting, mainly for one-way communication to them. On the alternating weeks, we have a training meeting. The whole personnel department also meets every week.

"Less formally, we have many sales meetings about, for example, new products. We have combination sales and production meetings, which are called on an as-needed basis. Team meetings on the production line are also called whenever needed.

"All these formal meetings are supplemented by many company-sponsored activities. We have a company bowling league, tennis matches, softball, fishing and skiing. We often organize discount tickets. We're planning the Christmas party. Each employee can bring a guest, so it costs us about $40,000. Our company picnic costs $29,000."

"It sounds very well-worked out for the non-exempts," said John. "What about for the exempts?"

Sales Force

The company started with the largely American sales force. "They're a very different species. They have tremendous professional pride. Most of the American sales engineers have a very arrogant take-it-or-leave-it attitude. Our attitude is almost the complete opposite. We try to serve our customer's needs. Almost like a geisha girl, who makes her customer feel that he is the only one served by her," explained one of the Chiba managers.

"We try to communicate the following motto to them:

S	incerity
A	bility
L	ove
E	nergy
S	ervice

"Sincerity is the basic attitude you have to have as well as the ability to convince the customer. You must love the products that you sell, or you can't convince the customer. You must have energy because, at the end of the day, it's always the case that you could have done one more thing or made one more sales call. Finally, the mentality of serving the customer is the most important.

"We communicate that to our sales force and they like it, especially when they don't have to tell white lies to customers or put up with harassment from customers. We also want them to be honest with us, even about their mistakes. Quite often, we depend on input from the salespeople for our understanding of customers, so an objective daily report by telex or phone is very important to us.

"No one in our company works on a commission basis, not even salesmen. We would lose market share for products that are difficult to promote. Also, the nature of different sales territories would make commissions unfair.

"Although we pay on straight salary only, we don't just have a unilateral sales quota. The salespeople discuss targels with their boss. They are purposely set high, so good performance against goals is grounds for a merit increase the next year.

"We don't really have a marketing department. We feel that it is, an expensive luxury. We have a vice president in charge of marketing, but this is almost a corporate sales staff function."

US Management

John was curious about how American line managers reacted to working in a Japanese company. A Japanese manager explained. "When Americans join us, they expect the usual great deal of internal politicking. They scan people in meetings, looking for those with real power; looking, to use our expression, for whose apple they should polish. It takes time for them to realize that it's unnecessary.

"When we interview American executives for a job, we do it collectively, so five to ten interviewers are present. That usually puzzles the interviewees. They wonder whom they will report to. We reply that they will be hired by the *company,* although they may report to one individual. As in Japan, the company will take care of them, so it does not depend on their loyalty to one individual."

"What about your company criteria for hiring managers?" asked John.

"We focus on a manager's way of thinking, not necessarily on ability. Although a Harvard MBA is welcomed, it is not essential. In fact no one here has one. We don't provide an elegant fit to his or her social elite. There are no private offices. Salary and benefits are up to par for the location (and industry), but not especially high. We work long hours.

"We're looking for devotion and dedication as well as an aggressive attitude. We conduct two or three long interviews for an important position. We ask questions like 'what is your main shortcoming?' We're interested not in the answer itself but in the kind of thinking behind it. We do make mistakes sometimes, but our batting average is good.

"Sometimes there's a very deep communication gap between Japanese management and US management because we believe in dedication and devotion to the company. They do too, but only up to a certain point. We often tell them that the joy of working for the company can be identical to personal happiness with the family. I ask my wife for her understanding of that, and I work six days a week from seven o'clock to ten o'clock. Their wives place demands on them to come home at six o'clock. US executives put personal and family happiness first. I'm not telling you which is right. But it is second nature for me to think about the future of the company. So long as I have challenging assignments and job opportunities, I will put the company before my personal happiness."

"What do American interviewees feel about all this?" inquired John.

"One problem is that they ask, 'What's my real future? Can I be considered for president?' There's no real answer because it probably will be a Japanese. However, we don't like to close those doors to a really capable American.

"The issue of communication between Japanese and Americans is still a problem. After the Americans go home, the Japanese get together at seven or eight o'clock and talk in Japanese about problems and make decisions without the Americans present. Naturally, this makes the Americans feel very apprehensive. We're trying to rectify it by asking the Japanese managers not to make decisions alone and by asking the Americans to stay as late as possible.

"More important, if we could really have our philosophy permeate the American managers, we Japanese could all go back to Japan and not worry about it. Our mission is to expedite that day by education and training.

"So far, however, there is a gap. Americans are more interested in individual accomplishment, remuneration, and power. When they are given more responsibility, they don't feel its heavy weight, rather they feel that it extends their sovereign area so that they have more of a whip. That creates power conflicts among US managers."

"Let me tell you, though," summarized the American personnel manager. "I like it. I was recruited by a headhunter. Now, I've been with the company five years and the difference from my former employer is astounding. I don't have to get out there and be two-faced, fudging to keep the union out, hedging for the buck. In general, it's hard to find an American employer that really, sincerely cares for the welfare of the low-level employee. This company went almost too far in the opposite direction at first. They wanted to do too much for the employees too quickly, without their earning it. That way, you don't get their respect."

Financial Principles

"Our financial people throughout the company are proud because of our impressive company performance," said one of Chiba team. "Only 20 percent of our financing is through debt, in contrast to many Japanese companies. We also have a rather unique way of treating some of our raw materials internally. We try to expense everything out. It's derived from our founder's very conservative management. We ask the question: 'If we closed down tomorrow, what would our liquid assets be?' In line with that, for example, internally we put our inventory at zero.

"We follow the 'noodle peddler theory.' The noodle peddler is an entrepreneur. He has to borrow his cart, his serving dishes and his pan to make ramen. He has to be a good marketer to know where to sell. He has to be a good purchasing director and not overbuy noodles, in case it rains. He could buy a fridge, but he would need a lot of capital, the taste of the noodles would deteriorate, and he would need additional manpower to keep an inventory of the contents of the fridge. The successful noodle peddler puts dollars aside at the end of the day for depreciation and raw materials for tomorrow. Only then does he count profits. That's also why we don't have a marketing department. The successful peddler doesn't have time to examine opportunities in the next town.

"This is the way a division manager has to operate. In order to maximize output with minimum expenditure, every effort is made to keep track on a daily basis of sales, returns, net shipment costs, and expenses."

Open Communication

"I understand all that you've said so far," mused John, "but how exactly do you take all these abstract philosophical ideas and make them real?"

"Oh, open communications is the key. We have a fairly homogenous workforce. Most are intelligent, some are even college graduates. Most are also very stable types with dependents or elderly parents they send money to.

"We're lucky, but of course, it's not as homogeneous as in Japan, where everyone has experienced one culture. So here, the philosophy has to be backed up by a great deal of communication.

"We mentioned the meetings. We also have a suggestion box, and we answer all the suggestions in print in the company newspaper. Also, one person from personnel tours the plant all day, for all three shifts, once a week, just chatting and getting in touch with any potential problems as they arise. It's kind of a secondary grievance systems. We're not unionized and I guess we'd rather stay that way as it helps us so much with flexibility and job changes among our workforce.

"In the fall, when work is slow, we have many *kompas*. You may not know about this, John. A *kompa* is a small gathering off-premises after work. Eight to eighteen people participate, and the company pays for their time and for refreshments. They're rarely social: they have an objective. For example, if two departments don't get along and yet they need to work together, they might hold a *kompa*. A *kompa* can take place at all levels of the company. Those groups that do it more frequently tend to move on from talking about production problems to more philosophical issues."

Appraisal and Reward Systems

"It all sounds great," sighed Ken, "just as good as Japan. But tell me, how does it tie in with wages and salaries, because people here are used to such different systems?"

Exhibit 2.1 Semiannual performance review

Employee's name	Clock no.	Dept.	Shift	Over last six-month period			
				Days absences	Number tardies	Number early exits	Work days leave of absence
Employee's job title	Anniversary						

Rate on factors below:		Numerical score			
		L	S	M	F
1. Loyalty/Dedication:	Faithful to the company cause, ideals, philosophy, and customers; devoting or setting aside, time for company purposes.				
2. Spirit/Zeal:	Amount of interest and enthusiasm shown in work; full of energy, animation, and courage; eagerness and ardent interest in the pursuit of company goals.				
3. Cooperation:	A willingness and ability to work with leaders and fellow employees toward company goals.				
4. Quantity of work:	Volume of work regularly produced; speed and consistency of output.				
5. Quality of work:	Extent to which work produced meets quality requirements of accuracy, thoroughness, and effectiveness.				
6. Job knowledge:	The fact or condition of knowing the job with familiarity gained through experience, association and training.				
7. Safety attitude:	The willingness and ability to perform work safely.				
8. Creativeness:	The ability to produce through imaginative skill.				
9. Attendance:	Includes all types of absence (excused or unexcused), tardies, early exits, LOAs from scheduled work.				
10. Leadership:	The ability to provide direction, guidance, and training to others.				

Overall evaluation of employee performance:

Supervisor's approval	Manager's approval	Personnel dept. approval

Do not write below this line – for human resource department use only

Present base rate	New base rate	Effective date of increase	Refer to instructions on the back side of this paper.

"Well, we don't have lifetime employment, but we do have an explicit no-layoff commitment. We are responsible for our employees. This means that employees also have to take responsibility and have broad job categories, so we don't have to redo paperwork all the time. We have tried to reduce the number of job classifications to the raw minimum, so we have two pay grades covering 700 workers. At the higher levels, we have three pay grades for craftsmen and two for technicians."

John ventured: "I guess an example of your job flexibility in action is the mechanic you mentioned when we toured the plant."

"Yes, the person you spoke with was a dry press mechanic. He's doing menial labor this week, but his pay hasn't been cut and he knows he wouldn't be taken off his job if it weren't important."

"We don't hire outside, if we can avoid it," added the personnel manager, "only if the skill is not available in-house. The bulk of our training is on the job. We don't utilize job postings. We promote when a person's skills are ripe or when there is a need.

"The job of a 'lead' or team leader is the stepping-stone to supervisor. It's not a separate job status within our system, but the lead is given a few cents an hour extra and wears a pink, not a yellow, smock. Leads are carefully groomed for their position, and although a lead might be demoted because a specific need for them no longer existed, a lead would rarely be demoted for lack of skills or leadership ability.

"Rewards are for service and performance. Plant workers, unskilled and semiskilled, are reviewed every six months. The lead completes the evaluation form [see exhibit 2.1]. This is checked or confirmed by the supervisor, and the overall point score translates into cents per hour. There are two copies, one for the supervisor and one for the employee. Depending on the supervisor, some employees get a copy, some don't.

"The office clerical staff are all reviewed on April 1st and October 1st. The review form for managers [see exhibit 2.2] is used to determine overall letter scores. All the scores are posted on a spread sheet and compared across departments, through numerous meetings of managers and personnel people, until the scores are consistent with one another. Then the scores are tied to dollars. Some managers provide feedback, some don't.

"Salaried staff are reviewed on April 1st and, as a separate process, the spread procedure just outlined is carried out. Af least two managers review any exempt employee, but feedback is usually minimal. The reason is that we encourage feedback all year. If there are no surprises for your subordinate at review time, then you've managed well.

Exhibit 2.2 Example of completed performance review

DOE. John

Values

| | Below average | | Average | Above average | |
Unsatis-factory	Fair		Good	Very good	Excellent
E–	D–	C–		B+	A–
E	D	C		B	A
	D+	C+		B–	

E–	E	D–	D	D+	C–	C	C+	B–	B	B+	A–	A
1	2	3	4	5	6	7	8	9	10	11	12	13

Factors

Factor			
1. Loyalty/Dedication:	Faithful to the company cause, ideals, philosophy, and customers; a devoting or setting aside time for company purposes.	B+	11
2. Spirit/Zeal:	Amount of interest and enthusiasm shown in work; full of energy, animation, and courage; eagerness and ardent interest in the pursuit of company goals.	C	7
3. Consultation:	The ability to consult and listen to subordinates, fellow employees and superiors in an effort to arrive at the best possible decision.	C–	6
4. Communications:	The ability to communicate effectively with subordinates, fellow employees, superiors and business associates.	C+	8
5. Philosophy:	The willingness to learn and practice company philosophy; the ability to train others regarding company philosophy	B–	9
6. Method of thinking:	The ability, good sense and judgment to discern inner qualities and relationships to determine the best course of action.	D	4
7. Cooperation:	A willingness and ability to work with leaders and fellow employees toward company goals.	A	13
8. Job knowledge:	The fact or condition of knowing the job with familiarity gained through experience, association and training.	B–	9
9. Attendance:	This factor includes reliability, dependability and punctualness; one's ability to be "on-the-job".	A–	12
10. Results:	The efforts which have brought about a beneficial effect in line with company goals.	E	2

$$\frac{81}{10} = 8.1$$

Overall comment C+

"Agreements on reviews for exempt personnel take place in many meetings at various levels. The process is very thorough and exceptionally fair, and contributes to the levels of performance we get."

Quality and Service

A question from John as to how Chiba International was doing as a result of all this elicited much pride.

"Turnover is 2½ percent a month, which is very satisfactory for our kind of labor, given a transient society. We rarely have to advertise for new employees now. The community knows about us. But we do select carefully. The personnel department does the initial screening and then the production managers and supervisors get together and interview people.

"The lack of available, technically trained people used to be a big problem, but over the years, we've developed the expertise internally. Our productivity is now almost as high as in Japan."

Ken and John asked what other aspects of the company they had not yet discussed. They were told that quality, and hence customer service, was another central part of the philosophy. "Our founder, Mr Amano, firmly believes in zero defect theory. Doctor Deming taught us the concept of quality control. Unfortunately, many American companies did not emphasize this. During World War II, the concept of acceptable quality level was developed in the United States. The idea was that, with mass production, there will be some defects. Rather than paying for more inspectors on the production line, real problems, for example, with cars, could be identified by the consumer in the field and repaired in the field.

"We don't allow that. We have 100 percent visual inspection of all our tiny parts, which only cost $50 per 1,000 units. We inspect every finished package under a microscope, so we have 130 inspectors, which is about one sixth of our production staff.

"Mr Amano, has said to us, 'We try to develop every item our customers want. Being latecomers, we never say no, we never say we can't.' Older manufacturers would evaluate a proposal on a cost basis and say no. Yet we have been profitable from the start."

As the interview drew to a close, one Japanese manager reflected, "Mr Amano has a saying:

Ability × philosophy × zeal = performance.

"If the philosophy is negative, performance is negative because it's a multiplicative relationship.

"But in our company, which now numbers 2,000, we must also start to have different kinds of thinking. The Japanese sword is strong because it is made of all different kinds of steel wrapped around one another. The Chinese sword is also very strong, but because it's all one material, it's vulnerable to a certain kind of shock. We must bear that in mind so that we have differences within a shared philosophy.

"We're thinking of writing a book on our philosophy, addressing such issues as what loyalty is, by piecing together events and stories from our company history. This would be a book that would assist us in training."

Ken and John walked out into the parking lot. "Whew!" sighed John. "It's more complicated than I thought."

"Oh yes! You need a great deal of patience," responded Ken paternally.

"So we'd better get started quickly," said John, enthusiastic. "Where shall we begin? Perhaps I should call the translator."

Ken wasn't sure what his answer should be.

3

Euro Disneyland

J. Stewart Black and Hal B. Gregersen

On January 18, 1993, Euro Disneyland chairperson Robert Fitzpatrick announced he would leave that post on April 12 to begin his own consulting company. Quitting his position exactly one year after the grand opening of Euro Disneyland, Fitzpatrick's resignation removed US management from the helm of the French theme park and resort.

Fitzpatrick's position was taken by a Frenchman, Philippe Bourguignon, who had been Euro Disneyland's senior vice president for real estate. Bourguignon, 45 years old, faced a net loss of FFr 188 million for Euro Disneyland's fiscal year which ended September 1992. Also, between April and September 1992, only 29 percent of the park's total visitors were French. Expectations were that closer to half of all visitors would be French.

It was hoped that the promotion of Philippe Bourguignon would have a public relations benefit for Euro Disneyland – a project that has been a publicist's nightmare from the beginning. One of the low points was at a news conference prior to the park's opening when protesters pelted Michael Eisner, CEO of the Walt Disney Company, with rotten eggs. Within the first year of operation, Disney had to compromise its "squeaky clean" image and lift the alcohol ban at the park. Wine is now served at all major restaurants.

Euro Disneyland, 49 percent owned by Walt Disney Company, Burbank, California, originally forecasted 11 million visitors in the first year of operation. In January 1993 it appeared attendance would be closer to 10 million. In response, management temporarily slashed prices at the park for local residents to FFr 150 ($27.27) from FFr

This case was prepared by Research Assistant Sonali Krishna under the direction of Professors J. Stewart Black and Hal B. Gregersen as the basis for class discussion. Reprinted by permission of the authors.

225 ($40.91) for adults, and to FFr 100 from FFr 150 for children in order to lure more French during the slow, wet winter months. The company also reduced prices at its restaurants and hotels, which registered occupancy rates of just 37 percent.

Bourguignon also faced other problems, such as the second phase of development at Euro Disneyland, which was expected to start in September 1993. It was unclear how the company planned to finance its FFr 8–10 billion cost. The company had steadily drained its cash reserves (FFr 1.9 billion in May 1993) while piling up debt (FFr 21 billion in May 1993). Euro Disneyland admitted that it and the Walt Disney Company were "exploring potential sources of financing for Euro Disneyland." The company was also talking to banks about restructuring its debts.

Despite the frustrations. Eisner was tirelessly upbeat about the project. "Instant hits are things that go away quickly, and things that grow slowly and are part of the culture are what we look for," he said. "What we created in France is the biggest private investment in a foreign country by an American company ever. And it's gonna pay off."

In the Beginning

Disney's story is the classic American rags-to-riches story which started in a small Kansas City advertising office, where Mickey was a real mouse prowling the unknown Walt Disney floor. Originally, Mickey was named Mortimer, until a dissenting Mrs Disney stepped in. How close Mickey was to Walt Disney is evidenced by the fact that when filming, Disney himself dubbed the mouse's voice. Only in later films did Mickey get a different voice. Disney made many sacrifices to promote his hero-mascot, including selling his first car, a beloved Moon Cabriolet, and humiliating himself in front of Louis B. Mayer. "Get that mouse off the screen!" was the movie mogul's reported response to the cartoon character. Then, in 1955, Disney had the brainstorm of sending his movie characters out into the "real" world to mix with their fans and he battled skeptics to build the very first Disneyland in Anaheim, California.

When Disney died in 1966, the company went into virtual suspended animation. Their last big hit of that era was 1969s *The Love Bug*, about a Volkswagen named Herbie. Today, Disney executives trace the problem to a tyrannical CEO named E. Cardon Walker who ruled the company from 1976 to 1983, and to his successor, Ronald W. Miller. Walker was quick to ridicule underlings in public and impervious to any point of view but his own. He made decisions according to what he thought Walt would have done. Executives clinched arguments by quoting Walt like the Scriptures or Marx, and the company eventually supplied a little book of the founder's sayings. Making the wholesome family movies Walt would have wanted formed a key article of Walker's creed. For example, a poster advertising the unremarkable *Condorman* featured actress Barbara Carrera in a slit skirt. Walker had the slit painted over. With this as the context, studio producers ground out a thin stream of tired, formulaic movies that fewer and fewer customers would pay to see. In mid-1983, a similar low-horsepower approach to television production led to CBS's cancellation of the hour-long program *Walt Disney*, leaving the company without a regular network show for the first time in 29 years. Like a reclusive hermit, the company lost touch with the contemporary world.

Ron Miller's brief reign was by contrast a model of decentralization and delegation. Many attributed Miller's ascent to his marrying the boss's daughter rather than to any special gift. To shore Miller up, the board installed Raymond L. Watson, former head of the Irvine Co., as part-time Chairperson. He quickly became full time.

Miller sensed the studio needed rejuvenation and he managed to produce the hit film, *Splash*, featuring an apparently (but not actually) bare-breasted mermaid, under the newly devised Touchstone label. However, the reluctance of freelance Hollywood talent to accommodate Disney's narrow range and stingy compensation often kept his sound instincts from bearing fruit. "Card [Cardon Walker] would listen but not hear," said a former executive. "Ron [Ron Miller] would listen but not act."

Too many box office bombs contributed to a steady erosion of profit. Profits of $135 million on revenues of $915 million in 1980 dwindled to $93 million on revenues of $1.3 billion in 1983. More alarmingly, revenues from the company's theme parks, about three quarters of the company's total revenues, were showing signs of leveling off. Disney's stock slid from $84.375 a share to $48.75 between April 1983 and February 1984.

Through these years, Roy Disney, Jr. simmered while he watched the downfall of the national institution that his uncle, Walt, and his father, Roy Disney, Sr., had built. He had long argued that the company's constituent parts all work together to enhance each other. If movie and television production weren't revitalized, not only would that source of revenue disappear but the company and its activities would also grow dim in the public eye. At the same time the stream of new ideas and characters that kept people pouring into the parks and buying toys, books, and records would dry up. Now his dire predictions were coming true. His own personal shareholding had already dropped from $96 million to $54 million. Walker's treatment of Ron Miller as the shining heir apparent and Roy Disney as the idiot nephew helped drive Roy to quit as Disney vice president in 1977, and to set up Shamrock Holdings, a broadcasting and investment company.

In 1984, Roy teamed up with Stanley Gold, a tough-talking lawyer and a brilliant strategist. Gold saw that the falling stock price was bound to flush out a raider and afford Roy Disney a chance to restore the company's fortunes. They asked Frank Wells, vice chairperson of Warner Bros, if he would take a top job in the company in the event they offered it. Wells, a lawyer and a Rhodes scholar, said yes. With that, Roy knew that what he would hear in Disney's boardroom would limit his freedom to trade in its stock, so he quit the board on March 9, 1984. "I knew that would hang a 'For Sale' sign over the company," said Gold.

By resigning, Roy pushed over the first of a train of dominoes that ultimately led to the result he most desired. The company was raided, almost dismantled, greenmailed, raided again, and sued left and right. But it miraculously emerged with a skilled new top management with big plans for a bright future. Roy Disney proposed Michael Eisner as the CEO but the board came close to rejecting Eisner in favor of an older, more buttoned-down candidate. Gold stepped in and made an impassioned speech to the directors. "You see guys like Eisner as a little crazy . . . but every studio in this country has been run by crazies. What do you think Walt Disney was? The guy was off the god-damned wall. This is a creative institution. It needs to be run by crazies again."[1]

Meanwhile Eisner and Wells staged an all-out lobbying campaign, calling on every board member except two, who were abroad, to explain their views about the company's future. "What was most important," said Eisner, "was that they saw I did not come in a tutu, and that I was a serious person, and I understood a P&L, and I knew the investment analysts, and I read *Fortune*."

In September 1984, Michael Eisner was appointed CEO and Frank Wells became president. Jeffrey Katzenverg, the 33 year old, maniacal production chief followed Eisner from Paramount Pictures. He took over Disney's movie and television studios. "The key," said Eisner, "is to start off with a great idea."

---

[1] Stephen Koepp, "Do You Believe in Magic?" *Time* (April 25, 1988): pp 66–73.

Exhibit 3.1   How the theme parks grew

1955	Disneyland
1966	Walt Disney's death
1971	Walt Disney World in Orlando
1982	Epcot Center
1983	Tokyo Disneyland
1992	Euro Disneyland

Disneyland in Anaheim, California

For a long time, Walt Disney had been concerned about the lack of family-type entertainment available for his two daughters. The amusements parks he saw around him were mostly filthy traveling carnivals. They were often unsafe and allowed unruly conduct on the premises. Disney envisioned a place where people from all over the world would be able to go for clean and safe fun. His dream came true on July 17, 1955, when the gates first opened at Disneyland in Anaheim, California.

Disneyland strives to generate the perfect fantasy. But magic does not simply happen. The place is a marvel of modern technology. Literally dozens of computers, huge banks of tape machines, film projectors, and electronic controls lie behind the walls, beneath the floors, and above the ceilings of dozens of rides and attractions. The philosophy is that "Disneyland is the world's biggest stage, and the audience is right here on the stage," said Dick Hollinger, chief industrial engineer at Disneyland. "It takes a tremendous amount of work to keep the stage clean and working properly.

Cleanliness is a primary concern. Before the park opens at 8 a.m., the cleaning crew will have mopped and hosed and dried every sidewalk, every street and every floor and counter. More than 350 of the park's 7,400 employees come on duty at 1 a.m. to begin the daily cleanup routine. The thousands of feet that walk through the park each day and chewing gum do not mix, and gum has always presented major clean up problems. The park's janitors found long ago that fire hoses with 90 pounds of water pressure would not do the job. Now they use steam machines, razor scrapers, and mops towed by Cushman scooters to literally scour the streets and sidewalks daily.

It takes one person working a full eight-hour shift to polish the

brass on the Fantasyland merry-go-round. The scrupulously mani-
cured plantings throughout the park are treated with growth retard-
ing hormones to keep the trees and bushes from spreading beyond
their assigned spaces and destroying the carefully maintained five-
eighths scale modeling that is utilized in the park. The maintenance
supervisor of the Matterhorn bobsled ride personally walks every foot
of track and inspects every link of tow chain every night, thus trusting
his or her own eyes more than the $2 million in safety equipment that
is built into the ride.

Eisner himself pays obsessive attention to detail. Walking through
Disneyland one Sunday afternoon, he peered at the plastic leaves on
the Swiss Family Robinson tree house noting that they periodically
wear out and need to be replaced leaf by leaf at a cost of $500,000. As
his family strolled through the park, he and his eldest son Breck
stooped to pick up the rare piece of litter that the cleanup crew had
somehow missed. This old-fashioned dedication has paid off. Since
opening day in 1955. Disneyland has been a consistent money-maker.

Disney World in Orlando, Florida

By the time Eisner arrived, Disney World in Orlando was already on
its way to becoming what it is today – the most popular vacation
destination in the US. But the company had neglected a rich niche in
its business: hotels. Disney's three existing hotels, probably the most
profitable in the US, registered unheard-of occupancy rates of 92
percent to 96 percent versus 66 percent for the industry. Eisner promptly
embarked on an ambitious $1 billion hotel expansion plan. Two ma-
jor hotels, Disney's Grand Floridian Beach Resort and Disney's Caribbean Beach Resort, were opened during 1987–9. Disney's Yacht
Club and Beach Resort along with the Dolphin and Swan Hotels,
owned and operated by Tishman Realty & Construction, Metropoli-
tan Life Insurance, and Aoki Corporation opened during 1989–90.
Adding 3,400 hotel rooms and 250,000 square feet of convention space,
this made it the largest convention center east of the Mississippi.

In October 1982, Disney made a new addition to the theme park –
the Experimental Prototype Community of Tomorrow or EPCOT
Centre. E. Cardon Walker, then president of the company, announced
that EPCOT would be a "permanent showcase, industrial park, and
experimental housing center." This new park consists of two large
complexes: Future World, a series of pavilions designed to show the
technological advances of the next 25 years, and World Showcase, a
collection of foreign "villages."

Tokyo Disneyland

It was Tokyo's nastiest winter day in four years. Arctic winds and eight inches of snow lashed the city. Roads were clogged and trains slowed down. But the bad weather didn't keep 13,200 hardy souls from Tokyo Disneyland. Mikki Mausu, better known outside Japan as Mickey Mouse, had taken the country by storm.

Located on a fringe of reclaimed shoreline in Urayasu City on the outskirts of Tokyo, the park opened to the public on April 15, 1983. In less than one year, over ten million people had passed through its gates, an attendance figure that has been bettered every single year. On August 13, 1983, 93,000 people helped set a one day attendance record that easily eclipsed the old records established at the two parent US parks. Four years later, records again toppled as the turnstiles clicked. The total this time: 111,500. By 1988, approximately 50 million people, or nearly half of Japan's population, had visited Tokyo Disneyland since its opening. The steady cash flow pushed revenues for fiscal year 1989 to $768 million, up 17 percent from 1988.

Exhibit 3.2   Investor's snapshot: The Walt Disney Company (December 1989)

Sales (latest four quarters)	$4.6 billion
Change from year earlier	Up 33.6%
Net profit	$703.3 million
Change	Up 34.7%
Return on common stockholders' equity	23.4%
Five year average	20.3%
Stock price average (last 12 months)	$60.50–$136.25
Recent share price	$122.75
Price/Earnings Multiple	27
Total return to investors (12 months to 11/3/89)	90.6%

Fortune, December 4, 1989

The 204 acre Tokyo Disneyland is owned and operated by Oriental Land under license from the Walt Disney Co. The 45 year contract gives Disney 10 percent of admissions and 5 percent of food and merchandise sales, plus licensing fees. Disney opted to take no equity in the project and put no money down for construction.

"I never had the slightest doubt about the success of Disneyland in Japan," said Masatomo Takahashi, president of Oriental Land Company. Oriental Land was so confident of the success of Disney in Japan that it financed the park entirely with debt, borrowing ¥180 billion ($1.5 billion at February 1988 exchange rates). Takahashi added, "The debt means nothing to me," and with good reason. According to Fusahao Awata, who co-authored a book on Tokyo Disneyland: "The Japanese yearn for [American culture]."

Soon after Tokyo Disneyland opened in April 1983, five Shinto priests held a solemn dedication ceremony near Cinderella's castle. It is the only overtly Japanese ritual seen so far in this sprawling theme park. What visitors see is pure Americana. All signs are in English, with only small *katakana* (a phonetic Japanese alphabet) translations. Most of the food is American-style, and the attractions are cloned from Disney's US parks. Disney also held firm on two fundamentals that strike the Japanese as strange – no alcohol is allowed and no food may be brought in from outside the park.

However, in Disney's enthusiasm to make Tokyo a brick-by-brick copy of Anaheim's Magic Kingdom, there were a few glitches. On opening day, the Tokyo park discovered that almost 100 public telephones were placed too high for Japanese guests to reach them comfortably. And many hungry customers found countertops above their reach at the park's snack stands.

"Everything we imported that worked in the US works here," said Ronald D. Pogue, managing director of Walt Disney Attractions Japan Ltd. "American things like McDonald's hamburgers and Kentucky Fried Chicken are popular here with young people. We also wanted visitors from Japan and Southeast Asia to feel they were getting the real thing," said Toshiharu Akiba, a staff member of the Oriental Land publicity department.

Still, local sensibilities dictated a few changes. A Japanese restaurant was added to please older patrons. The Nautilus submarine is missing. More areas are covered to protect against rain and snow. Lines for attractions had to be redesigned so that people walking through the park did not cross in front of patrons waiting to ride an attraction. "It's very discourteous in Japan to have people cross in front of somebody else," explained James B. Cora, managing director of operations for the Tokyo project. The biggest differences between

Japan and America have come in slogans and ad copy. Although English is often used, it's "Japanized" English – the sort that would have native speakers shaking their heads while the Japanese nod happily in recognition. "Let's Spring" was the motto for one of their highly successful ad campaigns.

Pogue, visiting frequently from his base in California, supervised seven resident American Disney managers who work side by side with Japanese counterparts from Oriental Land Co. to keep the park in tune with the Disney doctrine. American it may be, but Tokyo Disneyland appeals to such deep-seated Japanese passions as cleanliness, order, outstanding service, and technological wizardry. Japanese executives are impressed by Disney's detailed training manuals, which teach employees how to make visitors feel like VIPs. Most worth emulating, say the Japanese, is Disney's ability to make even the lowliest job seem glamorous. "They have changed the image of dirty work," said Hakuhodo Institute's Sekizawa.

Disney Company did encounter a few unique cultural problems when developing Tokyo Disneyland:

The problem: how to dispose of some 250 tons of trash that would be generated weekly by Tokyo Disneyland visitors?

The standard Disney solution: trash compactors.

The Japanese proposal: pigs to eat the trash and be slaughtered and sold at a profit.

James B. Cora and his team of some 150 operations experts did a little calculating and pointed out that it would take 100,000 pigs to do the job. And then there would be the smell . . .

The Japanese relented.

The Japanese were also uneasy about a rustic-looking Westernland, Tokyo's version of Frontierland. "The Japanese like everything fresh and new when they put it in," said Cora. "They kept painting the wood and we kept saying, 'No, it's got to look old.'" Finally the Disney crew took the Japanese to Anaheim to give them a first hand look at the Old West.

Tokyo Disneyland opened just as the yen escalated in value against the dollar and the income level of the Japanese registered a phenomenal improvement. During this era of affluence, Tokyo Disneyland triggered an interest in leisure. Its great success spurred the construction of "leisurelands" throughout the country. This created an increase in the Japanese people's orientation towards leisure. But demographics are the real key to Tokyo Disneyland's success. Thirty million Japanese live within 30 miles of the park. There is three times more than the number of people in the same proximity to Anaheim's

Disneyland. With the park proven such an unqualified hit, and nearing capacity, Oriental Land and Disney mapped out plans for a version of the Disney-MGM studio tour next door. This time, Disney talked about taking a 50 percent stake in the project.

Building Euro Disneyland

On March 24, 1987, Michael Eisner and Jacques Chirac, the French Prime Minister, signed a contract for the building of a Disney theme park at Marne-la-Vallee. Talks between Disney and the French government had dragged on for more than a year. At the signing, Robert Fitzpatrick, fluent in French, married to the former Sylvie Blondet and the recipient of two awards from the French government, was introduced as the president of Euro Disneyland. He was expected to be a key player in wooing support from the French establishment for the theme park. As one analyst put it, Disney selected him to set up the park because he is "more French than the French."

Disney had been courted extensively by Spain and France. The Prime Ministers of both countries ordered their governments to lend Disney a hand in its quest for a site. France set up a five-person team headed by a Special Advisor to Foreign Trade & Tourism Minister. Edith Cresson, and Spain's negotiators included Ignacio Vasallo, Director-General for the Promotion of Tourism. Disney pummeled both governments with requests for detailed information. "The only thing they haven't asked us for is the color of the tourists' eyes," moaned Vasallo.

The governments tried other enticements, too. Spain offered tax and labor incentives and possibly as much as 20,000 acres of land. The French package, although less generous, included spending of $53 million to improve highway access to the proposed site and perhaps speeding up a $75 million subway project. For a long time, all that smiling Disney officials would say was that Spain had better weather while France had a better population base.

Officials explained that they picked France over Spain because Marne-la-Vallee is advantageously close to one of the world's tourism capitals, while also being situated within a day's drive or train ride of some 30 million people in France, Belgium, England, and Germany. Another advantage mentioned was the availability of good transportation. A train line that serves as part of the Paris Metro subway system ran to Torcy, in the center of Marne-la-Vallee, and the French government promised to extend the line to the actual site of the park. The park would also be served by A-4, a modern highway that runs from Paris to the German border, as well as a freeway that runs to Charles de Gaulle airport.

Once a letter of intent had been signed, sensing that the French government was keen to not let the plan fail, Disney held out for one concession after another. For example, Disney negotiated for VAT (value added tax) on ticket sales to be cut from a normal 18.6 percent to 7 percent. A quarter of the investment in building the park would come from subsidized loans. Additionally, any disputes arising from the contract would be settled not in French courts but by a special international panel of arbitrators. But Disney did have to agree to a clause in the contract which would require it to respect and utilize French culture in its themes.

The park was built on 4,460 acres of farmland in Marne-la-Vallee, a rural corner of France 20 miles east of Paris known mostly for sugar beets and Brie cheese. Opening was planned for early 1992 and planners hoped to attract some 10 million visitors a year. Approximately $2.5 billion was needed to build the park making it the largest single foreign investment ever in France. A French "pivot" company was formed to build the park with starting capital of FFr 3 billion, split 60 percent French and 40 percent foreign, with Disney taking 16.67 percent. Euro Disneyland was expected to bring $600 million in foreign investment into France each year.

As soon as the contract had been signed, individuals and businesses began scurrying to somehow plug into the Mickey Mouse money machine – all were hoping to benefit from the American dream without leaving France. In fact, one Paris daily, *Liberation*, actually sprouted mouse ears over its front page flag.

The $1.5 to $2 billion first phase investment would involve an amusement complex including hotels and restaurants, golf courses, and an aquatic park in addition to a European version of the Magic Kingdom. The second phase, scheduled to start after the gates opened in 1992, called for the construction of a community around the park, including a sports complex, technology park, conference center, theater, shopping mall, university campus, villas, and condominiums. No price tag had been put on the second phase, although it was expected to rival, if not surpass, the first phase investment. In November 1989, Fitzpatrick announced that the Disney-MGM Studios, Europe would also open at Euro Disneyland in 1996, resembling the enormously successful Disney-MGM Studios theme park at Disney World in Orlando. The new studios would greatly enhance the Walt Disney Company's strategy of increasing its production of live action and animated filmed entertainment in Europe for both the European and world markets.

"The phone's been ringing here ever since the announcement," said Marc Berthod of EpaMarne, the government body that oversees the Marne-la-Vallee region. "We've gotten calls from big companies as well as small – everything from hotel chains to language interpreters – all asking for details on Euro Disneyland. And the individual mayors of the villages around here have been swamped with calls from people looking for jobs." he added.

Euro Disneyland was expected to generate up to 28,000 jobs, providing a measure of relief for an area that had suffered a 10 percent plus unemployment rate for the previous year. It was also expected to light a fire under France's construction industry which had been particularly hard hit by France's economic problems over the previous year. Moreover, Euro Disneyland was expected to attract many other investors to the depressed outskirts of Paris. International Business Machines (IBM) and *Banque National de Paris* were among those already building in the area. In addition, one of the new buildings going up was a factory that would employ 400 outside workers to wash the 50 tons of laundry expected to be generated per day by Euro Disneyland's 14,000 employees.

The impact of Euro Disneyland was also felt in the real estate

Exhibit 3.3 Chronology of the Euro Disneyland deal[2]

1984–85	Disney negotiates with Spain and France to create a European theme park Chooses France as the site
1987	Disney signs letter of intent with the French government
1988	Selects lead commercial bank lenders for the senior portion of the project Forms the *Societe en Nom Collectif* (SNC) Begins planning for the equity offering of 51% of Euro Disneyland as required in the letter of intent
1989	European press and stock analysts visit Walt Disney World in Orlando Begin extensive news and television campaign Stock starts trading at 20–25 percent premium from the issue price

[2] From Geraldine E. Willigan, "The value-adding CFO: an interview with Disney's Gary Wilson," *Harvard Business Review*, January–February 1990, pp. 85–93.

market. "Everyone who owns land around here is holding on to it for the time being, at least until they know what's going to happen," said Danny Theveno, a spokesman for the town of Villiers on the western edge of Marne-la-Vallee.

Disney expected 11 million visitors in the first year. The break-even point was estimated to be between seven and eight million. One worry was that Euro Disneyland would cannibalize the flow of European visitors to Walt Disney World in Florida, but European travel agents said that their customers were still eagerly signing up for Florida, lured by the cheap dollar and the promise of sunshine.

Protests of Cultural Imperialism

Disney faced French communists and intellectuals who protested the building of Euro Disneyland. Ariane Mnouchkine, a theater director, described it as a "cultural Chernobyl." "I wish with all my heart that the rebels would set fire to Disneyland," thundered a French intellectual in the newspaper *Le Figaro*. "Mickey Mouse," sniffed another, "is stifling individualism and transforming children into consumers." The theme park was damned as an example of American "neoprovincialism."

Farmers in the Marne-la-Vallee region posted protest signs along the roadside featuring a mean looking Mickey Mouse and touting sentiments such as "Disney go home," "Stop the massacre," and "Don't gnaw away our national wealth." Farmers were upset partly because, under the terms of the contract, the French government would expropriate the necessary land and sell it without profit to Euro Disneyland development company.

While local officials were sympathetic to the farmers' position, they were unwilling to let their predicament interfere with what some called "the deal of the century." "For many years these farmers have had the fortune to cultivate what is considered some of the richest land in France," said Berthod. "Now they'll have to find another occupation."

Also less than enchanted about the prospect of a magic kingdom rising among their midst was the communist dominated labor federation, the *Confédération Générale du Travail* (CGT). Despite the job-creating potential of Euro Disney, the CGT doubted its members would benefit. The union had been fighting hard to stop the passage of a bill which would give managers the right to establish flexible hours for their workers. Flexible hours were believed to be a prerequisite to the profitable operation of Euro Disneyland, especially considering seasonal variations.

However, Disney proved to be relatively immune to the anti-US virus. In early 1985, one of the three state-owned television networks signed a contract to broadcast two hours of dubbed Disney programming every Saturday evening. Soon after, *Disney Channel* became one of the top rated programs in France.

In 1987, the company launched an aggressive community relations program to calm the fears of politicians, farmers, villagers, and even bankers that the project would bring traffic congestion, noise, pollution, and other problems to their countryside. Such a public relations program was a rarity in France, where businesses make little effort to establish good relations with local residents. Disney invited 400 local children to a birthday party for Mickey Mouse, sent Mickey to area hospitals, and hosted free trips to Disney World in Florida for dozens of local officials and children.

"They're experts at seduction, and they don't hide the fact that they're trying to seduce you," said Vincent Guardiola, an official with *Banque Indosuez*, one of the 17 banks wined and dined at Orlando and subsequently one of the venture's financial participants. "The French aren't used to this kind of public relations – it was unbelievable." Observers said that the goodwill efforts helped dissipate initial objections to the project.

Financial Structuring at Euro Disneyland

Eisner was so keen on Euro Disneyland that Disney kept a 49 percent stake in the project, while the remaining 51 percent of stock was distributed through the London, Paris, and Brussels stock exchanges. Half the stock under the offer was going to the French, 25 percent to the English, and the remainder distributed in the rest of the European community. The initial offer price of FFr 72 was considerably higher than the pathfinder prospectus estimate because the capacity of the park had been slightly extended. Scarcity of stock was likely to push up the price, which was expected to reach FFr 166 by opening day in 1992. This would give a compound return of 21 percent.

Walt Disney maintained management control of the company. The US company put up $160 million of its own capital to fund the project, an investment which soared in value to $2.4 billion after the popular stock offering in Europe. French national and local authorities, by comparison, were providing about $800 million in low interest loans and poured at least that much again into infrastructure.

Other sources of funding were the park's 12 corporate sponsors, and Disney would pay them back in kind. The "autopolis" ride, where kids ride cars, features coupes emblazoned with the "Hot Wheels" logo. Mattel Inc., sponsor of the ride is grateful for the boost to one of its biggest toy lines.

The real payoff would begin once the park opened. The Walt Disney Company would receive 10 percent of admission fees and 5 percent of food and merchandise revenue, the same arrangement as in Japan. But in France, it would also receive management fees, incentive fees, and 49 percent of the profits.

A Saloman Brothers analyst estimated that the park would pull in three to four million more visitors than the 11 million the company expected in the first year. Other Wall Street analysts cautioned that stock prices of both Walt Disney Company and Euro Disney already contained all the Euro optimism they could absorb. "Europeans visit Disneyworld in Florida as part of an 'American experience,'" said Patrick P. Roper, marketing director of Alton Towers, a successful British theme park near Manchester. He doubted they would seek the suburbs of Paris as eagerly as America and predicted attendance would trail Disney projections.

The Layout of Euro Disneyland

Euro Disneyland is determinedly American in its theme. There was an alcohol ban in the park despite the attitude among the French that wine with a meal is a God-given right. Designers presented a plan for a Main Street USA based on scenes of America in the 1920s, because research indicated that Europeans loved the Prohibition era. Eisner decreed that images of gangsters and speak-easies were too negative. Though made more ornate and Victorian than Walt Disney's idealized Midwestern small town, Main Street remained Main Street. Steam ships leave from Main Street through the Grand Canyon Diorama en route to Frontierland.

The familiar Disney Tomorrowland, with its dated images of the space age, was jettisoned entirely. It was replaced by a gleaming brass and wood complex called Discoverland, which was based on themes of Jules Verne and Leonardo da Vinci. Eisner ordered $8 or $10 million in extras to the "Visionarium" exhibit, a 360 degree movie about French culture which was required by the French in their original contract. French and English are the official languages at the park and multilingual guides are available to help Dutch, German, Spanish, and Italian visitors.

With the American Wild West being so frequently captured on film, Europeans have their own idea of what life was like back then.

Exhibit 3.4 The Euro Disneyland Resort[3]

5,000	acres in size
30	attractions
12,000	employees
6	hotels (with 5,184 rooms)
10	theme restaurants
414	cabins
181	camping sites

Frontierland reinforces those images. A runway mine train takes guests through the canyons and mines of Gold Rush country. There is a paddle wheel steamboat reminiscent of Mark Twain, Indian explorer canoes, and a phantom manor from the Gold Rush days.

In Fantasyland, designers strived to avoid competing with the nearby European reality of actual medieval towns, cathedrals, and chateaux. While Disneyland's castle is based on Germany's Neuschwanstein and Disney World's is based on a Loire Valley chateau. Euro Disney's *Le Château de la Belle au Bois Dormant*, as the French insisted Sleeping Beauty be called, is more cartoon-like with stained glass windows built by English craftsmakers and depicting Disney characters. Fanciful trees grow inside as well as a beanstalk.

The park is criss-crossed with covered walkways. Eisner personally ordered the installation of 35 fireplaces in hotels and restaurants. "People walk around Disney World in Florida with humidity and temperatures in the 90s and they walk into an air-conditioned ride and say, 'This is the greatest,'" said Eisner. "When its raining and miserable, I hope they will walk into one of these lobbies with the fireplace going and say the same thing."

Children all over Europe were primed to consume. Even one of the intellectuals who contributed to *Le Figaro*'s Disney-bashing broadsheet was forced to admit with resignation that his ten year old son "swears by Michael Jackson." At Euro Disneyland, under the name "Captain EO," Disney just so happened to have a Michael Jackson attraction awaiting him.

---

[3] Roger Cohen, "Threat of strikes in Euro Disney debut," *The New York Times*, April 10, 1992, p. 20.

Food Service and Accommodations at Euro Disneyland

Disney expected to serve 15,000 to 17,000 meals per hour, excluding snacks. Menus and service systems were developed so that they varied both in style and price. There is a 400-seat buffeteria, six table service restaurants, 12 counter service units, ten snack bars, one Discovery food court seating 850, nine popcorn wagons, 15 ice-cream carts, 14 specialty food carts, and two employee cafeterias. Restaurants were, in fact, to be a showcase for American foods. The only exception to this is Fantasyland which recreates European fables. Here, food service will reflect the fable's country of origin: Pinocchio's facility having German food; Cinderella's, French; Bella Notte's, Italian; and so on.

Of course recipes were adapted for European tastes. Since many Europeans don't care much for very spicy food, Tex-Mex recipes were toned down. A special coffee blend had to be developed which would have universal appeal. Hot dog carts would reflect the regionalism of American tastes. There would be a ball park hot dog (mild, steamed, a mixture of beef and pork), a New York hot dog (all beef, and spicy), and a Chicago hot dog (Vienna-style, similar to bratwurst).

Euro Disneyland has six theme hotels which would offer nearly 5,200 rooms on opening day, a campground (444 rental trailers and 181 camping sites), and single family homes on the periphery of the 27 hole golf course.

Exhibit 3.5 What price Mickey?[4]

	Euro Disneyland	Disney World, Orlando
Peak season hotel rates		
4-Person Room	$97 to $345	$104–$455
Campground space		
	$48	$30–$49
One-day pass		
Children	$26	$26
Adults	$40	$33

4 *Business Week*, March 30, 1992.

Disney's Strict Appearance Code

Antoine Guervil stood at his post in front of the 1,000 room Cheyenne Hotel at Euro Disneyland, practicing his "Howdy!" When Guervil, a political refugee from Haiti, said the word, it sounded more like "Audi." Native French speakers have trouble with the aspirated "h" sound in words like "*hay*" and "*Hank*" and "Howdy." Guervil had been given the job of wearing a cowboy costume and booming a happy, welcoming Howdy to guests as they entered The Cheyenne, styled after a Western movie set.

"Audi," said Guervil, the strain of linguistic effort showing on his face. This was clearly a struggle. Unless things got better, it was not hard to imagine objections from Renault, the French car company that was one of the corporate sponsors of the park. Picture the rage of a French auto executive arriving with his or her family at the Renault-sponsored Euro Disneyland, only to hear the doorman of a Disney hotel advertising a German car.

Such were the problems Disney faced while hiring some 12,000 people to maintain and populate its Euro Disneyland theme park. A handbook of detailed rules on acceptable clothing, hairstyles, and jewelry, among other things, embroiled the company in a legal and cultural dispute. Critics asked how the brash Americans could be so insensitive to French culture, individualism, and privacy. Disney officials insisted that a ruling that barred them from imposing a squeaky-clean employment standard could threaten the image and long-term success of the park.

"For us, the appearance code has a great effect from a product identification standpoint," said Thor Degelmann, vice president for human resources for Euro Disneyland. "Without it we wouldn't be presenting the Disney product that people would be expecting."

The rules, spelled out in a video presentation and detailed in a guide handbook, went beyond height and weight standards. They required men's hair to be cut above the collar and ears with no beards or mustaches. Any tattoos must be covered. Women must keep their hair in one "natural color" with no frosting or streaking and they may make only limited use of make-up like mascara. False eyelashes, eyeliners, and eye pencil were completely off limits. Fingernails can't pass the end of the fingers. As for jewelry, women can wear only one earring in each ear, with the earring's diameter no more than three-quarters of an inch. Neither men nor women can wear more than one ring on each hand. Further, women were required to wear appropriate undergarments and only transparent pantyhose, not black or anything with fancy designs. Though a daily bath was not specified in the rules, the applicant's video depicted a shower scene and informed applicant's that they were expected to show up for work "fresh and clean each day." Similar rules are in force at Disney's three other theme parks in the US and Japan.

In the US, some labor unions representing Disney employees have occasionally protested the company's strict appearance code, but with little success. French labor unions began protesting when Disneyland opened its "casting center" and invited applicants to "play the role of [their lives]" and to take a "unique opportunity to marry work and magic." The CGT handed out leaflets in front of the center to warn applicants of the appearance code which they believed represented "an attack on individual liberty." A more mainstream union, the *Confédération Française Démocratique du Travail* (CFDT) appealed to the Labor Ministry to halt Disney's violation of "human dignity." French law prohibits employers from restricting individual and collective liberties unless the restrictions can be justified by the nature of the task to be accomplished and are proportional to that end.

Degelmann, however, said that the company was "well aware of the cultural differences" between the United States and France and as a result had "toned down" the wording in the original American version of the guidebook. He pointed out that many companies, particularly airlines, maintained appearance codes just as strict. "We happened to put ours in writing," he added. In any case, he said that he knew of no one who had refused to take the job because of the rules and that no more than 5 percent of the people showing up for interviews had decided not to proceed after watching the video which also detailed transportation and salary.

Fitzpatrick also defended the dress code, although he conceded that Disney might have been a little naive in presenting things so directly. He added, "Only in France is there still a communist party. There is not even one in Russia any more. The ironic thing is that I could fill the park with CGT requests for tickets."

Another big challenge lay in getting the mostly French "cast members," as Disney calls its employees, to break their ancient cultural aversions to smiling and being consistently polite to park guests. The individualistic French had to be molded into the squeaky-clean Disney image. Rival theme parks in the area, loosely modeled on the Disney system, had already encountered trouble keeping smiles on the faces of the staff, who sometimes took on the demeanor of subway ticket clerks.

The delicate matter of hiring French citizens as opposed to other nationals was examined in the more than two year long pre-agreement negotiations between the French government and Disney. The final agreement called for Disney to make a maximum effort to tap into the local labor market. At the same time, it was understood that for Euro Disneyland to work, its staff must mirror the multicountry make-up of its guests. "Casting centers" were set up in Paris, London, Amsterdam, and Frankfurt. "We are concentrating on the local labor market, but we are also looking for workers who are German, English, Italian, Spanish, or other nationalities and who have good communication skills, are outgoing, speak two European languages – French plus one other – and like being around people," said Degelmann.

Stephane Baudet, a 28 year old trumpet player from Paris refused to audition for a job in a Disney brass band when he learned he would have to cut his ponytail. "Some people will turn themselves into a pumpkin to work at Euro Disneyland," he said. "But not me."

The Opening Day at Euro Disneyland

A few days before the grand opening of Euro Disneyland, hundreds of French visitors were invited to a pre-opening party. They gazed perplexed at what was placed before them. It was a heaping plate of spare ribs. The visitors were at the Buffalo Bill Wild West Show, a cavernous theater featuring a panoply of "Le Far West," including 20 imported buffaloes. And Disney deliberately didn't provide silverware. "There was a moment of consternation," recalls Fitzpatrick. "Then they just kind of said, 'The hell with it,' and dug in." There was one problem. The guests couldn't master the art of gnawing ribs and applauding at the same time. So Disney planned to provide more napkins and teach visitors to stamp with their feet.

On April 12, 1992, the opening day of Euro Disneyland, *France-Soir* enthusiastically predicted Disney dementia. "Mickey! It's madness," read its front page headline, warning of chaos on the roads and suggesting that people may have to be turned away. A French government survey indicated that half a million might turn up with 90,000 cars trying to get in. French radio warned traffic to avoid the area.

By lunch time on opening day, the Euro Disneyland car park was less than half full, suggesting an attendance of below 25,000, less than half the park's capacity and way below expectations. Many people may have heeded the advice to stay home or, more likely, were deterred by a one day strike that cut the direct rail link to Euro Disneyland from the center of Paris. Queues for the main rides such as Pirates of the Caribbean and Big Thunder Mountain railroad, were averaging around 15 minutes less than on an ordinary day at Disney World, Florida.

Disney executives put on a brave face, claiming that attendance was better than at first days for other Disney theme parks in Florida, California, and Japan. However, there was no disguising the fact that after spending thousands of dollars on the pre-opening celebrations, Euro Disney would have appreciated some impressively long traffic jams on the auto route.

Other Operating Problems

When the French government changed hands in 1986, work ground to a halt, as the negotiator appointed by the Conservative government threw out much of the ground work prepared by his Socialist predecessor. The legalistic approach taken by the Americans also bogged down talks, as it meant planning ahead for every conceivable contingency. At the same time, right-wing groups who saw the park as an invasion of "chewing-gum jobs" and US pop-culture also fought hard for a greater "local cultural context."

On opening day, English visitors found the French reluctant to play the game of queuing. "The French seem to think that if God had meant them to queue, He wouldn't have given them elbows." They commented. Different cultures have different definitions of personal space, and Disney guests faced problems of people getting too close or pressing around those who left too much space between themselves and the person in front.

Disney placed its first ads for work bids in English, leaving smaller and medium sized French firms feeling like foreigners in their own land. Eventually, Disney set up a data bank with information on over 20,000 French and European firms looking for work and the local Chamber of Commerce developed a video text information bank with Disney that small and medium sized companies through France and Europe would be able to tap into. "The work will come, but many local companies have got to learn that they don't simply have the right to a chunk of work without competing," said a Chamber official.

Efforts were made to ensure that sooner, rather than later, European nationals take over the day-to-day running of the park. Although there were only 23 US expatriates amongst the employees, they controlled the show and held most of the top jobs. Each senior manager had the task of choosing his or her European successor.

Disney was also forced to bail out 40 subcontractors, who were working for the Gabot-Eremco construction contracting group which had been unable to honor all of its commitments. Some of the subcontractors said they faced bankruptcy if they were not paid for their work on Euro Disneyland. A Disney spokesperson said that the payments would be less than $20.3 million and the company had already paid Gabot-Eremco for work on the park. Gabot-Eremco and 15 other main contractors demanded $157 million in additional fees from Disney for work that they said was added to the project after the initial contracts were signed. Disney rejected the claim and sought government intervention. Disney said that under no circumstances would they pay Gabot-Eremco and accused its officers of incompetence.

As Bourguignon thought about these and other problems, the previous year's losses and the prospect of losses again in the current year, with their negative impact on the company's stock price, weighed heavily on his mind.

4

Computex Corporation

Martin Hilb

Mr Peter Jones
Vice President—Europe
Computex Corporation
San Francisco / USA

Göteborg, May 30, 1985

The writers of this letter are the headcount of the sales department of Computex Sweden, AS, except for the sales manager.

We have decided to bring to your attention a problem which, if unsolved, probably will lead to a situation where the majority among us will leave the company within a rather short period of time. None of us want to be in this situation, and we are approaching you purely as an attempt to save the team for the benefit of ourselves as well as Computex Corporation.

We consider ourselves an experienced, professional, and sales-oriented group of people. Computex Corporation is a company which we are proud to work for. The majority among us have been employed for several years. Consequently, a great number of key customers in different areas of Sweden see us as representatives of Computex Corporation. It is correct to say that the many excellent contacts we have made have been established over years; many of them are friends of ours.

These traits give a very short background because we have never met you. What kind of problem forces us to such a serious step as to contact you?

Reprinted by permission of the author.

Problems arise as a result of character traits and behavior of our general manager, Mr Miller.

Firstly, we are more and more convinced that we are tools that he is utilizing in order to "climb the ladder." In meetings with us individually, or as a group, he gives visions about the future, how he values us, how he wants to delegate and involve us in business, the importance of cooperation and communication, etc. When it comes to the point, these phrases turn out to be only words.

Mr Miller loses his temper almost daily, and his outbursts and reactions are not equivalent to the possible error. His mood and views can change almost from hour to hour. This fact causes a situation where we feel uncertain when facing him and consequently are reluctant to do so. Regarding human relationships, his behavior is not acceptable, especially for a manager.

The extent of the experience of this varies within the group due to our location. Some of us are seldom in the office.

Secondly, we have experienced clearly that he has various means of suppressing and discouraging people within the organization.

The new "victim" now is our sales manager, Mr Johansson. Because he is our boss, it is obvious that we regret such a situation, which to a considerable extent influences our working conditions.

There are also other victims among us. It is indeed very difficult to carry through what is stated in our job descriptions.

We feel terribly sorry and wonder how it can be possible for one person almost to ruin a whole organization.

If this group consisted of people less mature, many of us would have left Computex Corporation already. So far only one has left the company due to the above reasons.

From September 1, two new sales representatives are joining the company. We regret very much that new employees get their first contact with the company under the present circumstances. An immediate action is therefore required.

It is not our objective to get rid of Mr Miller as general manager. Without going into details, we are thankful for what he has done to the company from a business point of view. If he could control his mood, show some respect for his colleagues, keep words, and stick to plans, we believe that we can succeed under his leadership.

We are fully aware of the seriousness of contacting you, and we have been in doubt whether or not to contact you directly before talking to Mr Miller.

After serious discussions and considerations, we have reached the conclusion that a problem of this nature unfortunately cannot be solved without some sort of action from the superior. If possible, direct confrontation must be avoided. It can only make things worse.

We are hoping for a positive solution.

Six of your sales representatives in Sweden

Peter Jones let out a long sigh as he gazed over the letter from Sweden. "What do I do now?" he thought, and began to reflect on the problem. He wondered who was right and who was wrong in this squabble, and he questioned whether he would ever get all the information necessary to make a wise decision. He didn't know much about the Swedes, and was unsure whether this was strictly a work problem or a "cross-cultural" problem. "How can I tease those two issues apart?" he asked himself, as he locked his office and made his way down the hallway to the elevator.

As Peter pulled out of the parking garage and on to the street, he began to devise a plan to deal with the problem. "This will be a test of my conflict management skills," he thought, "no doubt about it!" As he merged into the freeway traffic from the on-ramp and began his commute home, he began to wish that he had never sent Miller to Sweden in the first place. "But would Gonzalez or Harris have done any better? Would I have done any better?" Few answers seemed to come to him as he plodded along in the bumper-to-bumper traffic.

5

Ellen Moore in Bahrain

*Gail Ellement, Martha Maznevski, and
Henry W. Lane*

"The general manager had offered me a choice of two positions in the
operations area. I had considered the matter carefully, and was about
to meet with him to tell him I would accept the accounts control position.
The job was much more challenging than the customer services post,
but I knew I could learn the systems and procedures quickly and I would
have a great opportunity to contribute to the success of the operations
area."

It was November 1989, and Ellen Moore was just completing her
second year as an expatriate manager at the offices of a large American financial institution in Manama, Bahrain. After graduating with
an MBA from a leading business school, Ellen had joined her husband, who was working as an expatriate manager at an offshore bank
in Bahrain. Being highly qualified and capable, she had easily found a
demanding position and had worked on increasingly complex projects
since she had begun at the company. She was looking forward to the
challenges of the accounts control position.

Gail Ellement and Martha Maznevski prepared this case under the supervision of Professor
Henry W. Lane solely to provide material for class discussion. The authors do not intend to
illustrate either effective or ineffective handling of a managerial situation. The authors may
have disguised certain names and other identifying information to protect confidentiality.

Ellen Moore

Ellen graduated as the top female from her high school when she was 16, and immediately began working full time for the main branch of one of the largest banks in the country. By the end of four years, she had become a corporate accounts officer and managed over 20 large accounts.

> "I remember I was always making everything into a game, a challenge. One of my first jobs was filing checks. I started having a competition with the woman at the adjacent desk who had been filing for years, except she didn't know I was competing with her. When she realized it, we both started competing in earnest. Before long, people used to come over just to watch us fly through these stacks of checks. When I moved to the next job, I used to see how fast I could add up columns of numbers while handling phone conversations. I always had to do something to keep myself challenged."

While working full time at the bank, Ellen achieved a Fellowship in the Institute of Bankers after completing demanding courses and exams. She went on to work in banking and insurance with one of her former corporate clients from the bank. When she was subsequently promoted to manage their financial reporting department, she was both the first female and the youngest person the company had ever had in that position.

Since the time she had begun working full time, Ellen had been taking courses, contributing towards a Bachelor's degree, at night in one of the city's universities. In 1983 she decided to stop working for two years to complete the degree. After she graduated with a major in accounting and minors in marketing and management, she entered the MBA program.

> "I decided to go straight into the MBA program for several reasons. First, I wanted to update myself. I had taken my undergraduate courses over ten years and wanted to obtain knowledge on contemporary views. Second, I wanted to tie some pieces together – my night school degree left my ideas somewhat fragmented. Third, I wasn't impressed with the interviews I had after I finished the Bachelor's degree, and fourth I was out of work anyway. Finally, my father had already told everyone that I had my MBA, and I decided I really couldn't disappoint him."

Just after Ellen had begun the two year MBA program, her husband was offered a position in Bahrain with an affiliate of his bank, begin-

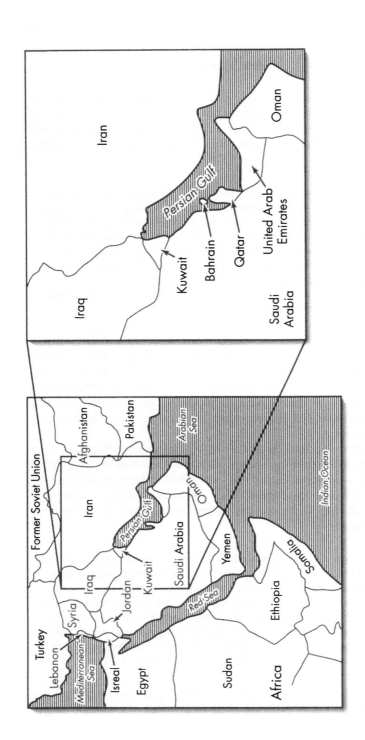

Exhibit 5.1 The Middle East

ning the next spring. They sat down and examined potential opportunities that would be available for Ellen once she completed her MBA. They discovered that women could work and assume positions of responsibility in Bahrain, and decided they could both benefit from the move. Her husband moved to Bahrain in March, while Ellen remained to complete her masters. Ellen followed, with MBA in hand, 18 months later.

Bahrain

Bahrain is an archipelago of 33 islands located in the Persian Gulf (see exhibit 5.1). The main island, Bahrain, comprises 85 percent of the almost 700 square kilometres of the country and is the location of the capital city, Manama. Several of the islands are joined by causeways, and in 1987 the 25 kilometre King Fahad Causeway linked the principal island to the mainland of Saudi Arabia, marking the end of island isolation for the country. In 1971, Bahrain gained full independence from Britain, ending a relationship that had lasted for almost a century. Of the population of over 400,000 people, about one third were foreigners.

Bahrain has had a prosperous history. Historically, it has been sought after by many countries for its lush vegetation, fresh water, and pearls. Many traditional crafts and industries were still practiced, including pottery, basket-making, fabric-weaving, pearl- diving, chow (fishing boat) building, and fishing. Bahrain was the pearl capital of the world for many centuries. Fortunately, just as the pearl industry collapsed with the advent of cultured pearls from Japan, Bahrain struck its first oil.

Since the 1930s, the oil industry had been the largest contributor to Bahrain's gross national product. The country was the first in the Persian Gulf to have an oil industry, established with a discovery in 1932. Production at that time was 9600 barrels a day. Eventually, crude output had reached over 40,000 barrels a day. Bahrain's oil products included crude oil, natural gas, methanol, ammonia, and refined products like gasoline, jet fuels, kerosene, and asphalts.

The Bahraini government had been aware for several years that the oil reserves were being seriously depleted. It was determined to diversify the country's economy away from a dependence on one resource. Industries established since 1971 included aluminum processing, shipbuilding, iron and steel processing, and furniture and door manufacturing. Offshore banking began in 1975. Since Bahraini nationals did not have the expertise to develop these industries alone, expatriates from around the world, particularly from western Europe and North America, were invited to conduct business in Bahrain. By the late 1980s, the country was a major business and financial centre, housing many Middle East branch offices of international firms.

Expatriates in Bahrain

Since Bahrain was an attractive base from which to conduct business, it was a temporary home to many expatriates. Housing compounds, schools, services, shopping and leisure activities all catered to many international cultures. Expatriates lived under residence permits, gained only on the basis of recruitment for a specialist position which could not be filled by a qualified and available Bahraini citizen.

To Ellen, one of the most interesting roles of expatriate managers was that of teacher. The Arab nations had been industrialized for little more than two decades, and had suddenly found themselves needing to compete in a global market. Ellen believed that one of her main reasons for working in Bahrain was to train its nationals to eventually take over her job.

"Usually the teaching part was very interesting. When I first arrived in the office, I was amazed to see many staff members with micro computers on their desks, yet they did not know the first thing about operating the equipment. When I inquired about the availability of computer courses, I was informed by a British expatriate manager that 'as these were personal computers, any person should be able to use them, and, as such, courses aren't necessary.' It was clear to me that courses were very necessary when the computer knowledge of most employees consisted of little more than knowing where the on/off switch was located on a microcomputer.

"Although it was outside of office policy, I held 'Ellen's Introduction to Computers' after office hours, just to get people comfortable with the machines and to teach them a few basics.

"Sometimes the amount of energy you had to put into the teaching was frustrating in that results were not immediately evident. I often worked jointly with one of the Bahraini managers who really didn't know how to develop projects and prepare reports. Although I wasn't responsible for him, I spent a great deal of time with him, helping him improve his work. Initially there was resistance on his part, because he was not prepared to subordinate himself to an expatriate, let alone a woman. But eventually he came around and we achieved some great results working together."

The range of cultures represented in Bahrain was vast. Expatriate managers interacted not only with Arabic nationals, but also with managers from other parts of the world, and with workers from developing countries who provided a large part of the unskilled labor force.

"The inequality among nationalities was one issue I found very difficult to deal with during my stay in Bahrain. The Third World immigrants were considered to be the lowest level possible in the pecking order, just slightly lower than nationals from countries outside the Gulf. Gulf Arabs, being of Bedouin origin, maintained a suspicious attitude towards 'citified' Arabs. Europeans and North Americans were regarded much more highly. These inequalities had a major impact on daily life, including the availability of jobs and what relations would develop or not develop between supervisors and subordinates. Although I was well acquainted with the racial problems in North America, I hadn't seen anything comparable with the situation in Bahrain. It wasn't unusual for someone to be exploited and discarded, as any expendable and easily replaceable resource would be, because of their nationality."

Although many expatriates and their families spent their time in Bahrain immersed in their own cultural compounds, social groups, and activities, Ellen believed that her interaction with the various cultures was one of the most valuable elements of her international experience.

Managing in Bahrain

Several aspects of the Middle Eastern culture had a tremendous impact on the way business was managed, even in Western firms located in Bahrain. It seemed to Ellen, for example, that "truth" to a Bahraini employee was subject to an Arab interpretation, which was formed over hundreds of years of cultural evolution. What Western managers considered to be "proof" of an argument or "factual" evidence could be flatly denied by a Bahraini: if something was not believed, it did not exist. As well, it seemed that the concept of "time" differed between Middle Eastern and Western cultures. Schedules and deadlines, while sacred to Western managers, commanded little respect from Bahraini employees. The two areas that had the most impact on Ellen's managing in a company in Bahrain were the Islamic religion and the traditional attitude towards women.

Islam[1]

Most Bahrainis are practicing Muslims. According to the Muslim faith, the universe was created by Allah who prescribed a code of life called Islam and the Koran is the literal, unchanged Word of Allah preserved exactly as transcribed by Muhammad. Muhammad's own acts as a prophet form the basis for Islamic law, and are second in authority only to the Koran. The five Pillars of Islam are belief, prayer, fasting, almsgiving and pilgrimage. Muslims pray five times a day. During Ramadan, the ninth month of the Islamic calendar, Muslims must fast from food, drink, smoking and sexual activity from dawn until dusk, in order to master the urges which sustain and procreate life. All Muslims are obliged to give a certain proportion of their wealth in alms for charitable purposes: the Koran stresses that the poor have a just claim on the wealth of the prosperous. Finally, if possible, all Muslims should make a pilgrimage to Mecca during their lives, in a spirit of total sacrifice of personal comforts, acquisition of wealth and other matters of worldly significance.

"Certainly the Muslim religion had a tremendous impact on my daily working life. The first time I walked into the women's washroom at work I noticed a tap about three inches off the floor over a drain. I found this rather puzzling: I wondered if it was for the cleaning crew. When a woman came in, I asked her about the tap, and she explained that before going to the prayer room, everyone had to wash all uncovered parts of their bodies. The tap was for washing their feet and legs.

"One time I was looking for one of my employees, Mohammed, who had a report due to me that afternoon. I searched for him at his desk and other likely spots throughout the office, but to no avail, he just wasn't around. I had had difficulties with Mohammed's work before, when he would submit documents long after deadlines, and I was certain he was attempting to slack off once again. I bumped into one of Mohammed's friends, and asked if he knew Mohammed's whereabouts. When he informed me that Mohammed was in the prayer room, I wasn't sure how to respond. I didn't know if this prayer room activity was very personal and if I could ask questions, such as the length of time one generally spends in prayer. But I needed to know how long Mohammed would be away from his desk. Throwing caution to the wind, I asked the employee how long Mohammed was likely to be in prayers and he told me it usually takes about ten minutes. It wasn't that I felt I didn't have the right to know where my employee was or how long he would be away, I just wasn't certain my authority as a manager allowed me the right to ask questions about such a personal activity as praying.

[1] *Resident in Bahrain* (Bahrain: *Gulf Daily News*, 1987), vol. 1, pp. 61–63.

"During Ramadan, the hours of business are shortened by law. It is absolutely illegal for any Muslim to work past two o'clock in the afternoon, unless special permits are obtained from the Ministry of Labor. Unfortunately, business coming in to an American firm does not stop at two, and a majority of the non-Muslim workers are required to take up the slack."

Unlike religion in Western civilization, Islam permeates every function of human endeavor. There does not exist a separation of church, state and judiciary. Indeed, in purist circles, the question does not arise. The hybrid systems existing in certain Arab countries are considered aberrations created by Western colonial influences. Accordingly, to function successfully, the expatriate must understand and learn to accept a very differently structured society.

Women in Bahrain

Bahrain tended to be more progressive than many Middle Eastern countries in its attitude towards women. Although traditions were strong, Bahraini women had some freedom. For example, all women could work outside the home, although the hours they could work were restricted both by convention and by the labor laws. They could only work if their husbands, fathers, or brothers permitted them, and could not take potential employment away from men. Work outside the home was to be conducted in addition to, not instead of, duties performed inside the home, such as child-rearing and cooking. Most women who worked held secretarial or clerical positions; very few worked in management.

Bahraini women were permitted to wear a variety of outfits, from the conservative full length black robe with head scarf which covers the head and hair, to below-the-knee skirts and dresses without head covering.

"Arabic women who sincerely want change and more decision-making power over their own lives face an almost impossible task, as the male influence is perpetuated not only by men, but also by women who are afraid to alter views they understand and with which they have been brought up all their lives. I once asked a female co-worker the reason why one of the women in the office, who had previously been 'uncovered', was now sporting a scarf over her head. The response was that this woman had just been married' and, although her husband did not request that she become 'covered', she personally did not feel as though she was a married woman without the head scarf. So she simply asked her husband to demand that she wear a scarf on her head. It was a really interesting situation, some of the more liberal Bahraini women were very upset that she had asked her husband to make this demand. They saw it as negating many of the progressive steps the women's movement had made in recent years."

Although Bahrainis had been exposed to Western cultures for the two decades of industrial expansion, they were still uncomfortable with Western notions of gender equality and less traditional roles for women.

"One day a taxi driver leaned back against his seat and, while keeping one eye on the road ahead, turned to ask me, "How many sons do you have?" I replied that I didn't have any children. His heartfelt response of 'I'm so sorry' and the way he shook his head in sympathy were something my North American upbringing didn't prepare me for. My taxi driver's response typifies the attitude projected towards women, whether they are expatriates from Europe or North America, or are Bahrainis. Women are meant to have children, preferably sons. Although Bahrain is progressive in many ways, attitudes on the role of women in society run long and deep, and it is quite unlikely these sentiments will alter in the near, or even distant, future.

"Another time I was greeted with gales of laughter when I revealed to the women in the office that my husband performed most of the culinary chores in our household. They assumed I was telling a joke, and when I insisted that he really did most of the cooking, they sat in silent disbelief. Finally, one woman spoke up and informed the group that she didn't think her husband even knew where the kitchen was in their house, let alone would ever be caught touching a cooking utensil. The group nodded in agreement. Although these women have successful business careers – as clerks, but in the workforce nonetheless – they believe women should perform all household tasks without the assistance of their husbands. The discovery that this belief holds true in Bahrain is not remarkable as I know many North American and European businesswomen who believe the same to be true. What is pertinent is these women allow themselves to be completely dominated by the men in their lives.

"The one concept I faced daily but never accepted was that my husband was regarded as the sole decision-maker in our household. He and I view our marriage as a partnership in which we participate equally in all decisions. But when the maintenance manager for our housing compound came by, repairs were completed efficiently only if I preceded my request with 'my husband wants the following to be completed.' It's a phrase I hated to use as it went against every rational thought I possess, but I frequently had to resort to it."

These attitudes also affected how Ellen was treated as a manager by Bahraini managers.

"One manager, I'll call him Fahad, believed that women were only capable of fulfilling secretarial and coffee-serving functions. One day I was sitting at my desk, concentrating on some documents. I didn't notice Fahad having a discussion with another male manager nearby. When I looked up from my papers, Fahad noticed me and immediately began talking in French to the other manager. Although my French was a bit rusty, my comprehension was still quite serviceable. I waited for a few moments and then broke into their discussion in French. Fahad was completely dismayed. Over the next few years, Fahad and I worked together on several projects. At first, he was pompous and wouldn't listen to anything I presented. It was a difficult situation, but I was determined to remain above his negative comments. I ignored his obvious prejudice towards me, remained outwardly calm when he disregarded my ideas, and proceeded to prove myself with my work. It took a lot of effort and patience but, in time, Fahad and I not only worked out our differences, but worked as a successful team on a number of major projects. Although this situation had a happy ending, I really would have preferred to have directed all that energy and effort towards more productive issues."

Bahraini nationals were not the only ones who perpetuated the traditional roles of women in society. Many of the expatriates, particularly those from Commonwealth countries, tended to view their role as "the colonial charged with the responsibility to look after the developing country." This was reflected in an official publication for new expatriates that stated: "Wives of overseas employees are normally sponsored by their husbands' employers, and their Residence Permits are processed at the same time . . ."[2] However, wives were not permitted to work unless they could obtain a work permit for themselves.

"The first question I was often asked at business receptions was 'What company is your husband with?' When I replied that I worked as well, I received the glazed-over look, as they assumed I occupied myself with coffee mornings, beach, tennis, and the other leisure activities pursued by the majority of expatriate wives.
"Social gatherings were always risky. At typical business and social receptions the men served themselves first, after which the women selected their food. Then women and men positioned themselves on opposite sides of the room. The women discussed 'feminine' topics, such as babies and recipes, while the men discussed the fall (or rise) of the dollar and the big deal of the day. At one Bahraini business gathering, I hesitated in choosing sides: should I conform and remain with the women? But most of these women did not work outside their homes,

[2] *Resident in Bahrain* (Bahrain: *Gulf Daily News*, 1987), vol. 1, p. 57.

and, consequently, they spoke and understood very little English. I joined
the men. Contrary to what I expected, I was given a gracious welcome.

"However, on another occasion I was bored with the female conversation, so I ventured over to the forbidden male side to join a group of
bankers discussing correspondent banking courses. When I entered the
discussion, a British bank general manager turned his nose up at me.
He motioned towards the other side of the room, and told me I should
join the women. He implied that their discussion was obviously over my
head. I quickly informed him that although I personally had found the
banking courses difficult to complete while holding a full-time banking
position, I not only managed to complete the program and obtain my
Fellowship but also, at the time, was the youngest employee of my bank
ever to be awarded the diploma. The man did a quick turnabout, was
thoroughly embarrassed, and apologized profusely. Although it was
nice to turn the tables on the man, I was more than a little frustrated with
the feeling that I almost had to wear my résumé on my sleeve to get any
form of respect from the men, whether European, North American, or
Arab."

A small percentage of Bahraini women had completed university degrees in North America and Europe. While residing in these Western
cultures, they were permitted to behave in the same way as their
Western counterparts. For example, they could visit or phone friends
when they wished without first obtaining permission. After completing their education, many of these women were qualified for management positions. However, upon returning to Bahrain they were required
to resume their traditional female roles.

"The notion of pink MBA diplomas for women and blue for men is very
real. Although any MBA graduate in North America, male or female, is
generally considered to have attained a certain level of business sense,
I had to constantly 'prove' myself to some individuals who appeared to
believe that women attended a special segregated section of the university with appropriately tailored courses."

Ellen discovered that, despite being a woman, she was accepted by
Bahrainis as a manager because of her Western nationality, her education, and her management position in the company.

"Many of my male Arabic peers accepted me as they would any expatriate manager. For example, when a male employee returned from a
holiday, he would typically visit each department, calling upon the other
male employees with a greeting and a handshake. Although he might
greet a female co-worker, he would never shake her hand. However,
because of my management position in the company and my status as

a Western expatriate, male staff members gave me the same enthusiastic greeting and handshake normally reserved for their male counterparts."

Ellen also found herself facilitating Bahraini women's positions in the workplace.

"As I was the only female in a senior management position in our office, I was often asked by the female employees to speak to their male superiors about problems and issues they experienced in their departments. I also had to provide a role model for the women because there were no female Bahraini managers. Some of them came to me not just to discuss career issues but to discuss life issues. There was just no one else in a similar position for them to talk to. On the other hand, male managers would ask me to discuss sensitive issues, such as hygiene, with their female staff members."

The government of Bahrain introduced legislation that restricted the amount of overtime hours women could work. Although the move was being praised by the (female) Director of Social Development as recognition of the contribution women were making to Bahraini industry, Ellen saw it as further discriminatory treatment restricting the choices of women in Bahrain. Her published letter to the editor of the *Gulf Daily News* read:

"... How the discriminatory treatment of women in this regulation can be seen as recognition of the immense contribution women make to the Bahrain workforce is beyond comprehension. Discrimination of any portion of the population in the labor legislation does not recognize anything but the obvious prejudice. If the working women in Bahrain want to receive acknowledgement of their indispensable impact on the Bahrain economy, it should be through an increase in the number of management positions available to qualified women, not through regulations limiting the hours they work. All this regulation means is that women are still regarded as second class citizens who need the strong arm tactics of the government to help them settle disputes over working hours. Government officials could really show appreciation to the working women in Bahrain by making sure that companies hire and promote based on skill rather than gender. But there is little likelihood of that occurring."

The letter was signed with a pseudonym, but the day it was published one of Ellen's female employees showed her the letter and claimed: 'If I didn't know better, Ellen, I'd think you wrote this letter.'

Career Decisions

When Ellen first arrived in Bahrain, she had great expectations that she would work somewhere where she could make a difference. She received several offers for positions and turned down, among others, a university and a high-profile brokerage house. She decided to take a position as a special projects coordinator at a large American financial institution.

> "In fact, the records will show I was actually hired as a 'financial analyst,' but this title was given solely because, at that time, the government had decided that expatriate women shouldn't be allowed to take potential positions away from Bahraini nationals. The expertise required as a financial analyst enabled the company to obtain a work permit for me as I had the required experience and academic credentials, although I performed few duties as an analyst."

In her special projects role, Ellen learned a great deal about international finance. She conducted efficiency studies on various operating departments. She used her systems expertise to investigate and improve the company's microcomputer usage, and developed a payroll program which was subsequently integrated into the company's international systems. She was a member of the strategic review committee, and produced a report outlining the long-term goals for the Middle East market, which she then presented to the senior vice president of Europe, Middle East and Africa.

After one year, Ellen was rewarded for her achievements by a promotion to manager of business planning and development, a position which reported directly to the vice president and general manager. She designed the role herself, and was able to be creative and quite influential in the company. During her year in this role, she was involved in a diverse range of activities. She managed the quality assurance department, coordinated a product launch, developed and managed a senior management information system, was an active participant in all senior management meetings, and launched an employee newsletter.

At the end of her second year in Bahrain, Ellen was informed that two positions in operations would soon be available, and the general manager, a European expatriate, asked if she would be interested in joining the area. She had previously only worked in staff positions, and quickly decided to accept the challenge and learning experience of a line post. Both positions were in senior management, and both had responsibility for approximately 30 employees.

The first position was for manager of accounts control, which covered the credit, collection and authorization departments. The manager's role was to ensure that appropriate information was used to authorize speeding by clients, to compile results of client payment, and to inform management of non-payment issues. The manager also supervised in-house staff and representatives in other Gulf countries for the collection of withheld payments.

The second post was manager of customer services, new accounts, and establishment services. The manager's role was to ensure that new clients were worthy and that international quality standards were met in all customer service activity. The manager also worked with two other departments: with marketing to ensure that budgets were met, and with sales to manage relationships with the many affiliate outlets of the service.

After speaking with the two current managers and considering the options carefully, Ellen decided that she would prefer working in the accounts control area. The job was more oriented to financial information, the manager had more influence on operations at the company, and she would have the opportunity to travel to other countries to supervise staff. Although she was not familiar with the systems and procedures, she knew she could learn them quickly. Ellen went into her meeting with the general manager excited about the new challenges.

Ellen Meets with the General Manager

Ellen told the general manager she had decided to take the accounts control position, and outlined her reasons. Then she waited for his affirmation and for the details of when she would begin.

"I'm afraid I've reconsidered the offer," the general manager announced. "Although I know you would probably do a terrific job in the accounts control position, I can't offer it to you. It involves periodic travel into Saudi Arabia, and women are not allowed to travel there alone." He went on to tell Ellen how she would be subject to discriminatory practices, would not be able to gain the respect of the company's Saudi Arabian clients, and would experience difficulty traveling there.

Ellen was astonished. She quickly pointed out to him that many businesswomen were representatives of American firms in Saudi Arabia. She described one woman she knew of who was the sole representative of a large American bank in the Eastern Province of Saudi Arabia who frequently traveled there alone. She explained that other women's experiences in Saudi Arabia showed professional men there treated professional women as neither male nor female, but as business people. Besides, she continued, there were no other candidates in the company for either position. She reminded the general manager of the pride the company took in its quality standards and how senior management salaries were in part determined by assuring quality in their departments. Although the company was an equal opportunity employer in its home country, the United States, she believed the spirit of the policy should extend to all international offices.

The general manager informed her that his decision reflected his desire to address the interests of both herself and the company. He was worried, he said, that Ellen would have trouble obtaining entry visas to allow her to conduct business in Saudi Arabia, and that the customers would not accept her. Also, if there were ever any hostile outbreaks, he believed she would be in danger, and he could not have lived with that possibility.

Ellen stated that, as a woman, she believed she was at lower risk of danger than her Western male counterparts since in the event of hostility, the Saudi Arabians would most likely secure her safety. There was much greater probability that a male representative of the firm would be held as a hostage.

The General Manager was adamant. Regardless of her wishes, the company needed Ellen in the customer service position. New accounts had only recently been added to the department, and the bottom line responsibility was thus doubled from what it had been in the past. The general manager said he wanted someone he could trust and depend upon to handle the pressure of new accounts, which had a high international profile.

Ellen was offered the customer service position, then dismissed from the meeting. In frustration, she began to consider her options.

Take the Customers Services Position

The general manager obviously expected her to take the position. It would mean increased responsibility and challenge. Except for a position in high school where she managed a force of 60 student police, Ellen had not yet supervised more than four employees at any time in her professional career. On the other hand, it went against her values to accept the post since it had been offered as a result of gender roles when all consideration should have been placed on competence.

She knew she had the abilities and qualifications for the position. She viewed the entire situation as yet another example of how the business community in Bahrain had difficulty accepting and acknowledging the contributions of women to international management, and didn't want to abandon her values by accepting the position.

Fight Back

There were two approaches which would permit Ellen to take the matter further. She could go to the general manager's superior, the senior vice president of Europe, Middle East and Africa. She had several dealings with him, and had once presented a report to him with which he was very impressed. But she wasn't sure she could count on his sympathy regarding her traveling to Saudi Arabia as his knowledge of the region was limited, and he generally relied on local management's decisions on such issues. She could consider filing a grievance against the company. There were provisions in Bahraini Labor Law that would have permitted this option in her case. However, she understood that the Labor Tribunals, unlike those held in Western countries, did not try cases based on precedents or rules of evidence. In other words, the judge would apply a hodgepodge of his own subjective criteria to reach a decision.

Stay in the Business Planning and Development Job

Although the general manager had not mentioned it as an option, Ellen could request that she remain in her current position. It would mean not giving in to the general manager's prejudices. Since she had been considering the two operations positions, though, she had been looking forward to moving on to something new.

Leave the Company

Ellen knew she was qualified for many positions in the financial centre of Bahrain and could likely obtain work with another company. She was not sure, though, whether leaving her present company under these circumstances would jeopardize her chances of finding work elsewhere. Furthermore, to obtain a post at a new company would require a letter of permission from her current employer, who, as her sponsor in Bahrain, had to sanction her move to a new employer who would become her new sponsor. She was not sure that she would be able to make those arrangements considering the situation.

"I always tell my employees: 'If you wake up one morning and discover you don't like your job, come to see me immediately. If the problem is with the tasks of the job, I'll see if I can modify your tasks. If the problem is with the department or you want a change, I'll assist you in getting another position in the company. If the problem is with the company, then I'll help you write your resume.' I have stated this credo to all my employees in every post I've held. Generally, they don't believe that their manager would actually assist with resume writing, but when the opportunity arises, and it has, and I do come through as promised, the impact on the remaining employees is priceless. Employees will provide much more effort towards a cause that is supported by someone looking out for their personal welfare."

Ellen's superior did not have the same attitude towards his employees. As she considered her options, Ellen realized that no move could be made without a compromise either in her career or her values. Which choice was she most willing to make?

6

TDK de Mexico

Manab Thakur

"I want to be the main supplier of magnets for South and North America," proclaimed Fumio Inouye, general manager of TDK de Mexico, located in Cd. Juarez, a border city of millions close to El Paso, Texas. "To help gain this status, our operating targets need to be met, and that might include expansion of present plant facilities and more automation. Increasingly I feel, though, that people here don't want to see expansion . . . They seem to enjoy excuses! Whether you call it Japanese or American management, I cannot accept delays, wastes, and excuses! Culture to me is important only when the process of production and the importance of work are clearly understood. Make no mistake, my parent company (TDK of Japan) wouldn't stand for anything other than making acceptable margins. I am having difficulty in putting the reasons for all the problems on culture . . . I refuse to take it as a dumping ground."

Production Methods and Technology

TDK de Mexico produced ceramic ferrite magnets of various shapes and sizes that were used for speakers, generators, and motors. It was one of the few plants in its area that produced a final product from the raw material. Production was based on job orders – in other words, production was scheduled as TDK de Mexico received orders for X number of Y type of magnet. The raw material used to make the final product was black powder called ferrite powder. The ferrite powder, a critical raw material, was imported although it was available in the Mexican market. But to ensure quality, TDK of Japan insisted on using ferrite powder from Japan. The manufacturing process started by wetting and mixing the powder in large containers. The mixture was dried and then fed into the press machines that gave the shape to the magnets. The shape was determined by the mold inserted into the press machine. All of the molds used also came from Japan. The various molds for the different shapes and sizes were stored at the plant and used as needed.

Two distinct methods, were used during the press stage of the production process, the dry method and the wet method. The basic difference between the two was that the wet method, installed at TDK de Mexico in 1983 after Inouye took charge, utilized water during the pressing of the raw material. It made stronger magnets, but it took more time. With the wet method, the worker collected the magnets just pressed and placed them in a temporary drying area before they were baked in the ovens. With the dry method, the worker collected the magnets just pressed, and they were sent straight to the ovens for baking. While collecting the magnets, the worker visually checked each magnet for cracks or other defects. Defective ones were thrown out for scrap. It was important to spot defective magnets at this stage because it was much harder to convert them into scrap after they were baked. All scrap materials were broken down and used again in the raw material mixture.

After pressing, the magnets were mechanically moved through a series of ovens. One set of pressed magnets was placed in the oven every 12 hours. The magnets were baked at progressively higher temperatures from entrance to exit. After their exit from the ovens, the magnets continued moving to a temporary storage area to cool. The ovens presently in use were electrically powered, but there was a plan to convert them to gas ovens to take advantage of the lower cost of gas. Once cooled, each magnet was subject to process inspection by workers. This was one of two main quality control checkpoints in the production process.

Cooled magnets were taken to the scraper machine. The scraper machine smoothed the rough edges and surface of the magnets. The scrapings were collected and used again in the raw material mixture. From the scraper machine, the workers placed the magnets in water to be cleaned. After cleaning, the magnets were sent through the drying machine. At the exit point of the drying machine, the magnets were collected by workers and placed in boxes. The boxes of magnets were taken to the final process department where each magnet was given a final check. This stage was called the shipping inspection, and it represented the second main quality control checkpoint. Quality control and specification requirements adhered to at this stage included measurement of weight, length, and appearance of magnets.

About 85 percent of production was exported to the United States – to TDK of America facilities in Chicago, Los Angeles, New York, and Indiana. The remaining 15 percent was exported to Hong Kong. The sales offices and warehouse facilities in these cities were in charge of all selling, shipping, and billing functions. TDK of America sold most of its products to Briggs and Stratton of Milwaukee, Wisconsin, and to Buehler Products of Kingston, North Carolina.

TDK of Mexico had encountered no bureaucratic delays or customs problems in shipping out final products, even though other companies in the area were having difficulties arranging for timely shipment of their merchandise out of Mexico. Inouye was proud that he had been able to secure the necessary clearances and paperwork for getting the product out of the country without much hassle. His explanation was, "You don't create systems when you simply need some people who can do things for you. You need to get out and find them. You create systems where systems are accepted . . . It is not here!"

Hiratzuka, TDK's production manager, commented, "We hear that the Mexican government may change the rules of the game. There are rumors that we may have to buy 20 to 25 percent of our raw materials from Mexican suppliers. Other than what the government will and will not do, I think you also need to understand that our primary concern is to attract quality labor, since our production process demands it . . We can't just hire anyone who walks in."

TDK de Mexico had not looked into possible changes in the Mexican government's local procurement rules to any extent, but had expressed its apprehension to Mexican officials if the firm was forced to buy ferrite powder locally. On another issue, Hiratzuka stated, "As you know, border plants in Mexico like ours have a 'no sale' rule where all goods produced must be exported. But the government is considering a compulsory selling rule whereby 20 percent of a border plant's goods must be sold locally." Such a rule was potentially more troublesome to TDK de Mexico because it was not clear that there was much of a market in Mexico for TDK's products.

The Mexican Maquiladoras

In 1965 the United States, working in conjunction with the Mexican government, set up the maquiladora program to create jobs for unemployed and underemployed Mexican workers. The idea was to get US companies to open light assembly plants just across the Mexican border and to use cheap Mexican labor to assemble American-made parts into finished goods. In many cases, the components were manufactured in plants located on the US side of the border; this allowed the components to be easily and quickly transported to the Mexican side for final assembly. The effect was to create twin plants a few miles apart – the US plant being used for capital-intensive/skilled-labor operations and the Mexican plant being used for labor-intensive, assembly operations.

When the finished products were shipped back into the United States, US companies were taxed only on the value added in Mexico (mostly labor costs) rather than on the total value of the goods being imported. When the Mexican government experienced a debt crisis in 1982 and the value of the Mexican peso collapsed against the dollar, cheap Mexican wages triggered a maquiladora explosion. By early 1987, there were over 630 plants employing over 178,000 people along the Mexican side of the US border. These plants, known as maquiladoras (or "in-bond" or twin plants), were all engaged in assembling components in Mexico for reexport in the United States and elsewhere and had become an important economic force along the US–Mexican border. Juarez, where TDK de Mexico's plant was located, had a big concentration of maquilas. (Some of the features of the maquiladoras program are presented in the appendix.)

Maquiladoras operated within a highly volatile political environment, one that affected every aspect of their existence. They were dependent upon the Mexican government continuing to permit raw materials and components to enter duty free and the US government simultaneously permitting finished products to return with duty paid only on the value added in Mexico. Any major change in these policies by either country could shut down most maquiladoras overnight by making assembly operations on the Mexican side of the border uneconomical. Both countries had strong political groups opposed to the maquiladora concept. Opponents labeled such operations as sweatshops and claimed that workers were being exploited by capitalistic interests.

The average age of the maquiladora workers was 24, with a relative dearth of workers over 30. Seventy percent were young women and teenage girls. Workers lived under crowded conditions – the mean household size of maquiladora workers was 7.8 persons. Their wages averaged about $0.80 per hour, barely more than half the 1987 average Mexican manufacturing wage of $1.57 an hour (including benefits). The low wages made it very attractive for mass assembly operations requiring low-skill labor to be located on the Mexican side of the US border. Managers of the maquiladoras expressed a preference for hiring "fresh or unspoiled" workers who had not acquired "bad habits" in other organizations. The work was so low-skilled that workers received very little training. The turnover rate ran 59 percent to 100 percent a year in many plants.

However, many of the large multinational companies with maquiladoras paid more than the wage minimums, and their overall compensation package was more attractive than the lowest-paying operations. Some of the multinationals also spent substantial amounts in training and employee development.

The location of twin (or maquiladora) plants along the northern border of Mexico was increasing at a phenomenal speed, and unemployed Mexicans were flocking to northern border towns to fill the rapidly expanding number of job openings. By the end of 1988, it was predicted that maquiladoras would employ 350,000 workers, one tenth of Mexico's industrial workforce, and that the plants would import $8 billion in US components, add $2 billion in value (mostly labor), and ship $10 billion in finished goods back to the United States for sale in the United States and other world markets. A number of Japanese-based companies had begun to set up maquila operations to handle the production and sale of their products in US markets – TDK de Mexico was one of these companies.

Despite concerns over the maquiladoras, the program was central to the Mexican government's economic revival plans. Mexican leaders were most enthusiastic about a new kind of maquiladora. These were plants built in the interior of Mexico that were geared to exports, like the border plants, but unlike the border operations, they undertook in-house manufacture of many of the components used in the final assembly process. These plants used more highly skilled employees and paid wages much closer to the average manufacturing wage in Mexico, and they did not rely so heavily on the use of female labor. They also depended more on Mexican companies for raw material supplies and services.

TDK's Internal Management

TDK de Mexico had 183 employees (158 women and 25 men). Inouye, before he came to TDK de Mexico, operated machines in a Taiwan plant to help gain a better understanding of workers at that level. After his move to Mexico in 1983, Inouye organized the workforce into teams consisting of workers, subleaders, and leaders. Leaders were not entrusted with the job of supervision; all supervisory responsibilities remained with individuals having a title of supervisor. It

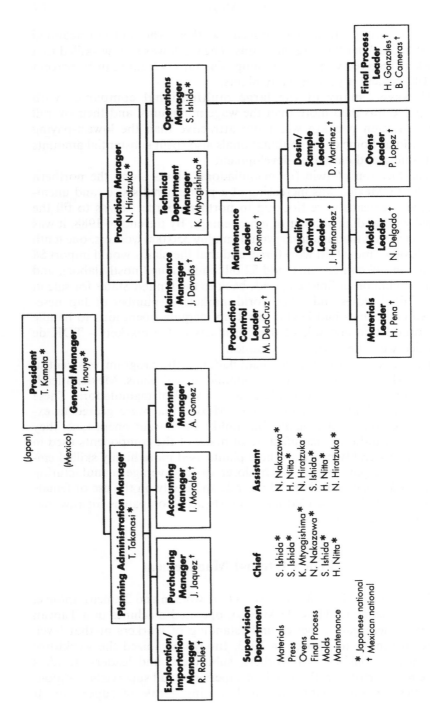

(Japan)

President
T. Kamata *

(Mexico)

General Manager
F. Inouye*

Planning Administration Manager
T. Takanasi*

Exploration/Importation Manager
R. Robles †

Purchasing Manager
J. Jaquez †

Accounting Manager
I. Morales †

Personnel Manager
A. Gomez †

Production Manager *

Operations Manager
S. Ishida*

Maintenance Manager
J. Davalos †

Technical Department Manager
K. Miyagishima*

Production Control Leader
M. DeLaCruz †

Maintenance Leader
R. Romero †

Quality Control Leader
J. Hernandez †

Desin/Sample Leader
D. Martinez †

Materials Leader
H. Pena †

Molds Leader
N. Delgado †

Ovens Leader
P. Lopez †

Final Process Leader
H. Gonzales †
B. Cameras †

Supervision Department	Chief	Assistant
Materials	S. Ishida*	N. Nakazawa*
Press	S. Ishida*	H. Nitta*
Ovens	K. Miyagishima*	N. Hiratzuka*
Final Process	N. Nakazawa*	S. Ishida*
Molds	S. Ishida*	H. Nitta*
Maintenance	H. Nitta*	N. Hiratzuka*

* Japanese national
† Mexican national

Exhibit 6.1   TDK de Mexico organization chart

took an average of two years for a worker to become a subleader. All subleaders at TDK de Mexico were Mexican; they had a median age of 28.2 years. Only three were women.

There were 11 leaders. The specifics of their job were dependent upon their department. Generally, they oversaw workers and machines in their respective departments but were given little authority and were not accountable for achieving set objectives. They were also in charge of training new workers. The leaders at TDK de Mexico had been at the company for an average of 6.4 years. The average time it took to become a leader was about three years. All of the leaders at TDK de Mexico were Mexican. Very few had ever been promoted to the supervisory level.

Five Japanese filled the 12 positions of supervisors and assistant supervisors (see exhibit 6.1). Like the leaders, their jobs varied based on the department they supervised. Primarily their duties included supervision of the leaders as well as the teams under the leaders. They determined production plans for their respective departments. Although there were Mexican nationals in higher positions, all Japanese employees, irrespective of their job titles, reported directly to Inouye. Because most of the Japanese could not speak Spanish, Inouye thought it was wise to have this direct reporting relationship. However, some of the managers of Mexican origin did not accept this line of reasoning (one manager called it "clannish behavior"); their protests to Inouye had not met with much success.

Wage Policies

TDK de Mexico paid higher wages than most other companies located in the Juarez industrial park plants. TDK de Mexico had several pay incentives available to the workers. They received a bonus after 30 days on the job. There was extra pay for overtime, night shifts, weekend work, and also generous incentives for attendance. Yet, Alfred Gomez, personnel manager for TDK de Mexico, stated, "Absenteeism and lateness are becoming problems. In some cases, when a worker decides to leave her job, she just stops coming to work without any notice. One reason for this problem is that the Juarez public health hospital gives out medical excuses to workers to miss work for the slightest illness . . . There is very little we can do about it."

Training

TDK had invested a lot of resources in training its employees; most of its training, however, had been confined to leaders and subleaders. Gomez, the head of personnel, did not go through any systematic training need analysis but professed to know "who needed training and who did not by sight." Inouye's position was, "We will spend money on training, of course, but only with those who show promise." Asked how did he see promise, he replied, "I have been working for 25 years . . . I know!" A leader who had just finished an in-house training program on motivation commented, "Whenever we face a major crisis, the six Japanese managers get together with Mr Inouye and decide what course of action to take. It seems like the only decisions I am allowed to participate in are of routine nature that are easily solved. What do I do with what I learned from the training sessions?"

Fumio Inouye's Concerns

In March 1988, Inouye met with all the managers (Mexican and Japanese) and presented the plant's most recent operating statistics (see exhibit 6.2). He was clearly unhappy with the data. A senior manager from Japanese headquarters also attended the meeting along with two other managers from TDK of America. Inouye laid out several options that could be pursued:

1. Downsize the labor force, to correct for the decline in sales and the increase in expenses.
2. Try to avoid downsizing and try to reduce operating costs by buying ferrite powder locally. Since it was not known where and how ferrite powder could be obtained from Mexican sources, Inouye suggested that immediate consideration be given to making the material locally or acquiring a native company.
3. Send some senior managers (Inouye emphasized Mexican nationals) to Japan for further training.

The Mexican managers thought the concerns expressed in the meeting were addressed specifically to them. One Mexican manager said after the meeting, "If these people would live in Mexico and not run to their comfortable homes on the other side of the border after five o'clock, maybe they would understand us a little better!"

Exhibit 6.2 Operating statistics of TDK de Mexico, 1984–87

	1984	1985	1986	1987
Total sales (US dollars)	$4,168,000	$3,774,000	$3,837,000	$3,168,000*
Employees	112	128	140	183
Sales per person	$29,000	$22,000	$20,000	$23,000
Efficiency rate	82%	81%	80%	80%
Labor turnover rate	16%	47%	46%	39%†
Selling/administrative expenses	$1,623,000	$1,529,000	$1,698,000	$1,878,000
Cost of raw materials	$1,052,000	$1,071,000	$1,099,000	$1,181,000

Shipping cost = 0.01¢ per gram or 2–10% of total costs
Price of magnets = 0.5¢ per gram
Average production for a year = 5,100,000 grams
Production figure for 1987 = 6,900,000
Plant is presently at full capacity

* Based on the then exchange rate
† Other maquilas in the park ranged from 25 to 170 percent per year

Several Mexican managers again suggested to Inouye that the Japanese managers learn the language and work closely with the workers. Inouye was sympathetic to the suggestion but questioned whether learning the language was essential. He advised them to examine "the pockets of inefficiency" and lectured them about the value of hard work.

The manager from TDK Japan left with a stern warning for imminent improvement or else. He explained to the casewriter:

"You see, I came over here in late 1983, after spending years in Singapore, Taiwan, and Hong Kong. I don't know how useful it is to have a grand strategy or any plan per se for an operation like this. . . What it boils down to is SHOOTEN (focus), SHITSU (quality), and BUNAI (distribution). . . I'm not about to give up because of cultural differences or any such nonsense. Maybe, and just maybe, I will ask these people here: 'What do you have to do to earn more money?' And if the answer is anything but work harder, I have problem!"

Inouye began to contemplate what actions he should take.

APPENDIX

The Maquiladora Program: Legal and Regulatory Requirements Imposed by the Mexican Government

Foreign investment
As a rule, a foreign company may subscribe and own only up to 49 percent of the stock in Mexican corporations with the exception of maquilas, which may be totally owned by foreigners. Except for wearing apparel, all items may be produced by in-bond assembly enterprises. Wearing apparel, due to the restriction of textile imports into the United States, is subject to a quota.

Import duties
In-bond plants are not required to pay import duties, but the product assembled or manufactured may not be sold in Mexico. Bonds are generally posted by bonding companies and are renewed yearly.

Taxes
The maximum income tax on corporate profits is 42 percent on taxable income of $500,000 or more in a fiscal year, and employees' share in profits before taxes is at the rate of 8 percent. There are other taxes such as the Social Security Tax based on salaries earned and state taxes.

Maquiladora versus joint venture
A comparison of the different rules and practices for joint ventures between Mexican and foreign companies is summarized opposite:

Concept	Maquiladora	Joint venture
Doing business in Mexico	To operate in Mexico under a maquila program, a company must be incorporated under Mexican laws (i.e., Sociedad Anonima)	To carry out industrial or commercial activities for the Mexican market, a corporation or other recognized corporate entity must be organized
Equity ownership	100% foreign ownership is allowed	The general rule is that foreigners may not hold more than 49% of the stock of a corporation doing business in the Mexican market. Exceptions to allow higher percentages of foreign ownership, up to 100%, may be authorized by the Mexican government under special circumstances
Special Operating authorizations	To operate under maquila (in-bond) status, the Ministry of Commerce (SOCOFINO) must authorize a maquila program, setting forth the products or activities the company may manufacture/assemble or carry out. Certain commitments must be made, the compliance with which shall be reviewed periodically	Unless the company intends to work within a branch of regulated industry, a joint venture company may freely operate without the need to obtain any special operating permits
Importation of equipment	All production equipment may be imported free of all duties, under bond, subject to it being exported once the company ceases to operate under its maquila program	The importation of raw materials and supplies for the production of items that are to be sold in the Mexican market requires an import permit to be obtained and normal duties to be paid thereon

Concept	Maquiladora	Joint venture
Importation of raw materials	All raw materials and supplies may be imported free of all duties under bond, subject to them being exported within an extendable six-month period, shrinkage and wastage excepted. Under special circumstances, maquiladoras may be authorized to sell up to 20% of a specific product within the Mexican market	The importation of raw materials and supplies for the production of items that are to be sold in the Mexican market requires an import permit to be obtained and normal duties to be paid thereon. In all cases, import permits are granted on an absolutely discretionary basis. Currently such permits are quite restricted. Under certain conditions, the negotiation of a manufacturing or integration program with the government may be required
Currency Exchange controls	Any operating expense, including rent, payroll, taxes, etc., must be paid in Mexican pesos that must be obtained from a Mexican bank by selling dollars thereto at the controlled rate of exchange. Fixed assets may be paid for in dollars at the free rate of exchange	There are no specific exchange controls on domestic transactions. If the company exports, it will, in general, be required to sell foreign currencies received to a Mexican bank at the controlled rate of exchange
Labor law requirements	Subject to the Federal Labor Law	Equally subject to the Federal Labor Law
Acquisition of real estate	Real estate to establish a production facility may be freely bought in the interior of the country. In the border areas or coasts, it may be acquired through a trust	Same as a maquiladora

Concept	Maquiladora	Joint venture
Leasing of real estate	Real estate may be leased under freely negotiated items, up to a maximum of 10 years	Same as a maquiladora, although the term may be longer
Immigration requirements	Foreign technical or management personnel are readily granted work visas, subject to very lenient requirements	Work visas for foreign technical or management personnel are granted on a very limited basis. Requirements for the obtainment thereof are significantly more stringent
Transfer of technology	For tax purposes it is advisable that a Technical and/or Management Assistance Agreement be executed between the maquiladora and its parent. Such agreement would need to be registered with the National Transfer of Technology Registry (NTTR), which registration would be readily obtained	If technical or management assistance is granted to a domestic company from a foreign source and royalties or fees are to be paid therefor, an agreement must be registered with the NTTR. To obtain such registration the agreement must meet certain criteria and the amounts which may be charged are limited
Taxes	A maquiladora is in principle subject to the payment of all Mexican taxes. However, since such operations are intended to be cost centers rather than profit centers, the income taxes to be paid are limited. Also, any value added tax paid by the maquiladora shall be refunded to it upon its request	A domestic company is subject to all normal taxes such as income tax and value added tax (maximum corporate income tax rate = 42%

7

IKEA: Managing Cultural Diversity

P. Grol, C. Schoch, and CPA

After firmly attaining leadership within Sweden, where it holds more than 20 percent of the overall market, IKEA has succeeded over the last 25 years in doing what no furniture distributor has ever attempted: to become a global player in an industry formerly considered by nature to be local.

Today IKEA delivers low-priced quality furniture to key markets throughout the world. It is the only distributor in its field to have successfully established itself in all parts of Europe, including southern and eastern Europe, and more notably in North America, including the USA. It has stores today in the Middle East, Singapore, and Hong Kong and is preparing to enter the Chinese market some time in the early part of the next century. Recently Ingvar Kamprad, the company's founder, secured his position in Europe with the acquisition of British-based Habitat, IKEA'S chief rival in the UK and France.

To provide some idea of its worldwide presence, IKEA receives annually over 120 million visitors in its 125 stores, and distributes 35 million catalogs. Its sales revenues increased steadily over the last 10 years by an average of 12 percent annually, in spite of the flattening out of its business in Western Europe which still represents nearly 80 percent of its annual volume (see exhibit 7.1).

Ingvar Kamprad's stubborn insistence that people would buy more furniture if the price was low enough and the furniture was of decent quality, with no delays in delivery has gradually revolutionized the conservative national furniture markets in Europe and beyond.

Kamprad intuitively anticipated the rise of consumerism in the 1950s
and 1960s, and virtually invented the practices of cash and carry, self-
service, and volume buying in Europe.

IKEA was to invent many other concepts and new ways of dealing
with logistics, sourcing, and retailing. Many of these innovations have
become industry standards: knock-down furniture that can be stored
and shipped in flat boxes, the involvement of customers in the
value-adding process of handling the transportation and doing
home-assembly themselves; and turning shopping into a family event
by creating attractive open store environments that contain IKEA
trademarks like the children's areas with brightly colored plastic balls
and the buffet style restaurants where you can eat Swedish meatballs.

IKEA has affected the way furniture is sold and distributed in
every country where it is doing business, inspiring imitation and drawing
respect, sometimes begrudgingly, from traditional furniture dealers.

One aspect of IKEA'S success has been the development of unique
product design capabilities, based on an almost religious dedication
to the simple yet graceful design of contemporary Swedish furniture.
In so doing, it has introduced millions of households around the world
to the Swedish style that it, more than others, has come to typify.

IKEA's strength today comes from its mastery of three key aspects
of the value chain: unique design capabilities, unique sourcing, and
tightly controlled logistics. This means the company is able to produce products that are distinctive enough to provide market recognition, secure sourcing for long runs at profitable levels, and reduce
inventory costs through regional warehouses which work very closely
with stores. In this way it has been able to buck industry trends and
steadily increase its share of slow growth, sometimes shrinking, markets.

IKEA has become a household name as much in Warsaw as in Los
Angeles, attracting customers who just want to come to a store, look
around, and have some fun. Something universally irresistible about
IKEA makes it very difficult for people to come away from one of its
stores without making a purchase and instills unprecedented loyalty
among its customers and employees.

IKEA'S successful development, particular organizational capaci-
ties, and the bold and inspired leadership of its entrepreneur-founder
have all been largely written up and commented. Its organization,
communication, marketing, product range, and store layouts, all tell
the same story – the story of the "IKEA Way." A way strongly rooted
in the personality of founder Ingvar Kamprad and the Swedish (regional) culture that he grew up in.

The "IKEA Way": Doing Things Differently

What is it that makes IKEA so different? Is it just a matter of "quality goods at affordable prices"? Or is there a deeper explanation? When asked these questions, IKEA managers and personnel become mystical and somewhat vague. "It is really a winning combination of price and a merry feeling, a feeling of delight," a Dutch marketing manager answers. This feeling and a conscious awareness that, in addition to the competitive advantage, there is something strong and intangible at IKEA that drives and motivates its success, is shared by Ikeans throughout the organization. Could it be that the "IKEA Way's" combination of vision, charismatic leadership, sound business principles is subtly reinforced by the influence of Swedish culture? Could it be that Swedish, or Scandinavian, culture contains elements that facilitate international expansion?

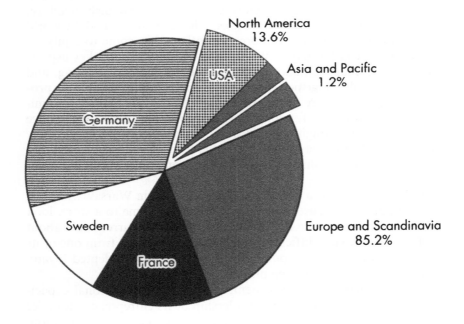

Number of active articles: 11,400
Number of suppliers: 2,353 in 65 countries
Number of distribution centres: 14

Exhibit 7.1 IKEA's sales by region, 1995–1996

Can a company's national culture in this case be a competitive advantage? Throughout our investigation of IKEA we have kept these questions in the back of our minds, and we invite you to consider them as we explore the "IKEA Way" more closely.

How It All Started

IKEA's name is derived from the initials of the company's founder, architect, and driving force' Ingvar Kamprad, those of the farm where he was raised, Elmtaryd, and those of his native village Agunnaryd, located in Smaland, a poor farming region in the south-east of Sweden. Coming from a modest background, Kamprad began as a trader in everything from matches to Christmas cards. He got into the furniture business almost accidentally after buying out a furniture plant which had to close down in the early 1950s. He demonstrated from the very beginning a combination of strong salesmanship, practical business acumen, thrift, an identity with ordinary people, and an unconventional perseverance in the face of adversity. Always modest he was nonetheless a true entrepreneur, and, more significantly, a non-conformist who was not the least bit restrained by the conventions and traditions of the contemporary Swedish furniture trade.

His habit of staying close to his customers and his reluctance to own manufacturing furniture plants gave him the freedom to focus and innovate on all the facets of distribution. With nearby furniture producers he co-designed furniture to meet very specific requirements for quality products that average customers could afford, and then printed them up in catalogues, which he had discovered as an economical and effective way of marketing to a growing customer base in his early days as a trader.

In 1953 he opened his first showroom at the furniture plant he had bought earlier in Almhult which has become the heart of his furniture empire. The only transportation link to the factory was by road but, at a time when more and more working class Swedes were purchasing their first automobiles, what was originally a problem would become a solution.

Kamprad was obsessed with low prices and the only way to offer them was to keep costs as low as possible – this conviction became a driving force of his business development. He would constantly seek new ways to lower prices. For example, he bought fabrics for his furniture directly from textile mills, placing large orders and then supplying the material himself to his network of small furniture manufacturers. In this way at the same time he was able to cut costs a bit more, and ensure that his customers would have a wider selection of upholstery to choose from in the catalogue. Unwittingly he had introduced the notion of vertical integration, which provided IKEA even then with a strong competitive advantage compared to traditional distributors who only displayed and sold furniture.

Such practices enabled him to maintain close contact with his suppliers, and eventually to learn intimately the parameters of furniture production. The relationship between Kamprad and his suppliers was so good that to obtain their commitment he needed only to draw rough sketches of the furniture he wanted and discuss with them how to adapt production to their capabilities. In so doing, he established over the years another cornerstone of his business philosophy: marrying the customers' need for low prices with the suppliers need for profit through efficiency and long production runs. This was a strong departure from the kind of relationship that distributors traditionally maintained with their suppliers, buying furniture as it was ordered piece by piece at high paces with long waiting periods for delivery.

Balancing customers' requirements and producers' needs, which enabled him to sell furniture at prices 30 to 50 percent below traditional distributors, is now the foundation of the "IKEA Way." This notion is so basic and imperative that a store manager in Germany told me, when walking through the accessories department where some Chinese gadgets were displayed, that this balancing of optimal product design with the supplier with the needs of the customer is the "Yin and Yang" of the IKEA strategy. It was already present in the way Ingval Kamprad developed his business through the 1950s when his innovative ways provoked stubborn counterattacks from his more established Swedish competitors.

A legendary showdown took place at the Sankt Erik's Fair in Stockholm where, for the first time, IKEA introduced its products. Feeling threatened by Kamprad's unexpected success and many new customers, the Swedish furniture cartel tried to block IKEA's entry at the fair. They failed, but soon thereafter managed a successful boycott of IKEA by Swedish furniture manufacturers, accusing Kamprad of unfair practices. Undaunted by this seemingly insurmountable obstacle, Kamprad looked for and found-new suppliers in Poland at the height of the Cold War.

Although Polish manufacturers were willing to sell at prices well below their counterparts in Sweden, the cost of transportation-offset this advantage. This new obstacle was at the origin of yet another IKEA invention, as Kamprad discovered that by "knocking down" furniture into disassembled parts it could be packed and shipped in flat cardboard cartons, reducing by more than 80 percent the cost of transportation. To further save on costs, the furniture could be sold directly to customers in these same flat boxes. To help customers participate in the distribution cycle, IKEA offered to rent roof racks and invented the simple assembly tool which has become another of its trademarks.

To reach the largest possible market and benefit fully from volume sales, in 1964 IKEA opened Europe's first large "warehouse scale" store in Stockholm. Unexpectedly large crowds of people attended the grand opening causing yet another problem. Seemingly endless queues formed at the checkout stands as employees scurried to the storage areas to fetch the purchased furniture. Instead of hiring more employees, Kamprad simply opened the storage area to customers and invited them to fetch the furniture themselves. Such practices were unheard of then, but understanding that this would lead to lower prices, customers willingly complied. In just a few years IKEA had invented the concept of "prosumers," whereby customers actively participate in the distribution cycle.

Suddenly the whole system was in place: customers were able to purchase attractive quality furniture at low prices; furniture suppliers benefitted from long production runs, and IKEA, through volume sales, was able to make a considerable profit from small margins.

IKEA's business strategy did not evolve from "strategic planning," which is still scorned today in the company as "too sophisticated." It evolved from creative responses to difficult problems, turning them into solutions pragmatically and often with considerable risk. Not going by the book, or adopting conventional solutions, and learning by doing appears to be a distinguishing trait of Ingvar Kamprad's and IKEA's intuitive way of doing business.

The IKEA Mission

As IKEA grew, Ingvar Kamprad found ways to explain his unique way of doing business, always using simple language and metaphors. He has consistently maintained that IKEA's mission is *to offer "a wide range of home furnishing items of good design and function, at prices so low that the majority of people can afford to buy them."* This statement is at the heart of the IKEA's philosophy and has shaped all of the phases of its business, particularly product range. The concept is protected through numerous guidelines and special legal entities. Changes in the criteria for product range can only be made by joint decisions of INGKA Holding BV and Inter IKEA Systems BV, both of which are outside the sphere of management.

The essential guidelines appear in a 1976 publication, *Testament of a Furniture Dealer*, in which Kamprad emphasizes the company's ambition to cover the furnishing and decorative needs of the total home area with a distinctive style that reflects "our thoughts and is as simple and straightforward as ourselves." The guidelines also express such modern ideals as furniture that is durable and easy to live with, reflects a natural and free life style, and appeals to youthfulness with color and joy. Most of IKEA's products are designed by Swedes in Almhult, who consciously reproduce designs that reflect these values – values which are very consistent with Swedish culture. At the same time there is something in that specific design which has universal appeal throughout the markets of the world.

Business Principles

IKEA has developed unique competencies and an ability to deliver products which are distinctly Swedish, attractively presented in warm value-adding environments, and at prices consistently lower than its competitors.

What has made IKEA so different from other distributors is the balanced focus it has maintained on product range, sourcing, vertical integration, mass marketing, cost leadership, and a distinctive image. As such, the company is not market driven, and tends to react rather slowly to new consumer trends, studying them to see how they can be fitted into its operating systems and what value IKEA can add within its proven framework before adopting them into the company's range. The issue of range is vital for IKEA as, when it introduces new products, it must insure that the volumes it produces are leveraged from within: sourcing–logistics–store layouts.

The Yin/Yang metaphor, mentioned earlier, illustrates the imperative balance of strategic sourcing and marketing mix.

The balance and complementariness of:

Strategic Sourcing   and   the Marketing Mix

In the area of strategic sourcing, IKEA has established a long-standing competitive advantage. The durable partnerships that it has developed with furniture producers and other suppliers is based on the producers' capacity to provide long runs of parts, and their willingness to comply with IKEA's quality standards, and IKEA's guaranteed purchase of all parts produced. IKEA considers its producers as key stakeholders and provides them with technical assistance to increase their productivity, sometimes underwriting investments in new technology. Together they actively contribute to both cost reduction and quality enhancement, which in turn optimizes the marketing mix.

Through such partnerships IKEA has virtually integrated production into its value-added chain without the heavy investments of actually owning and running its own furniture plants.

Management Style and Practices

IKEA's management style is described by non-Swedish members as informal, open, and caring. Hierarchy is not emphasized and in a typical store there are only three levels of responsibility between the store manager and co-workers (which is what employees are called).

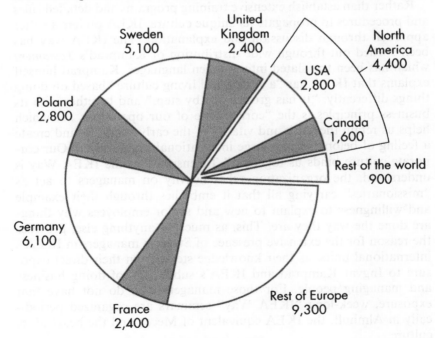

Exhibit 7.2 Distribution of IKEA's co-workers

A pragmatic approach to problem solving and consensus-based decision making are also strongly imbedded in IKEA management practice.

Co-workers at all levels are encouraged to take initiatives, and making mistakes is considered a necessary part of "learning by doing." Managers are expected not only to share information with co-workers but also their knowledge and skills. IKEA wants its co-workers to feel important: they can express their ideas, and should feel responsible for improving the way things are done.

An entrepreneurial zeal for getting the job done in the most direct way and a distaste for bureaucratic procedures are basic managerial attitudes that have long been promoted within IKEA. Managers are expected to be close to their co- workers, with few if any status barriers, and not to take themselves seriously. This egalitarian approach to management has also made it easy for motivated employees to work their way up the organization with little formal training. It is significant that Swedish managers' titles do not appear on their business cards, and that company cars are the same economy models for all of those who need them for work or business regardless of their position.

Rather than establish extensive training programs and detailed rules and procedures to propagate its unique culture, IKEA prefers a softer approach through discussion and explanation. The IKEA way has been spelled out through wide distribution of Kamprad's *Testament* which has been translated into a dozen languages. Kamprad himself explains that IKEA has "a strong and living culture" based on doing things differently. "It has grown step by step," and together with its business principles is the "cornerstone of our operations . . . which helps us retain the spirit and vitality of the early years . . . and create a feeling of belonging in a large international organization. Our corporate culture binds us together." To ensure that the IKEA Way is understood, the organization relies heavily on managers to act as "missionaries" carrying all that it embodies through their example and willingness to explain to new and senior employees why things are done the way they are. This, as much as anything else, provides the reason for the extensive presence of Swedish managers in IKEA's international units, as their knowledge stems from their direct exposure to Ingvar Kamprad and IKEA's subtle way of doing business and managing people. For those managers who do not have that exposure, week-long "IKEA Way" seminars are organized periodically in Almhult, the IKEA equivalent of Mecca and the heart of its culture.

IKEA's Strategy of International Expansion: Flexibility Within Established Parameters

Patterns of International Expansion

IKEA's international expansion has taken place progressively over the last 25 years, with a focus on markets in countries with growth potential (see exhibit 7.3). Expansion outside of Scandinavia was driven by Ingvar Kamprad's intuitive quest for new opportunities, and his previous successful search for suppliers outside of Sweden more than by any formal development strategy. Some insights are provided by one of IKEA's Swedish executives, an early companion of Ingvar Kamprad. "When we opened our first store outside Scandinavia, in Switzerland, people asked why there? It was a difficult market. Ingvar said that if we could succeed there, we should succeed anywhere. He had intuitions, he spoke to people on the streets to learn what they were looking for." Such an empirical experiential approach goes against the orthodox rules of international retailing, which preach extensive market studies before entering a new market, catering to local tastes, and gaining expertise through acquisitions and joint ventures.

When IKEA expanded into Germany, competition was strong and German distributors didn't take them seriously. "They called us 'those crazy Swedes,' but we didn't mind; we even used this label in our advertising. It took them five years to really react, but by then we had eight stores and were setting the standards."

Charting its own course, IKEA has developed internationally by

Exhibit 7.3 The IKEA expansion

	No. of outlets	No. of countries	No. of co-workers	Turnover (NLG)[d]
1954	1	1	15	2,200,000
1964	2	2	250	55,500,000
1974	10	5	1,500	372,900,000
1984	66	17	8,300	2,678,700,000
1994	120 (125[a])	25 (26[a])	26,600[b]	8,350,000,000
1996	129 (136[a])	27 (28[a])	33,400[b]	9,626,000,000[c]

[a] Including stores opening after September 1, 1996.

[b] 20% of co-workers are part time.

[c] Corresponding to net sales of the IKEA Group of companies.

[d] The holding company is in the Netherlands which explains the use of NLG.

finding cheap land for stores, checking sourcing possibilities and proximity to central warehouses, or lowering marketing costs. When, in
the late 1970s, the company decided to go into Belgium because it was
cost effective to serve that country from its central warehouse in Germany, it ran into problems with building permits and so decided to
develop in France instead. The preference has been for leveraging
market costs by concentrating several stores in the same area. This
explains why IKEA opened four stores in the Philadelphia/Washing-
ton DC/New Jersey area, sometimes in locations that were rather
isolated. Similarly, the company also preferred to concentrate four
stores in the Paris area, even if this could dilute individual store sales
and create potential competition between stores.

Typically development has been done on a store-by-store basis.
IKEA opens a beachhead in a given country with a group of trusted
and experienced Swedish "Missionaries." Together they form a
tight-knit group which can solve problems and make decisions quickly.
They supervise the building work, lead operational teams who open
the store, and run the store until local management has learned how
the system works. After a short time, store management is turned
over to local managers, while most of the key national positions remain in the hands of Swedes until the operation and market have
reached maturity.

Adapting to National Markets

Adapting to new markets in western Europe throughout the 1970s
and early 1980s was fairly simple. Catalog offerings were virtually the
same. However, concessions had to be made, particularly in bedroom
furnishings since bedding could be substantially different from country to country.

"When we entered a new country we did things our way. The idea
was to be IKEA everywhere: after all, our furniture is a cultural
statement. But as the years went by we learned to be more flexible,
particularly when demand in Sweden declined and we became more
dependent on our non-Scandinavian markets," recalls one IKEA
manager.

Adapting to the US market was a real learning experience for IKEA,
since many standards were different. Few product managers from
IKEA of Sweden had traveled to North America because the price of
air travel was prohibitive in terms of IKEA's cost-conscious policies.
They expected their European range to sell just as easily in the US,
but this did not turn out to be the case. As a former US country
manager explains: "IKEA ran into problems in the US so we had to

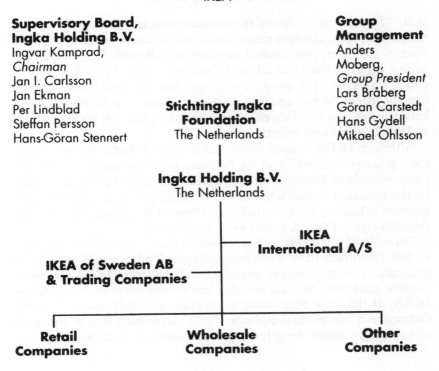

Supervisory Board, Ingka Holding B.V.
Ingvar Kamprad,
Chairman
Jan I. Carlsson
Jan Ekman
Per Lindblad
Steffan Persson
Hans-Göran Stennert

Stichtingy Ingka Foundation
The Netherlands

Group Management
Anders Moberg,
Group President
Lars Bråberg
Göran Carstedt
Hans Gydell
Mikael Ohlsson

Ingka Holding B.V.
The Netherlands

IKEA International A/S

IKEA of Sweden AB & Trading Companies

Retail Companies

Wholesale Companies

Other Companies

Exhibit 7.4 The organization of the IKEA Group

ask ourselves what we could offer to Americans. Should we become an American company, or merely adapt our merchandising to American customers? We finally decided on a solution: merchandising to the American customer by speaking English with a Swedish accent; capitalizing on our strengths as an outsider."

Development of the range is now closely monitored by IKEA of Sweden (IOS) and the board of directors of INGKA Holding. The issue of range is vital for them as, when they introduce new products they must insure that the volumes they produce are balanced from within (sourcing–logistics–store layouts). It took IKEA of Sweden several years to introduce "futons" in "Europe, and American store managers had to work hard to convince the company that a "Home Entertainment" line was feasible in North America.

As a former French country manager described, obtaining concessions from product managers to take into account specific national preferences was a consensual process that required many negotiation skills. "Some room is allowed for national considerations in our catalog range. But, since changes mean that it will be more expensive for the country manager, only limited numbers are allowed. Still, 90 percent of our range is the same all over the world: only 5 to 10 percent is country specific. The product manager has the final word, but he usually listens to the country manager. There is a healthy tension between the two and this enables us to adapt but not to over-adapt and weaken our cost effectiveness."

Although IKEA's stated mission is to provide home furnishing for the "greatest number" and its business is conducted on a volume basis, outside of Scandinavia it is in reality a niche player, appealing to the educated population with mid- to upper level incomes. This segment is looking for non-traditional lines of furniture, and finds the Swedish style of IKEA suited to its modern taste.

"In spite of our image as the 'common man's stored,' the majority of our customers have a university degree," admits a French store manager. This may appear paradoxical considering IKEA's avowed mission statement, but the paradox has proven successful as it keeps IKEA, at the same time, close to its roots and still makes it highly distinctive in foreign marketplaces. It also plays neatly into its strengths of sourcing, volume, long runs, and cost-efficient distribution.

Human Resource Management

Management of international operations has largely followed the IKEA Way and its strong Swedish flavor. The belief of those in IKEA is that their way of managing people has universal appeal. "People like to participate in making decisions. They like to feel respected, and that they can take responsibility," one Swedish expatriate states.

When recruiting, IKEA looks for people who have good communication skills, open minds, positive work attitudes, and good potential without necessarily having diplomas. It attracts people with its pleasant working environment, job security, and the caring attitude it shows towards the individual. IKEA employees, regardless of nationality, are more than likely to have strong preferences for cooperative informal relations, with a high degree of independence, and have tolerant approach to others. "We look for people who know how to listen, and who are able to transmit their knowledge to others. They should not feel they are better than others and be curious about what is going on around them."

Being an IKEA manager overseas isn't solely about running the stores and distribution systems smoothly. He or she must be able to explain to employees and managers why things are done in the way they are and win people's hearts and minds to the "IKEA Way." They are expected to be ambassadors and must educate their non-Swedish co-workers through patience, common understanding, and example. It is not always easy to transmit IKEA's egalitarian management style. While it goes down easily in the Netherlands, it is less acceptable in Germany or France, and for different reasons. In the United States, long-term employees generally feel more comfortable with Scandinavian managers than with Americans – younger American managers don't seem to know how to show "equalness."

The challenge IKEA may be facing is that, with its extended international network, it is becoming more difficult to find enough Swedish IKEA managers who are willing to work overseas for long periods. IKEA has had to hire Swedes from outside the company. Also in the past the company has not systematically searched out and developed at an early stage its international "high potentials," although it does send its most loyal and successful foreign managers to week-long seminars in Sweden and encourage its co-workers to learn something about the culture.

It is still very difficult for non-Scandinavians to work their way up the corporate ladder. To do so they need to have learned all of IKEA's key trades: retailing, logistics, product design, and purchasing. Non-Swedes can work their way up in retailing through the national organizations and sometimes in the logistical organizations which are run regionally, but very few have gone into product management because this function is part of IKEA of Sweden in Almhult, where IKEA's product managers and furniture schools are located. It is a very remote area and only Swedish is spoken. So, speaking the language as well and knowing the culture become pre-requisites that very few managers from foreign branches have been able to fulfill.

There are no formal career paths, as a long-term Swedish expatriate executive admits. "To get ahead in IKEA you first have to know the range intimately, then you have to know and use the informal internal network, and then you have to understand the subtleties of the 'IKEA Way,' its cultural roots. It is really difficult for outsiders to know their way around. In reality it is a difficult company to understand. Humbleness is not a sign of weakness. It comes from Ingvar. People are expected to learn from their experience, and this takes time and patience. You can't be in a hurry to move up the ladder."

Dealing with the Europeans

Germany

Germany is the largest national organization in the IKEA group, accounting for ±30 percent of the total group sales through more than 20 stores, including the newly opened stores in former East Germany.

Although IKEA has been established in Germany for more than two decades (its first store was opened in Munich in 1974), Swedish management is still perceived by German IKEA members as peculiar. As described by Thomas Larson, the store manager in Cologne: "Some senior co-workers still have problems addressing me by my first name, or using the German *du* (the informal equivalent for you, like *tu* in French). "*Dutzen*," using the informal you, is often felt as undermining the respect and prestige of the boss. As Heike Oestreich, the personnel manager said: "There are two different *du*'s, the IKEA *du* and the *du* which is used between friends."

The Germans are very disciplined and precise. They do exactly what the boss asks them to do and what is agreed or put down in writing. A problem is that the Swedish notion of "taking on responsibilities for yourself," the cornerstone of their work policy, is not perceived in the same way by the Germans, who have a tendency to adhere very closely to precisely defined rules and instructions. When IKEA translated the corporate brochure *The IKEA Way* into German, a need was felt to sharpen and make more explicit the original Swedish text which presented key IKEA concepts in sometimes vague terms in order to give freedom to people to adapt them and take personal responsibility for carrying them out. Once, Anders Moberg, Kamprad's successor, suggested in a letter that certain merchandising displays could be used in a variety of places. In Germany, department managers interpreted this as an order, and systematically set up the displays in every part of their stores.

In general, German employees feel that the Swedes are more result-oriented and treat every problem as a challenge that should be met. However, they believe that Swedish management does not sufficiently assess risks before taking action. According to Heike Oestreich: "The Swedes, to reduce bureaucracy, would like to dump all our office desks in the back yard." The lack of formality is also dismaying to Germans. To implement a decision "some notes on the back of a cigarette packet are often sufficient" for the Swedes. In contrast, Germans are more comfortable adhering to formal procedures: "We need procedures and forms. Germans love administration because it provides us with security."

France

Development in France, which has fewer than half the number of stores in Germany, was always considered problematic because of the numerous administrative regulations on the retail trade, and a hostile attitude towards discounters that prevailed in the late 1970s and early 1980s. By carefully avoiding too much public attention and with only a limited number of store openings IKEA managed to secure a safe place for itself in the market and develop an 8 percent share.

The main challenge for IKEA management in France is the French tendency to judge informality as a sign of weakness, or indecisiveness. French people are accustomed to formal rules and strong hierarchy. In the words of a former Swedish country manager, when IKEA first started in France: "Some French managers felt that the Swedish informality meant they could do whatever they wanted. When we told them that they should inform their subordinates they did not take us seriously." Some aspects of the informality can even be irritating to the French, such as the lack of formal job descriptions and written procedures. Whereas Swedish managers will justify this by saying that they don't like to limit responsibility, and that they get more out of people with an informal approach, the French tend to be suspicious of informality for the same reasons.

In the view of IKEA's French human resource manager: "Working here isn't for everyone. It is particularly difficult for people over 35 because IKEA is different from all other workplaces in France. When you join IKEA, you enter another world – we do not behave like a normal French company. Status is not recognized, which can cause an identity problem: everyone is put on the same level – no one stands out, and you can get lost in the crowd. It is hard to explain what IKEA is, everyone will give a different answer. One shouldn't freeze the system, it is flexible, and it should stay that way."

Two of the main reasons given for IKEA's appeal to French candidates are :

1. The esthetics of the stores – they look nice and are pleasant to work in.
2. The intelligent way in which IKEA works – it makes sense.

To make things clearer to employees, a formal communication platform has been developed in France to spell things out in facts and figures by comparing IKEA's benefits with those of competitors. Also, more formal training programs are being developed because in France "learning by doing" is not perceived as a credible way of developing competency. Typically, a boss would not be trusted to develop one's skills in France, and more faith is placed in "off-site programs." In France tolerance has its limits and when IKEA hired "too many" people of non-French origin, the company received complaints from customers, so now it makes a point of keeping non-French workers to a minimum.

Some years ago, relations with unions were hostile. There was a bitter strike and widespread discontent. French labor unions did not trust or understand IKEA's Swedish management style, with its tendency to seek consensus. More recently, IKEA's management has taken a more affirmative attitude, and relations have improved notably. They may continue to improve now that IKEA France is run by a Frenchman, Jean Louis Baillot, whose wife is Swedish and who has worked in Almhult.

Doing Things Differently in The United States

Expanding into the US market was certainly the boldest developmental decision that IKEA had made up to that time. From an historical perspective the venture seemed unlikely to succeed. First, the culturally specific requirements for home furnishing in the United States are considerably different than the European markets, particularly in terms of the size and functions of furniture. Second, the American market had come to be known as the "graveyard" of European retailers with a long list of unfortunate ventures by such successful firms as Casino, Carrefour, and Marks & Spencer. But, somehow, IKEA seemed confident that going about it in their own way would prove an exception to the laws of failure that seemed to doom European entrants to the US market.

Initially, development in the US was quite consistent with IKEA's pattern in Europe: identify prime markets with volume potential; purchase cheap land on the periphery of big cities; use mass advertising with a unique message emphasizing IKEA's Swedishness; focus on range and price through the catalogue, establishing a beachhead from which to launch and develop the organization. Also, its approach was empirical and pragmatic. It did not set out to take the US by storm, but merely to test its existing formula and learn through experience how success could be achieved. In fact, from the mid-1970s to the early 1980s IKEA opened a series of franchised stores in Canada, developing during this time its logistics capabilities and demonstrating that its European range could sell in America's back yard, before it finally entered the US market in 1985.

Its first stage of development in the US began on the East Coast with the opening of Plymouth Meeting in Philadelphia's northwest suburbs, followed by a cluster of four other stores. "Development was initially based on the potato field approach. Find some place where there is cheap land, build, and the people will follow." This approach ignored the rule of American retailing based on fine-tuned segmentation and targeting. The choice of locations, driven by cost-consciousness, led IKEA to establish its stores in shopping centers that had no prestige "anchor stores" to draw the high-income customers that IKEA appeals to. This should have been a relative disadvantage, since competitors like Home Depot locate their stores in prime centers with "anchor stores" like Nordstroms and Macy's. But by maintaining the profile of a "different kind of store," very Swedish, with a wide range of products, it apparently has overcome this obstacle. Here, the catalogue has served them well, as people can plan their purchases before they come and thus optimize their time investment.

Up until the late 1980s IKEA enjoyed a honeymoon of sorts. The American public was attracted by the novelty of Scandinavian style, and IKEA's unique merchandising, which resembles in many ways a European village marketplace. Its advertising was a success. People drove six to eight hours to come to the stores and they initially came in large numbers. Riding on a high dollar, IKEA had appeared to have gotten off to as fast a start as they had in Germany and other European markets. The honeymoon ended suddenly when the dollar went down, revealing multiple weaknesses.

First and foremost, even though Americans were initially attracted by IKEA's advertising and novelty, the company's range of furniture was unsuited to American standards and sold poorly. One often told anecdote illustrates just how far from those standards they really were: customers would purchase flower vases thinking they were American-size drinking glasses. Americans furnish their master bedrooms with king size beds, whereas IKEA's largest beds were five inches narrower. Also, Americans are harder on sitting room furniture, and IKEA's sofa and armchair offerings proved too lightly designed. Additionally, IKEA did not offer furniture suitable for the "home entertainment centers" that blossomed throughout the 1980s and into the 1990s in American households with the proliferation of widescreen televisions, VCRs, and hi-fi equipment. With declining sales revenues and shrinking profits, by 1989 the "graveyard effect" seemed to have caught up with IKEA.

A courageous decision was then made by Anders Moberg, and a new management team was brought in to head the US organization. Faced with the alternatives of holding on and waiting for better times, withdrawing humbly, or fighting back, the latter course of action was chosen. In 1990, the American retail management group, under the leadership of Göran Carstedt, recently hired from the Volvo, convinced the product managers at IKEA of Sweden that the IKEA European range had to be adapted and American-based sourcing stepped up. At the same time, he reassured them that IKEA would not prostitute itself. In the words of Carsted: "The IKEA strategy in North America will still be blue and yellow, but we will put more stars and stripes and more maple leaves in it."

It was not easy but they succeeded in changing the design of many household products. To make the point, one US manager brought a plastic American-size turkey with him to Almhult and before a surprised group of product managers placed it on one of the best-selling dining tables in the European range. Given the size of the bird there was only room for two table settings instead of the normal six. He had made his point.

However there was a condition attached to adapting the range, and that condition was volume. Lines of furniture specifically designed for the American market would have to be produced in long enough runs to meet IKEA's commitment to suppliers and be priced at the lowest levels possible.

A combination of luck and bold counterattacking led to an unexpected expansion on the West Coast that was to ease pressure on its pricing and provide much needed growth in its retail business. An imitator, "Stor," inspired by IKEA'S success, had illicitly acquired intimate knowledge of IKEA's floor plan and merchandising schemes and successfully opened four stores primarily around Los Angeles, far from IKEA's base on the East Coast. Responding as much to the threat to the company's image as to the opportunity to capitalize on Stor's advertising of Swedish style furniture, IKEA decided to counter attack. It opened a store in Los Angeles and eventually, through its price and sourcing advantage, drove Stor to the brink of bankruptcy. It then bought out its imitator at a bargain price and established a solid base in a prime market on the West Coast. If IKEA's low-profile stance stressed its humble origins and culture, it definitely did not mean that the company was a weakling. IKEA showed that it could be tough and decisive in that toughest of tough markets. The current US country manager, Jan Kjellman, in comparing the US market to his previous European experience used the following words: "The biggest difference is competition. Competitors are everywhere, and they are strong. The market is crowded, but still there always seem to be new competitors. Even with a million and a half customers, we are small. It is a total struggle for us, and it is tough to survive." Could IKEA adapt to such competition and still remain faithful to the "IKEA Way"?

Swedish managers are impressed with the professionalism of American salesmanship. "Over here, retailing is a profession. Sales persons are subjected to a lot of pressure for short-term results because large retailers are publicly owned and shareholders measure quarterly results. So they are very time-efficient and masters of the hard sell," relates Kjellman. IKEA has always maintained a soft approach, believing that people know what they want, so that sales personnel are there to help them find it. Moreover, the strategy is that most of the selling is done by the catalogue so that people arrive with specific purchases in mind. Impulse buying takes place for smaller items like candle holders, or accessories which are sought for as bargains. On this point IKEA has stood firm, and sales personnel from competitors such as Macy's or Bloomingdale have to unlearn the hard sell approach.

American's are always looking for convenience, which means more space, more information, anything that reduces effort and saves time. To respond to these demands, IKEA had to redesign its store layouts, providing more directions, and short cuts for people who don't want to just wander through the store. "Customers were screaming 'let us out' before we remodeled our layout," reported one store manager. "They couldn't find their way out of our maze of displays, there were no windows or signs, they felt lost and panicky." While making these adjustments in store layout, which have been criticized by IKEA International headquarters, IKEA has maintained its policy of minimal service. Customers who want home delivery or someone to assemble their furniture must pay the full add-on cost. In fact, IKEA stores carefully outsource these services to local providers and they never promote such services in their advertising. Instead, they encourage their customers to do it the "IKEA Way," which means renting a roof rack and assembling it yourself.

Adapting IKEA's floor plans and furniture to American dimensions paid off, and sales increased by 25 to 30 percent in comparison with the late 1980s. By 1994 IKEA had turned around the situation in the US. Through its acquisition of Stor and by adapting its range to US requirements, sales have increased steadily by about 10 percent annually, providing IKEA with the volume base necessary to sustain long production run and to keep prices low. Whereas at first only 15 percent of the furniture in American stores was produced locally, the figure is now about 50 percent.

In the view of several IKEA senior US managers, the key to this successful turn around was the granting of more autonomy to the American country management than their European counterparts had enjoyed. "You can't steer America from Europe," admitted Anders

Moberg in 1994. "When we went in we hadn't planned a clear strat-egy of how to supply the American market at a low cost." Learning how to succeed in the United States through its own painful expense took more than five years. Although its US operation showed a profit over the subsequent three years, it still has not recovered its initial investment. With flat growth in Europe, and heavy investment in longer term expansion into eastern Europe and China putting pres-sure on IKEA's capital reserves, the focus in the US is now on devel-oping sales and profit from its existing stores before expanding into new regions. Following its bold actions in the early 1990s, IKEA has entered a more conservative phase of consolidation. Perhaps it has also learned that the price of being different means that you also have to be more careful about where you invest.

Unresolved Issues: Management and Human Resource Development

From an American perspective, Swedish managers don't show emo-tion in the workplace. "Praise is given for looking calm in all situa-tions. They do not feel comfortable in conflictual situations. Also, they tend not to set themselves apart, and self-promotion is frowned upon. They don't like drum beating or cheerleading in a culture where both are common ways of motivating workers."

"The biggest conflicts here stem from the Americans who need to know who's in charge. People expect their managers to tell them what to do here." However, at IKEA the manager's role is more subtle and they tend to have a long-term approach to management. "It takes longer to do things our way but we want to train people to know how to do things the right way." Since there are few written procedures, the golden rule for managers is to help people understand why things are done in a particular way. This can be viewed as indecision by American employees new to IKEA who are more used to rules and procedures spelled out clearly and managers who take responsibility for quick decision making.

American employees perceive IKEA as being more employee-ori-ented than average American employers. IKEA attracts and selects people who value security, job enrichment, and benefits which are more generous than typical American employers (like five weeks of paid holiday) more than career advancement. However, with full em-ployment in the US it is becoming more difficult to find candidates, particularly for management positions, who have the necessary job qualifications and whose values match IKEA's.

Although IKEA has recently initiated an American style performance review procedure, which requires documenting employees' individual performance strengths and weaknesses, Swedish managers feel uncomfortable with the formality of the system and the need to provide negative feedback. Since they hold the more senior positions, their ambivalence has resulted in little real discrimination in pay increases which are directly linked to the reviews. Although turnover at IKEA is lower than the industry average, and co-workers generally appreciate IKEA'S caring environment, there is some latent discontent with the way pay increases are distributed, even among long-term employees who feel that their individual achievements are not always rewarded.

In the opinion of one American manager, "A lot of people have left IKEA because they can't move up fast enough here. Some left the store to go to the Service Center (IKEA's national headquarters) then left because it was too hard for them to adjust, there was no clear frame of reference in terms of policies and procedures. We have lost some key American managers because they didn't have a clear idea of their role or future in the organization."

Acknowledging that there are not enough American managers in senior positions, IKEA is trying to attract management trainees through presentations at business schools. However, its low-key image and lack of structured career paths are not easy to sell to "high potentials" more attuned to the packages offered by retailers such as Home Depot which forcefully push rapid promotion and individualize pay incentives. There is a general consensus that IKEA needs to develop young American managers who can play a bigger role in the organization than at present. However, there is no agreement yet on how critical the need is, nor on how to solve the problem.

Two differing views that could be overheard in a fictitious debate between two long-term Ikeans illustrate the unresolved issues facing IKEA USA at the end of 1996.

The view of a young American manager
There is a glass ceiling here. I am at a level at which my growth will stop because I'm not Swedish. IKEA should be made less complicated for Americans, easier for us to adapt to, and develop in. Our management needs to be much more professional in managing human resources. We need to bring new people into the organization, and reward individual accountability for results. This requires a better balance between the IKEA Way and American management. Becoming a successful manager at IKEA requires a lot of time and effort to understand how everything fits together. Yet not everyone can go to Sweden or learn Swedish, and today too many talented Americans

choose to go to competitors. Competition is catching up on us in terms of benefits, and with full employment we should be much more competitive than we are on the American job market."

The Swedish view
"Being the underdog, not doing things the traditional way over here is vital to IKEA's success in the United States. We must keep a unique image and work better at getting our message across to employees and customers so that they understand why we are successful. Pride in being a part of IKEA must be built locally and since our system is unique, this takes time. The real danger is assimilation. We are becoming too American. Giving people bonuses and pay incentives doesn't make them more intelligent; people are motivated by learning and improving in an organization that provides them with room to grow. Rewards should be more on a give and take basis – when the company makes more, it can give more – but we must remain flexible. Although we must seek a balance between adapting and sticking to our proven ways, we must protect our unique concepts and way of doing things. This means that we will always need a strong Swedish presence in the US. They are our "on-site missionaries" who can develop loyalty to an understanding of our uniqueness."

Clouds on the Horizon

By the mid-1990s, in spite of its undisputed international success and expansion over the past 25 years, signs appeared that the pattern of growth and steady profit were slowing down. Costs were rising, complaints on quality were more frequent, and unaccustomed delays appeared in product delivery. External factors had changed from the early times in Europe. Economic growth slowed as baby boomers moved into middle age, with new tastes and demands, and fewer new homes were being sold. Competitors had also learned from IKEA's pioneering distribution and were offering better furniture at lower prices, seeking low-cost furniture suppliers in eastern Europe, which put pressure on IKEA's unique sourcing.

IKEA had become a large international organization and, in an effort to adapt to the requirements of its many domestic markets, its product range had grown from 10,000 to 14,000 items, thus weakening returns from long production runs and overburdening logistic supply lines. Increasingly greater attention had to be given to bringing costs down, often through productivity gains which put unprecedented pressure on retail staffs to improve sales to staff ratios. During the years of rapid growth, many recruits were brought in from outside the company, and were therefore not steeped in IKEA culture. Its extended network made it difficult to provide employees and mid-level managers with a clear perception of how their local business impacted on the corporation as a whole. Local initiatives were taken without regard to their impact on the whole system. Was this the price of diversity or was IKEA suffering in many ways from too much decentralization?

In 1993, to cope with this situation, Andreas Mober and IKEA's senior management launched a company-wide operation "*Nytt Läge*" (New Situation), with the formation of task forces and project teams to suggest ways of improving communication and eliminating snags in distribution. Many suggestions were implemented, including the creation of new regional divisions in Europe for closer coordination of country operations, and the hiring of more professionals at headquarters to provide guidelines and more efficient corporate control systems. Although the *Nytt Lage* program met with a lot of enthusiasm and did achieve improvements in some areas, it soon became clear to Ingvar Kamprad that a more radical change in the organization was needed.

In early 1996, a major organizational change was introduced to "shorten the value chain" between customers and suppliers. Regional organizations were eliminated to bring stores in more direct contact with IKEA of Sweden. New emphasis was given to the importance of a living corporate culture based on the IKEA values of simplicity and self-discipline, rather than relying on formal policies and procedures. At the same time, IKEA's expansion plans in Europe and the United States were delayed. The fear at corporate headquarters was that IKEA had drifted too far away from the basic principles that were behind its legendary success.

Back to the Roots

In May, Ingvar Kamprad gathered IKEA's 250 worldwide store managers and senior managers at an important meeting in Poland to explain IKEA's need to refocus and redirect its efforts. He actually used the word "rejuvenate."

"Our product range and purchasing people often have an unequal battle with retailers and their far too many interests. Many of our suppliers got stuck in the middle. Our IKEA idea as one of the world's few production-oriented companies is under threat.

"Perhaps we were blinded by the booming years of the 1980s which increased the geographical spread of our operations to new markets, both on the retail and trading sides. Internal communication also became difficult, our administration expanded and our overheads became increasingly heavy. Our costs rose, and our customers and suppliers felt lost – many of them got in touch with me directly.

"Decision making took longer and longer, and endless discussions took place. It became more difficult to see the company as a whole. Far too much of our product development had too little to do with the tastes and wallets of the majority of people. Our product range expanded in every direction and could not be handled in a reasonable way on our sales floors. Our price advantage compared to competitors began to shrink. Even IKEA's soul, our fine corporate culture, was in danger. Have we forgotten to explain to our new workers about the IKEA Way? Have our desks prevented us from being involved enough in the commercial activity? Have we lost our way?"

The managers who attended that meeting felt galvanized by the founder's strong message, and their confidence and belief in the IKEA Way had been doubtlessly reinforced. In an increasingly complex world environment, simplicity indeed appeared to be a true virtue that had guided the company in the past. Several wondered, as they left, how Kamprad's intuitive ability to see through the complexity of a worldwide organization and reignite the dynamics of IKEA's success could be transmitted throughout the organization? Others wondered if they would have as much autonomy as they had previously enjoyed in adapting to very different markets. Some wondered if the company could regain its developmental thrust through the late 1990s?

8
Olivia Francis

Mark Mendenhall

Jim Markham did not know what to do. The more he tried to analyze the problem, the murkier it became. Normally, Jim felt confident in counseling his students – both past and present – but this time it was different. Olivia Francis had been one of the best students he had ever taught in the MBA program. She was bright and curious, one of those rare students whose thirst for knowledge was uppermost in her reasons for being in the program.

She had never disclosed much about her family or her past to him, but he knew from her student file and information sheet, and from bits and pieces of conversations with her, that she had come from a poor, somewhat impoverished neighborhood in St. Louis and had earned her way through college on academic scholarships and part-time jobs. Upon graduation from the MBA program, she left the Midwest, taking a job with a prestigious consulting firm in Los Angeles, and at the time he had felt sure she would travel far in her career. Perhaps that is why her phone call earlier that morning troubled him so.

Awaiting him on his arrival to his office was a message on his answering machine from Olivia. He returned her call and wound up talking to her for an hour. The salient portions of their conversation began to run through his mind again. What had struck him the most initially was the range and the depth of her emotions. Never had he spoken to anyone in his life who was seething with so much rage. After she had vented the rage, like air slowly being discharged from a balloon, she became almost apathetic, and her resignation to her situation almost frightened him – her only way out, as far as she could see, was to find another job. Jim could not recall ever being in a situation where he felt he had absolutely no control over what

This case was written especially for this book and is reprinted by permission of the author.

happened to him, where his input was meaningless to the resolution of a problem he faced.

Olivia had stated that her first performance appraisal had been below average, and two weeks ago, her second appraisal was only average. She felt that she had worked hard on her part of the team's projects and believed her work was first rate. The only reason for the appraisals, as far as she could see, was that she was black. She was the only black on the team – in the whole office for that matter. Jim believed her when she said that her work was excellent, for her work had always been excellent as a graduate student and as a research assistant. He had attempted to get her to analyze the situation further, but it was like pulling teeth; she seemed emotionally worn out and just wanted out.

"Surely they gave you more feedback about your performance than that it was below average?" he remembered asking. All she would say is that they mentioned something about her attitude, not being a team player, that her work was technically exemplary, but that she was part of a team and that working with others was as critical as the nature of the work she did by herself. Olivia felt that this was a smokescreen for the fact that she had been dumped on the office by a corporate recruiter with an EEO quota to fill, and that they were trying to get rid of her by using subjective criteria that she couldn't really defend herself against. The frustration came back to Jim as he remembered probing her for more information.

"What was the tone of your manager in the feedback session?"

"Condescending, false sincerity; there was a lot of talk on his part of 'my potential.' It was humiliating, actually."

"How do the other people in your team act toward you? Are they friendly, aloof, or what?"

"Oh, they're friendly on the surface – especially the project leader – but that's about as far as it goes."

"Is the project manager the person who gave you this feedback?"

"No, she is under the group manager. He is a long-time company guy. But obviously she gives him her evaluation and impressions of me, so I'm sure that they both pretty much see issues regarding me eye-to-eye."

"Tell me more about the group manager."

"Mr. Bresnan? I don't know much about him to tell you the truth. He oversees five project teams, and each project manager reports to him. He comes in and gives us a pep talk from time to time. Other than that I've never had occasion to really interact with him. He's always cracking jokes, putting people at ease. Kind of a 'Theory Y' type – at least on the surface."

"Do you ever go to lunch as a group?"

"Yes, they go to lunch a lot and they invite me along, but all they talk about are things I don't find very interesting – they're kind of a shallow bunch."

"What do you mean, shallow?"

"They couldn't care less about real issues – their discussions range from restaurants to social events around town to recent movies they've seen."

"Does the project manager go to these lunches?"

"Yes, she comes and even plans parties after work, too. Her husband is in the entertainment industry, a movie producer. Nothing big, documentaries and that type of thing, but they put on airs, if you know what I mean. She is really gregarious and always wants to be of help to people, but she strikes me as putting on a front, a mask. Obviously she isn't really sincere in wanting to help everyone 'be the best that they can be' – that's one of her little slogans by the way – after all, look what happened to me."

"Why do you think they're prejudiced against you?"

"Well, the poor appraisals for one thing – those are completely unfounded. They do other less obvious things, too. Twice I've overheard some of them from behind cubicles relaxing and telling racist jokes about 'wetbacks.'"

"Is it just a few of them that do this? I can't believe all of them are racist."

"I don't know, I don't enter the cubicle and say, 'Hi guys, tell some more jokes!' But it isn't just one or two of them. Look, I obviously don't fit in, do I? It's lily-white in the office, and I'm not."

"What do they do that is work-related that bothers you?"

"Well, when project deadlines get closer their anxiety level increases. They run around the office, yell at secretaries . . . it's like a volcano building up power to explode. They worry and agonize over the presentation to the client and have two or three trial presentation runs that everyone is required to go to. It's all so stupid."

"Why is that?"

"The clients always like what we produce, and with a few relatively small adjustments, our work is acceptable to the clients. So, it's as though all that wasted energy was needless. We could accomplish so much more if they would just settle down and trust their abilities."

"How do you act when they are like this?"

"I do my work. I respond to them rationally. I turn my part of the project in on time, and it is *good* work, Professor Markham. I guess I try to be the stabilizing force in the team by not acting as they do – I guess I just don't find the work pressures to be all that stressful."

"Why not?"

"Oh, I don't know really. Well maybe I do a little bit. I don't know if you know this or not, but my mother was a single parent with four kids. I was the oldest. She worked, and I looked after the kids when I came home from school. She worked two jobs to provide for us, so I would be in charge of the smaller kids sometimes upwards of nine o'clock at night. Doing your homework while taking care of a sick kid with the others listening to the television – that's stressful! These people at work, they don't know what stress is. Most of them are single, or if they are married they don't have any kids. They all seem very self-centered, like the universe revolves around them and their careers."

"What kind of behavior at work seems to get rewarded?"

"I guess doing good work doesn't. What seems to get rewarded is being white, being more or less competent, and being interested in insipid topics. Professor Markham, don't you know of any firms that are more enlightened I can send my resume to? I'm looking for a firm that will reward me for the work I do and not for who I am or am not."

Jim leaned back in his chair pondering what to do next. He had promised Olivia that he would call her back in a day or two with some advice. He sensed that he didn't quite understand her problem, that there was more to it than what appeared on the surface. But he felt he didn't have enough data to analyze it properly. He decided to go for a walk around the neighborhood to clear his mind. As he opened the front door and gazed down his street, he suddenly realized for the first time that his neighborhood was lily-white.

9

How Much Sleaze is Too Much?

Asbjorn Osland

Eric had returned to Africa as a field director assigned to Senegal after a failed rotation through the organization's headquarters. Now in Senegal, Eric was pleased that the program was going well but concerned that he had become too accommodating in his approach to ethical issues. Things that he would previously have judged as clearly wrong, he now tolerated. He wondered if his faded idealism had been supplanted by a realism that bordered on unethical. Should he continue to show flexibility in his handling of ethical dilemmas? Should he renew his youthful idealism and refuse to budge on behaviors that were clearly wrong by North American standards? Should he simply leave and no longer have to deal with the question of "how much sleaze is too much?"

Developmental International

Development International was founded in the 1930s to assist war orphans of the Spanish civil war. It is a child sponsorship agency that markets its appeal through the personal identification of the donor with a sponsored child and family. The agency experienced rapid growth from the 1970s through the 1990s, primarily funded by donors from Canada, the United States, and the Netherlands. Given the need to enroll more poor families, the program was established in Senegal in 1982. Control over the donors' contributions – used to finance development projects in the Third World – was a critical value expressed by Development International: field directors were regularly fired for failing to exert sufficient control.

Reprinted by permission of the author.

Eric

Eric began his career in international service as a Peace Corps volunteer in his mid-20s. After he left the Peace Corps, he worked for Development International in Latin America and French West Africa. In the process, he found that he enjoyed the process of building a new program more than managing one that was already established. He also enjoyed the autonomy of working thousands of miles away from the direct control of his superior. He liked the responsibility of establishing and managing a program without too much interference from his superiors. He felt that he was competent and experienced as a field director. Serving the needy of the Third World gave him a sense of meaning and he felt confident the development projects had a positive impact.

During Eric's rotation through headquarters, his superiors concluded that his political skills were better utilized overseas, where the challenge of dealing with different cultures obligated him to interact with others in a diplomatic manner. Eric had incorrectly assumed that while working in his home culture he could be himself and speak candidly to his bosses. They sometimes made assertions that reflected a lack of experience in the areas of the Third World where Eric had served (i.e., West Africa and Latin America), and Eric would correct them with less diplomacy than required. That, combined with the fact that Eric was used to running his own show, made it difficult for Eric to integrate into the headquarters. He lacked the political sensitivity to interact effectively in a headquarters environment. In contrast, while overseas he had learned to be very careful, as a rule, and present himself in a manner that was respectful of the foreign culture. Because Eric had insulted his superiors at headquarters and given them the impression that he regarded them as incompetent, the international director felt that Eric's skills could be utilized more effectively in Africa. He had previously served there and accomplished that which the organization desired – i.e., enrolled enough families so that contributions covered expenses as well as developed programs that were recognized by the host government officials as meeting the needs of the population served. Although he had enjoyed working in Africa, Eric was actually tired of working in the Third World. He found it exasperating and had lost much of his zeal or sense of mission for Development International. After the transfer had been announced, he saw the errors of his brutal candor but felt let down by his bosses whom he previously had admired a great deal. Therefore he tried to find another job but it proved impossible.

So off he went, his first task to negotiate the establishment of a program in Central Africa. However, the official with whom he had to arrange the details of the agreement repeatedly asked for substantial bribes. Eric refused to pay them and relayed this back to headquarters. Consequently, his boss arranged for him to go to Senegal, where the central government was highly cooperative and an agreement was signed in several weeks. Eric then returned to the US, reported to headquarters and received a conditional go-ahead, subject to the international board's approval, to begin operations in Senegal. He then returned to Senegal with his wife, Jennifer, and their children. Jennifer was very supportive about the move, though she was saddened that Eric felt so badly about the exile. Eric was worried by the prospect of illness for his children, based on previous experience in Africa, and the work his wife would have to undertake to establish a home in conditions of great hardship.

In Senegal, his coping strategy for the stress he suffered proved self-destructive. He and his expatriate friends would get together once or twice a week and indulge themselves in long bouts of jogging followed by rewarding themselves with a beer for each of the many kilometers jogged. This caused his wife great dismay.

Eric was unsure of his status within the organization, given his forced transfer from the headquarters. He was close to completing his ten years with Development International, which would guarantee him some retirement benefits, at which time he and Jennifer planned to return to graduate school. However, for the next two years, he would have to accomplish the organization's goals. He knew that he had to work closely with productive, though sometimes corrupt, indigenous leaders, such as Saidou.

Saidou

Eric found the Senegalese government amenable to the establishment of a program and the preliminary arrangements with the central government went smoothly. Eric then requested the necessary tax exoneration on a vehicle and was awaiting the approval. This process generally took six to eight weeks. It was worth the wait as excise taxes on vehicles were several hundred percent of the landed value. He had been in contact with the local development office in northern Senegal and had made arrangements to visit the rural areas where the program would begin. He and his family took up temporary residence in a local hotel built during the colonial era at the foot of the bridge on the Senegal River.

His contact, Saidou, had proven cooperative. Saidou was the assistant director of the regional office of the national government's ministry of social development, the branch of the national government with which Development International had signed its agreement. Eric enjoyed Saidou's company and his stories. Saidou was in his early 50s at that time. One morning, Eric entered his office, directly across from the hotel. In broken Wolof, the local African language spoken by many Senegalese, Eric said, "Good morning."

Saidou responded with a smile and a question that Eric didn't understand. Saidou noted that Eric hadn't understood and clarified, "I asked how your son was." Eric had noticed that Third World people always seemed to ask about his son but not his daughters.

Eric had been thinking about Saidou's stories of the post-independence period. "You once said you had been to Moscow. How did that come about?" he asked.

Saidou responded, "During the early years of independence we were fairly leftist in our sympathies. Also, there was lots of money available for training all over the place. I also went to Israel, before the boycott, and to France."

"How did you like France?" asked Eric. Eric noted that Saidou's demeanor changed, and he seemed to grow cold and distant.

Saidou looked away and said, "You have no idea how painful it was. People would run from me and point at me. They said I was a monkey."

Eric added, "I noticed that the waiters in the hotel treat the French guests with chilling distance. Yet with us, once they hear our American accents, they seem to warm up. Why is that?"

Saidou explained, "The Americans have a better reputation. During World War II, they provided relief, which was well received and is remembered by the older segment of the population. Also, Peace Corps Volunteers generally attempt to learn the local languages, something few French nationals do."

Saidou looked with warmth at Eric. He seemed to see some of that Peace Corps-like desire to assist in Eric. Over the next few months, Saidou guided Eric through the labyrinth of officialdom to get the program started. Eric often visited him in his office to consult about different concerns as they arose.

Saidou's assistance extended to the personal domain as well. Eric had fallen years before off a roof and suffered a herniated disc that became aggravated in Senegal, perhaps due to jogging. As it was evident that Eric was occasionally in great pain, Saidou thought he could best help his new friend by introducing him to a traditional healer. Eric was prepared to cooperate with incantations and dancing but was not about to drink the "prescribed" purgative that would provide the necessary "output," which the healer would then "read" to determine whether or not the problem had been cured. "How is it that a well-educated man like Saidou would trust such cures?" wondered Eric. However, Eric simply accepted this difference as one of many where he and Saidou clearly marched to a different drummer. Eric enjoyed these differences, which made it interesting to work in Africa. He also respected Saidou a great deal as a development professional.

Eric wanted to hire Saidou to head the program. He found him extremely knowledgeable about development and well connected with the traditional leaders of the villages in the surrounding area. He had confidence in Saidou's commitment to serving his people. He saw Saidou as a man possessed with a desire to serve – it was his last chance to make the contribution he had dreamed of as a young man during the heady days of independence. Then his career had somehow been derailed, and he was relegated to spending his time smoking and waiting for the day to end in his office. Eric also knew Saidou had the ability to generate solid program results. One day Eric asked him if he wanted a job: "Saidou, you have all the experience one could ever hope for. I wonder if you could somehow get the government to assign you to Development International? We'd pay you a good salary and provide you with a vehicle."

Saidou put down his newspaper and placed his cigarette holder in the overflowing ashtray. He then pulled out a Kola nut (a source of caffeine) from his tunic top and broke off a piece and began to chew it. Eric noted the pair of stub fingers that had resulted from an accident Saidou had suffered as an apprentice carpenter working for a Frenchman during the colonial era. Saidou spoke with bitterness about the incident, describing the conditions as unsafe. After what seemed like a few minutes, Saidou responded, "It'll take some doing but, yes, I'm interested." He rose and they shook hands.

During a subsequent visit, Eric noted that Saidou appeared very anxious and quietly asked, "Is something bothering you?"

Saidou responded, "I don't know how I'm going to make ends meet. I can't go to work for you until the government gives its approval, yet I don't have the money at the moment to buy the rice I need to feed my two families next month." Saidou had two wives who lived in separate homes and he was short of 100 kilograms of rice, the monthly ration for all the people he was expected to feed. Almost in the same breath, Saidou suggested, "Say, while we wait for your customs clearance on the vehicle to come through, we could repair a vehicle that the government has. It would only be about $75 dollars."

Eric was suspicious but agreed. Saidou looked away at the window and said, "God is great." Eric wondered what he meant, as the car never did appear, though it was always "almost" ready each time Eric questioned Saidou. Eventually Eric stopped asking.

After the government gave its approval and the customs clearance finally came through for Development International to purchase vehicles, Saidou went to work and proved to be an extremely industrious and effective program head. Since he was well connected to the informal network that ran the country, he could generally work out whatever problems occurred with the government. The official bureaucracy seemed to exist to provide jobs for the educated elite, in Eric's view. However, the informal network of kinship and collegial bonds was highly effective. With Saidou working the informal system, Eric and Development International were spared the onerous task of obtaining written approval for each specific project, though Saidou always obtained verbal approval from the local official.

Budget Planning and Changes

While at headquarters, Eric had developed a planning format called the Situation Assessment and Goal Establishment, the SAGE report. This was the core document on which the budget would be based. Eric enjoyed this period of planning. He would obtain reports from the US government in Senegal in which the development priorities and needs of the country were described and discussed, based on studies prepared by experts. Development International had also engaged the services of an American scholar who was an expert on Senegal. Armed with the information contained in such reports, Eric and Saidou would next speak with the various local officials and village leaders, conversations that generally proved very informative.

However, the villagers would present long lists of needs that were indeed apparent: education, health, infrastructure (i.e., public water sources, roads, schools, clinics, etc.) and jobs were all desperately needed. Nevertheless, Development International could not provide everything. This was also beyond the ability of the community to support and sustain. The communities that received assistance were generally asked to provide in-kind support – usually "sweat equity" (i.e., manual labor to complete the projects). The projects they were willing to support with hard work were the ones Saidou felt they should do. However, only future experience would show what villagers were willing to support. Because Eric had to present an annual budget and was unsure of what people would contribute their sweat equity toward, he included the lengthy list of requests made by the villagers. The budget had been approved and they were in the implementation phase, when the monthly financial statements would be monitored by the international controller.

Eric had experienced difficulty with the international controller in previous years when he had attempted to be responsive to changing development priorities due to natural disaster, political turmoil, and the need to substitute projects planned by Development International but then undertaken by other agencies. The controller had accused Eric of poor control and attempted to cause him to lose face with the international executive director. However, Eric's immediate supervisor had come to his aid and documented the approval he had given for such flexibility.

Eric enjoyed the flexibility of beginning a new program. One never knew what would occur. For example, while launching the program in Senegal, a drought occurred. The area served by Development International was at the northern-most limit of peanut cultivation in the country. Senegal depended on peanut exportation for foreign currency. During the colonial era, the French had encouraged the country to switch from subsistence crops, such as millet, that were well suited to the soil and growing conditions, to peanuts, a cash crop. To compensate for the food deficiency brought about by the abandonment of subsistence crops, the French imported broken rice from Indochina, also then under French rule. However, peanut cultivation exhausted the sandy soils in northern Senegal. During the period Eric served in Senegal, there was virtually a total peanut crop failure in the area just south of St. Louis due to the drought. Many of the able-bodied men, and some women, left home to work in the capital or other major cities in labor-intensive jobs. Some men traveled to other African nations and France as well. They sent money home to avert the starvation of their families.

One morning Saidou entered Eric's office. He sat down and smoked several cigarettes while discussing varied concerns. Then he observed, "These are desperate times for the villagers. We need to help them and I believe their desperation could serve as motivation to work hard on suitable projects related to food. Why don't we take a drive to visit the site of a community garden so you can see what I mean?" Eric agreed. He had wanted to see what had become of the community gardens, two of which had been budgeted. Eric loved this part of his job, when he and Saidou would drive throughout the rural area they served.

On the way they stopped at a small store so that Saidou could get a pack of cigarettes. Eric enjoyed these small stores because they sold one cigarette at a time, thereby permitting him a taste of indulgence without the embarrassment of bumming one from Saidou. These tiny stores were found in every small town and neighborhood of larger towns or cities. Saidou explained that the owners were Mauritanians, Arabs working in Black Africa. They used relatives to operate and live in the store in a bondage-like arrangement. The boss, a patriarch of the clan, would travel from store to store in an aging Mercedes Benz collecting the day's revenues. He would then go to the bank to make a cash deposit. Bank patrons were often forced to await such deposits to cash their checks, since the bank seldom had cash. The Mauritanians came in daily with their shopping bags full of dirty small bills to replenish the coffers of the bank. Eric appreciated such cultural explanations provided by Saidou as to why things were the way they were.

During village visits, Eric watched Saidou speak with the villagers. They sat for long periods, sipping very strong sweetened green tea made in an elaborate ceremony. Beautiful young women often served the tea. Though scarcely eighteen years old, one of them caught Saidou's eye. He later took her as his third wife. Eric enjoyed watching Saidou and the girl's relatives laugh and talk.

Eric was always struck by the contrast of such joy with the pathetic image presented in the American press of Africa. He became convinced that the Africans he had known were generally happier than most of his compatriots, though lacking in material wealth and other objective measures of development (i.e., infant mortality, life expectancy etc.). Like Saidou said, "There's more to life than life expectancy."

As they approached the village in the car, Saidou told Eric, "Yesterday I came here and told the villagers that they would have to choose a site and fence it off. We would then put in the wells they need for water." When Saidou stopped the car at the top of the hill, both Eric and Saidou were stunned to see about 50 people, both men and women, completing the perimeter of the garden. They had planted a living fence, a type of shrub. One often finds such fencing material in the tropics, sometimes with barbed wire attached after the shrubs had grown tall enough. Here, they didn't have the money for barbed wire and relied instead on thorn bushes to fill in the holes in the fence. Saidou exclaimed, "Look at that! In 24 hours they've almost completed what I thought would take them several weeks." The village elders approached and gathered around Saidou. He complimented them on their achievement and spoke with them about the next steps. They would have to house the well diggers as well as assist them in their work.

Saidou and Eric drove back to St. Louis in the late afternoon after completing their work. At that time, the softer light brought out colors and shapes that the sun of mid-day seemed to suffocate in its blaze. Appreciative of the shifting light, Eric felt a sense of comfort. Eric returned from his day-dreaming and asked, "Why do you think the villagers built the fence so quickly?"

"They simply don't have much hope in the peanut harvest. These community gardens are a potential source of vegetables for the families as well as a likely supplement to their income," replied Saidou.

"Too bad we didn't budget more of these gardens. It looks like something all 20 villages could use," observed Eric.

"That's true. Why can't we do more of the gardens and fewer schools and health projects?" asked Saidou. "We'd finance the gardens with those funds."

"That's logical, but I don't know if our headquarters will go for it. Let me think about it," said Eric. They drove the rest of the way in silence, interrupted by occasional small talk. Eric was preoccupied with his thoughts about the gardens. He wanted to spend the funds allocated to other projects on the gardens but worried that the controller and others at headquarters would object to major changes in the budget at mid-year. Also, the health and education projects were important. However, Eric saw for himself the almost desperate level of motivation displayed by the villagers for the gardens. He worried about his tentative status with the organization and if he had the political clout to get this budget change approved. He went to bed that night discussing the matter with his wife. His wife tried to help, but Eric found it difficult to believe in himself enough to feel influential. He didn't want to appear both disorganized (i.e., ask for a major change to the program budget) and too flexible in his response to the requests from the authorities for payments and Saidou's improper behavior.

More Control Problems

In mulling over Saidou's proposals, Eric thought about some of the problems with Saidou. He noticed that when he sent Saidou to the capital with the accountant, another Senegalese, to make major purchases, they would always be charged more than Eric found he would be charged for comparable purchases. Eric brought this up to the accountant: "How is it that when I make purchases I pay less than what you and Saidou pay?" Eric noted the smile on the accountant's face.

"I think you should make the purchases," came the reply.

Saidou was hypersensitive to Western style audits that Eric would periodically ask the accounting staff to perform. Saidou became extremely upset and indignant that Eric would have the "gall" to send a young female accountant to audit one of his projects. "How could you send a grandchild of mine to check on me?"

Eric didn't respond to Saidou but excused himself by saying he had to check on something in the donor services office. He didn't want to have this matter blow up into an argument. Besides, he thought to himself, "I don't see how Saidou is related to the accountant except as part of the same large clan." Though he needed Saidou to get the job done, he wondered how an eventual successor would deal with Saidou. Eric made a mental note to himself: "It seems that Africans tolerate my audits and follow-up memos, yet go ballistic when a compatriot does the same thing."

Though Saidou was opportunistic in his behavior regarding the resources of Development International, he proved very helpful to Eric in dealing with the tremendous frustration one can encounter in such settings.

One such instance that Saidou helped resolve was a contract that had not been fulfilled by a local cabinet-maker. Eric had worked with the cabinet-maker, Alioune, for a year, during which time he had made good furniture for the office. When funding was approved for a school desk project, Eric asked Alioune and several other local cabinet-makers to bid on the project. Eric used other low bids and added the additional leverage of a substantial advance for materials to pressure Alioune into lowering his bid. Eric liked working with Alioune and wanted to help him raise the funds to purchase a power saw. Alioune agreed to Eric's terms without objection. He would likely have protested had a compatriot of comparable class and age coerced him in this way. However, Alioune was a poor man with limited capital and opportunities. He perceived Eric as representing power and money. It was the chance of a lifetime for Alioune – he would never be able to save enough money to purchase a table saw, given the intense competition from other artisans and the demands on his cash made by family members.

However, after the saw had been installed and materials stockpiled, deliveries failed to meet the schedule. Alioune had actually cut himself on the saw, which was an acceptable excuse for a time. Eric realized how mean-spirited he had become when he met with Alioune and noticed the bandage. Rather than immediately feeling sympathy, Eric had felt scorn when Alioune asked for an extension. Eric granted his request but was alarmed at the hostility he felt inside. A few months passed, Alioune's wound healed and he still did not deliver the desks as promised.

Eric didn't know exactly how to proceed, but Alioune's failure to fulfill the contract signified a sizable control problem that the regional auditor from the international headquarters would have to be told of during his forthcoming visit. Directors were fired for such things. Saidou suggested that he apply family pressure on Alioune. He called a meeting of Alioune's family and used shame to get him to resume deliveries.

Eric feared the auditor's report regarding Alioune, as there was a potential loss of several thousand dollars. He wondered what a Western auditor would write in his or her report. It could read: "A seemingly reckless advance was made to an impoverished local cabinet-maker to fill a larger order than any he had ever delivered. He is now several months behind in deliveries. The field director claims to have taken appropriate action by holding a meeting with his father and other elders, a group of what appeared to be retired, frail men dressed in traditional garb." Eric winced at the thought of such a report reaching the international controller. On several occasions he had pushed the controller's limits and Eric felt the controller was waiting to nail him.

In Senegal things just didn't work the same way they did in developed countries, Eric would mutter to himself. One day he had been summoned to the office of Amadou, the regional director of social development. Amadou accused Eric of being uncooperative and threatened to denounce him to the minister. Eric never found out what he had done. Perhaps he had been too demanding of a few local contractors, who Eric had accused of incompetence for their inadequate services – the social network was tight and Amadou could have been told. At any rate, Eric concluded that he would have to satisfy Amadou to avoid difficulty since he could not afford to have the program fail in Senegal.

Thus, when Eric asked Amadou to go to the capital to speak with a visiting international board member of Development International, he decided to pay whatever expenses Amadou claimed, within reason. Eric knew that he needed to make a good impression on the board member – the go-ahead for the village garden program depended on it. After the meeting between Eric, Amadou and the board member, Amadou informed Eric that he had "lost" the money and could not pay his hotel bill nor get back to St. Louis. Eric suspected that the funds would be used for his personal benefit. However, since Amadou could make it very difficult for Eric to manage his program and had given an excuse, Eric paid for his expenses a second time and duly recorded the payments in the "other expenses" section of the monthly financial statement with a full explanation.

Another particularly galling situation, in Eric's view, involved the work inspector. All employees in Senegal had to be referred by the work inspector, a dubious legacy from the French. Given his position, the work inspector enjoyed considerable power over applicants. For example, all the initial candidates for secretarial positions were very attractive but none could type. Eric suspected they were required to perform sexual favors for the work inspector. One could keep rejecting candidates until a suitable one was sent, but this meant quite a number of rejections. The work inspector could also inspect an office at will and levy large fines for infractions, real or imagined. He would summon Eric to his office, make him wait all morning, and then extort gasoline coupons from Eric with the veiled threat of an inspection. The choice was pay or suffer an audit – Eric paid.

Though he succeeded in managing the relationship with the work inspector, Eric had become callused to the point where he wondered if he had not crossed the line from facilitation payments to bribery. According to the Foreign Corrupt Practices Act, Eric understood that a facilitation payment was a legal payment to speed the process for something that would eventually occur without the payment. On the other hand, a bribe was an illegal payment made so that something would happen that would otherwise not occur. "Were the gasoline coupons a bribe?" Eric wondered. He rationalized the incident to himself by concluding that he would have donated the coupons to the work inspector had he simply asked – he had done this before with another official and reported it as such in the financial statements. The work inspector's treatment left Eric with a bitter taste in his mouth but as time went on, the work inspector came to respect Eric as a decent employer and stopped calling on Eric for such assistance.

Once the local authorities had accepted him, Eric found that they didn't continue asking for favors. He asked Saidou about this.

Saidou responded in a fatherly tone: "You were kind of hard to get along with when you first came. You seemed bitter. However, over time you seem to have calmed down. Also, I think the authorities have recognized the contributions made to rural development by our programs. The other thing you always have to remember is that the French were very mean to us in school and when they were our colonial administrators. We've all grown up with tremendous hostility. Thus, when we can make a white man pay, we are tempted to do so." Saidou smiled mischievously and they both laughed at this last statement.

Eric enjoyed such moments with Saidou. Saidou could always explain why things were the way they were. However, Eric wondered if he hadn't been too flexible with the authorities and Saidou. Their behavior had been unethical by North American standards. "Have I crossed the line into unethical behavior?" Eric asked himself. He felt his frequent explanations to the international controller for such dubious payments weakened his influence in attempting to push for approval of the mid-year budget change. Yet he felt tremendous pressure to perform and achieve the program results the organization wanted from him. He spoke with Jennifer about his plight: "I don't know if I'm being practical or being unethical in paying the authorities and putting up with Saidou's requests. Sometimes I think I should be tougher and draw the line more clearly. But if I blow it and Saidou resigns, the program could stall or the authorities could shut us down. I suppose we could simply continue here for a while and then leave once I'm vested with the company after 10 years' service. Then you can attend grad school. I don't know. I'm just not sure what to do."

10
Chicago Medical Supplies Corporation: Explaining Sales in India

Lynne H. Rosansky

Chicago Medical Supplies Corporation was a privately owned company that sold medical devices, such as diagnostic and therapeutic catheters, to hospitals and practicing doctors. This corporation had been in existence for approximately 15 years and had been growing rapidly. Sales reached approximately $200 million dollars in 1991. Chicago Medical serves four major medical specialties (cardiology, radiology, gastroenterology, and urology) through separate product divisions. Each of these divisions had its own sales forces and marketing teams, while manufacturing, research and development, financing, and accounting were shared between the divisions. The company's sales are worldwide, with three subsidiaries in France, Germany, and Japan.

The medical devices industry is not the same as pharmaceuticals or medical equipment, their sole function being to make the produces necessary for medical procedures. Demand for medical devices, on the other hand, fluctuates with the health of the economy, although in comparison with other industries the fluctuation is minimal.

The Deal

With the rapid growth of the medical devices industry Chicago Medical Supplies Corporation was able to expand rapidly. After several years of this rapid and successful expansion, Chicago Medical reached a point where it was unable to generate working capital internally and had exhausted sources of finance from banks. The owners of Chicago Medical did not want to go public with stocks and similar financing, fearing loss of control and equity. Accordingly, they began searching for an investor to enable them to continue their expansion. After an in-depth search they found a willing, major player in the pharmaceuticals industry. This corporation was one of the elite *Fortune* 500 and had the finances that Chicago Medical needed.

The two companies' managements made a deal stating that the pharmaceutical corporation would invest a limited amount of capital in Chicago Medical, and in seven years the investor would have the option to buy the firm or let it carry on as a privately owned corporation. At the end of the seven years an appropriate price for Chicago Medical would be determined by multiplying the average after tax profits of 1990 and 1991 by the acquiring company's price/earnings ratio.

This deal would be very beneficial to Chicago Medical, giving them the opportunity to expand, but, on the other hand, there was tremendous pressure put on Chicago Medical employees by the owners to be one of the top performers in their industry. The owners wanted to drive profits as high as possible so that at the end of the seven years, when the time came for the investor to decide whether or not to buy, the company would be at the pinnacle of its success and the market.

Steve Jensen

Steve Jensen received his doctorate in management from Harvard in 1981. He taught in a local university for several years and then got involved with the medical devices industry.

Steve and his wife had their first child in 1987 and planned to have more in the future. His only regret was that he could not spend as much time as he wanted with his family due to the requirements of his job.

Steve entered Chicago Medical as a product manager in the gastroenterology division, but one year after the establishment of the International Division he was offered a position there in sales management. In the International Division, his title was director of export sales. The responsibilities of this job consisted of working with approximately 100 independent distributors in 65 countries with the aim of achieving sales targets. The predetermined sales targets were $12 million in 1988, $15 million in 1989, and $19.5 million in 1990. Steve was also responsible for building the distributor network and meeting expense targets.

The Scenario

Chicago Medical's international distributors and country markets were prioritized in three different groups: A, B, and C. At the end of each year the sales from the four divisions would be compared and ranked in descending order. A was the high-priority group of six to twelve distributors that received the maximum effort and support from Chicago Medical. The B group of another twelve distributors received considerable support, but less than the A, and the C group received whatever support Chicago Medical was able to give after the two higher priority classes had been seen to.

India had been in the C group from the lime that Steve had started in export sales. The country had always been operated in the same manner, with several small independent distributors all working for Chicago Medical on a non-exclusive basis. Since the distributors in India were ranked in the C group and had never given Chicago Medical much sales volume, India was not a priority to Steve.

One August afternoon Steve received a surprise phone call from Jamal, the president of one of these Indian distributors. Jamal expressed his desire to become the exclusive Indian distributor for Chicago Medical. Steve was hesitant at first, but when Jamal demonstrated his dedication by attending a worldwide training meeting in Chicago, Jensen saw the aggressiveness imperative in a great salesman. It was these qualities that led Steve to consider Jamal for the position as the sole Chicago Medical distributor in India. Furthermore, Jamal had demonstrated great perseverance in continually staying in contact with Steve, reassuring him that "he was the man" that would turn India into one of the company's biggest country markets. It was his desire to commit himself and steadfast determination that convinced Jensen to give Jamal the exclusive contract.

During that year, Steve was happy to see that Jamal was aspiring to the goals they had set and was working extremely hard. Steve was pleased with Jamal's work and had noticed that the sales figures for India had increased by 100 percent. But, despite the growth and Jamal's efforts, India remained a low to middle priority country in the ranking system.

The next years held many surprises in store for Steve Jensen. After the next full year's sales figures came out Steve was astonished by the numbers for India. India's sales had increased by approximately

Exhibit 10.1   Jamal's forecasted market and sales plan

Division	Product	Expected market ($)	Expected sales ($)
Cardiology	A	300,000	350,000
Cardiology	B	300,000	380,000
Cardiology	C	400,000	420,000
Cardiology	D	350,000	400,000
Cardiology	E	300,000	300,000
Radiology	F	100,000	120,000
Radiology	G	100,000	100,000
Radiology	H	150,000	150,000
Radiology	I	85,000	100,000
Radiology	J	50,000	75,000
Gastro/urology	K	180,000	180,000
Gastro/urology	L	90,000	100,000
Gastro/urology	M	120,000	130,000
Gastro/urology	N	100,000	100,000
Gastro/urology	O	85,000	100,000

$400,000 dollars especially marked rise in cardiology, and due to Jamal's hard work the country had moved into the top of the B distributors. But this was not the end of Jamal's success. The following year, even more substantial orders were placed, amounting to nearly $1 million. When Steve saw these figures he was completely amazed. He was aware of Jamal's persistency and aggressiveness when it came to sales, but this much of an increase was stunning. With the latest sales figures, India had moved into the A class and would now be a high-priority country. Steve felt that it was time for Jamal to come to Chicago Medical and give a presentation on the market size, future prospects, key physicians, marketing and sales plans, and plans for covering the entirety of India, a large and internally diverse nation.

The following spring Jamal came to the United States and gave his presentation to several important members of the International Department, including Steve. Jamal's presentation was thoroughly complete, excluding no details. Nevertheless, there was one part of Jamal's presentation that left Steve puzzled. When he had discussed the market and forecasted sales figures, Steve realized that the actual numbers were very different from what they should have been. Jamal listed the market for the product as X but, when he listed the forecasted sales dollars, he found the sales exceeded the market for the product (see exhibit 10.1). Steve was not sure what this meant: maybe the recent success in India had caused Jamal to embellish when it came down to actual dollars or maybe it was just a simple error. At any rate, Steve waited for the two of them to be alone to ask the questions he had concerning these numbers.

On Jamal's last day at Chicago Medical, Steve approached him and inquired about the market for the product and the unmatched forecasted sales dollars. Jamal seemed quite uneasy at first, but then responded with a straightforward answer: "This is a very unusual situation Steve. In India business is done very differently than it is here in the United States." Steve sat back and listened as Jamal explained that there were key physicians and players that he worked with directly. For each order of considerable size a certain percentage of its dollar value was given to people by Jamal. Furthermore, a great deal of India's medical supplies were funded by the Indian government, so Jamal was greasing the palms of everyone down the line, government officials, customs agents, accounting clerks, Purchasing agents, and, lastly, local physicians. This was the answer that Steve did not want to hear. The first thing that entered his mind was the Foreign Corrupt Practices Act – they were in violation of it. He knew that this matter would take a lot of thinking through and the consultation of colleagues at Chicago Medical, so he bid Jamal farewell and told him that he would be in touch.

Jensen's Decision

Steve Jensen found himself in very uncomfortable and unfamiliar territory. For the past two years he had done exceptionally well in the International Department, and the surprise of India moving from class C to class A made Steve look all the better. But now he was faced with an ugly situation. If Steve were to blow the whistle on Jamal, he would be losing a substantial amount of sales dollars for the company and with the internal pressure at Chicago Medical to have top performance in all areas, this might cost Steve his job. On the other hand, if Steve were to continue letting Jamal do business the way it is done in India and if someone were to discover that he was aware of the situation and had essentially participated in the violation of The Foreign Corrupt Practices Act, the penalties could be unthinkable.

Steve went to several colleagues, including his boss, and received the same response from everyone: at Chicago Medical they want sales any way they can get it. Steve's boss was frank with him; he told him that if anything were to be uncovered concerning the Foreign Corrupt

Practices Act, in no way would he admit to knowing or support him, and, in addition, Steve knew that if he failed to meet his specified quotas he would lose his job. So now Steve found himself in a Catch-22 situation. In these circumstances, a person will find it exceptionally hard to make the "right" decision. Steve knew that he was in a situation where whatever choice he made would have unfavorable ramifications. If he blew the whistle on Jamal, he would most likely lose his job, and if he let things go on as they were, he could possibly go to jail or be black-balled from the business world.

Steve Jensen was well educated, adequately experienced in public relations, and knowledgeable in the management field. As Director of Export Sales, he was very successful, always meeting or exceeding his monthly quotas. However, in spite of Steve's education and experience, he found himself in a situation that led him to break federal law.

11

Colgate Palmolive in Post-Apartheid South Africa

David T. Beaty

After a month of intense contemplation, Carol Lewis decided to accept the position of head of Colgate Palmolive Foundation (South Africa). Carol learned in her job interview that the American subsidiary, based in South Africa, was committed to extending its leadership role in generating social responsibility (SR) activities in a post-apartheid South Africa (see the appendix).

"Ever since 1967, when four dental educators first went into the surrounding black townships to educate residents about teeth that can be strong and healthy through receiving daily care and nourishment, investing in communities where the firm earns its living had been – and would continue to be – integral to its South African mission," vice president David Moore told her.

Indeed, Carol had studied the American firm and learned that Colgate Palmolive had achieved an outstanding Category 1 rating on the Sullivan Code for south Africa (see exhibit 11.1). She discovered that compliance to the code requires a firm to direct 12 per cent of its salary budget to social responsibility efforts. And she knew the company was serious about its SR activities. The firm had recently launched the $3 million Colgate Palmolive Foundation. Many South African firms believed this level of achievement was beyond even their financial reach. So Carol was glad to have been selected to lead Colgate Palmolive's SR initiatives. With over $100 million annual sales and a workforce of 600 employees, she believed that the American firm

Exhibit 11.1 Sullivan Code for South Africa

These were devised in 1977 by the Reverend Leon Sullivan of Philadelphia as a code of conduct for American multinationals in South Africa. They are:

Principle 1
Non-segregation of the races in all eating, comfort, locker room and work facilities.

Principle 2
Equal and fair employment practices for all employees

Principle 3
Equal pay for all employees doing equal or comparable work for the same period of time.

Principle 4
Initiate and develop training programs that will prepare blacks, coloured, and Asians in substantial numbers for supervisory, administrative, clerical and technical jobs.

Principle 5
Increase the number of blacks, coloured, and Asians in management and supervisory positions.

Principle 6
Improve the equality of employees' lives outside the work environment in such areas as housing, transportation, schooling, recreations and health facilities.

Principle 7
Work to eliminate laws and customs that impede social and political justice.

Exhibit 11.2 Colgate Palmolive's mission statement

Colgate Palmolive is committed, through its social investment program, to support social and socio-economic projects; in particular, those that promote the principles and structures of a non-racial society, equality of opportunity, advancement based on merit and freedom of association and speech.

We are dedicated to the upliftment of the quality of life for all South Africans through education, health and youthful sporting activities, which will encourage self-development and confidence-building to create an improved social climate in the South African community.

could continue to build on its stellar track-record. (See exhibit 11.2 for the mission statement.)

After a month spent doing MBWA (management by wandering around) on the job, Carol had listened to the opinions of individual and group stakeholders in the firm. She had learned about the kinds of SR initiatives they thought the firm should consider in a post-apartheid South Africa.

First, she discovered that Colgate Palmolive employees were the highest paid workers in the industry. In fact, she learned that the firm pays employees in excess of stipulations listed in the sullivan principles.

Second, she learned of the overwhelming support of all employees to the SR initiatives of colgate Palmolive. Indeed, she'd been frequently stopped in hallways and on factory floors by employees who thanked her and the company profusely for, inter alia, helping their kids with school bursaries, receiving funds for school fees for employees (on the condition they pass their subjects) and nutrional classes. She learned from her briefing by senior management that the primary mission of the firm's SR efforts was to "accelerate economic empowerment through education by developing formal and informal educational skills and motivating communities to become self-sufficient" (see a list and description of specific SR activities of Colgate Palmolive in the appendix). In fact, the firm, had "adopted" seven schools that could approach an employee committee with requests for anything from photocopying ink to teacher and pupil upgrading programs.

Third, she learned that Colgate Palmolive sponsors professional nurses to help day-care centers, schools, and community groups with primary health care education.

Fourth, she learned of the strategic initiative of top management to institute a formal "affirmative action" plan for black employees that would be implemented as a strategy to accelerate economic empowerment and remove any barriers to advancement into senior corporate positions.

Fifth, Carol listened to the appreciative comments from union leaders and community activities about the "social justice" role the firm had performed for its surrounding communities. She learned the firm had become politically active to assist neighboring communities in two ways. First, she discovered that Colgate Palmolive had provided legal assistance to members of a neighboring squatter camp who had been intimidated by the local council while steps were being taken to solve the squatter problem. Second, she discovered that although the American firm explicitly advocated nonalignment with any political party, initiatives were in place, at the request of community leaders, to provide "democracy training" as a social justice program. Indeed, materials she studied indicated that the firm sponsored lectures for the community by academics and other experts on specific subjects, such as voting procedures of issues connected with a bill of rights (these courses were offered for both white and black groups and communities).

Finally, Carol found that the SR projects that "worked" and achieved Colgate Palmolive's mission were ones in which people who were beneficiaries of the project were actively involved in formulating and implementing each activity. Colgate Palmolive followed the process of consultation with all stakeholders throughout their SR initiatives.

Carol paused, however, to reflect on a number of disturbing issues that had surfaced in personal interviews with some trade union leaders and community activists. In one of her meetings with trade union shop stewards, they argued that union leaders, not management, should direct and manage Colgate Palmolive's SR budget since they believed their constituency was the primary stakeholder group who were recipients of the firm's SR activities.

Carol countered that the SR budget should remain with the Foundation since Colgate Palmolive's unionized workforce comprised only 50 percent of employees and the firm had to ensure fair representation for all employees. Besides, Carol indicated to the shop stewards that the firm's SR activities were for "underprivileged" communities represented by all employee stakeholder race and ethnic groups.

Carol speculated on another issue that had surfaced with trade union leaders that made her uncomfortable. She wondered about the extent to which union leaders were genuinely interested in the needs of their community. She considered whether, based on her interviews with union leaders, they were more inclined to support issues to gain "political" favor with their followers inside the firm than the company's stakeholders and surrounding communities outside the firm than the company's stakeholders and surrounding communities outside the firm. For example, she remembered a discussion she'd had with union leaders about the best method to provide bursaries to the children of employees. Union leaders pressed hard to have ten bursaries that paid all fees. What's more, the union wanted to announce this decision to employees as a concession they'd obtained from management. On the other hand, she argued for shared responsibility of bursaries where parents paid a nominal amount and Colgate Palmolive contributed the remainder so that the budget would allow for an additional 20 bursaries and thus provide funding assistance to more in need. She believed this alternative was consistent with the notion that "shared help" is more effective than a "hand-out" in the firm's commitment to economic empowerment for underprivileged communities.

Finally, Carol reflected on an issue that several union representatives had raised during her interviews. Some leaders saw a dilemma for the firm. They pointed out that the firm was self-serving in promoting SR initiatives because a number of products were "sold" under the umbrella of social responsibility activities. For example, one leader described how the firm had supported primary health care education activities for a local community. He conceded that parents and children who received health care and nutritional handouts, posters, and other reading materials featuring a cartoon and logo depicting the "Colgate Smile" were helped by the program. On the other hand, they also received information promoting the "purchase" of oral care products sold by Colgate Palmolive. He questioned; "Is it right to help under privileged communities while at the same time also promoting your products to these communities?"

Carol frowned as she considered these issues; then the phone rang and she had to dash out, reminding herself to gain closure on the issues facing her.

APPENDIX

Social Responsibility Activities Through Education

Primary School   Colgate Palmolive was at the forefront of the adopted school initiative in South Africa. In 1977, Kutloanong Primary School in Vosloorus was the first school to receive assistance under this scheme and Colgate Palmolive now has five adopted primary schools in Vosloorus and Daveyton, all receiving assistance for teacher upgrade, media equipment, books, sports equipment, and even basics such as electricity and burglar-proofing.

High School   The St. Andrews Outreach and Bridging Program takes disadvantaged children from Daveyton to St. Andrews for additional and remedial tuition. Recreational days and fun events are also organized.

University   Pre-primary to tertiary level bursaries are offered to employees' dependents. The bursaries, which cover fees and text books, are also offered to dependents of retired and deceased employees.

Colgate Palmolive's assistance to the Academic Support Program at the University of the Witwaterrand is structured to supplement students' lectures, particularly at first-year level.

Colgate Palmolive recognizes the lack of adequate career guidance material and funds a high school career guidance program at the Medical University of South Africa.

An annual bursary donation is made to Medunsa and awarded by the university to dental students. A number of students also benefit each from bursary funding to the University of Cape Town.

Forty schools on the East Rand participated in the Deved Trust's Career Guidance Teachers' Program. Regular work shops and visits to industries give the teachers a better perception of the education necessary to enter identified careers.

The foundation supports teacher upgrade programs at the East Rand college of Education, Vista, and Promat. It also funds research surveys undertaken by Amcham's Policy Research Unit into Open, non-racial education in East Rand schools. This includes high school teacher training in cultural issues, and symposia for principals from TED and DET schools in the Boksburg area.

As part of their college diploma course, Technikon students are required to undertake six months' practical experience in industry. Colgate Palmolive has assisted many students to obtain their diplomas in analytical chemistry, chemical engineering, and production management through these six-month practical training periods.

Social Responsibility Activities Through Community Projects

The Colgate Palmolive Youth for South Africa program, started in January 1993, highlights the positive side of today's young people. It is aimed at encouraging youth groups to become more responsible to their communities, and rewards their efforts in diverse ways, as follows:

- Support is given to the Institute of Natural Resources project in KwaZulu, which includes water purification and basic sanitation work.
- Funding is provided for the St. Anthony's Aged Centre in Johannesburg.
- Colgate Palmolive organizes and manages the non-racial Colgate 15 km Road Race, which attracts over 4,500 runners each year. A percentage of the entrance money, matched by Colgate Palmolive, is given to the Retinitis Pigmentosa organization.
- Assistance is provided to the House of Mercy drug and alcohol rehabilitation center run by St. Anthony's
- Colgate Palmolive sponsors the running costs of the St. Francis House for the terminally ill.
- Aids Education Programs include sponsorship of an Aids aware-

ness page in school exercise books piloted by the Johannesburg City Council Health Department, as well as in-house programs for Colgate Palmolive employees.

- The Medunsa/Colgate Mobile Dental Unit provides treatment to underprivileged communities in northeastern Transvaal.
- Mobile Dental Units provide treatment to underprivileged communities in South Africa. Colgate Palmolive sponsorship has enabled the Departments of Community Dentistry at the Universities of Witwatersrand, Pretoria, and Medunsa to operate the three units currently providing this much-needed service in both rural and urban areas.
- The Business Development Training–East Rand Townships Project offers basic business skills training courses. This program gives opportunities to informal businesses to develop and create additional job opportunities in these areas of high unemployment.
- Colgate Palmolive supports the non-racial Eagle Tumbling Club, which offers gymnastics and tumbling training to children; it also covers transport and equipment costs.
- The Durban Lifesaver project sponsors the training and equipment needs of black lifesavers.
- Assistance and funding is provided to the Daveyton Physically Handicapped Training Center where a workshop offers sheltered employment.
- A Mobile Health Clinic has been built, using a bus, and is utilized in the expanding township of Vosloorus.
- Health education programs are provided by medical and dental students at rural clinics as part of the Medunsa Children's Clinic and Community Program. Funding is provided for a dental clinic located next to the children's medical ward at the provincial hospital adjoining Medunsa, and treatment is given free of charge by final-year Medunsa dental students.

12
Leadership of TQM in Autocratic Settings

Asbjorn Osland

Jim had returned to Central America, where he had worked for the previous two years (1990–2) as the company HR manager, to conduct some interviews which would help him better understand some research he had done earlier. Jim wondered how the latest company-change program, total quality management (TQM), would fare. He asked himself, "How can TQM be adopted in these old, company-town operations of the Tropical Export Company? How can one expect participation to flourish when the leaders are so autocratic?"

The Tropical Export Company is a family controlled, North American-based, multinational corporation with very extensive operations in Latin America that produce a labor-intensive tropical export goods for industrialized markets mainly in North America and Europe. There are a number of production divisions spread throughout Central and South America but Punta Blanca and Palo Amarillo are the two in which Jim had served.

Punta Blanca

Jim arrived in the late afternoon and would have to wait until the next day to speak to Julian, the general manager. He had dinner with another visitor to the guesthouse, a Latino information systems expert now assigned to the corporate office in the US. After chatting and watching TV, they decided to walk to the wharf to watch the loading process.

Reprinted by permission of the author.

From the wharf, Jim's companion, who had spent many years working at Punta Blanca early in his career, pointed to the modest wooden homes that lined the beach area and said: "See those houses there? That's where the Latinos lived. Only Americans and Europeans lived in the houses in the area surrounding the guesthouse, where the managers and supervisors now live. As late as 1970, there wasn't a single Latino manager or high-level supervisor."

Jim was surprised that he spoke with no bitterness. His companion had no doubt suffered from the "line," as they called it. The "line" referred to the social barrier to promotions of Latinos, erected during the 70 year neocolonial era when the company had dominated politics in the region. Jim hated to admit it but he enjoyed the deference that remained for foreign managers within the company. His companion added, "You know that Julian is the first general manager from the region – the first one to cross the line." They then returned to the guesthouse to retire for the night.

Jim enjoyed staying in the guesthouse at Punta Blanca. He enjoyed the camaraderie he felt with the other guests, people he had known when he worked for the company. The next morning, after he awakened to the blast of the ship's horn as it began its journey to Europe with a cargo produced by the Tropical Export Company in Punta Blanca, Jim remembered that he was to see Julian that morning. He left the comfortable guesthouse and made his way to the office. The shade of the old avocado and mango trees cooled the sidewalk and protected passers-by from the blazing tropical sun. It occurred to Jim that the shade was analogous to the strong traditions of the Punta Blanca operation that buffered it from the more trendy and ill-considered managerial innovations suggested by the corporate headquarters.

Julian

Julian, the general manager of Punta Blanca, is native to that community, a company town. He was educated in the US and completed a degree in the sciences. Early in his career he moved from research into production where he spent nearly his entire career of more than 25 years.

Jim entered the office and greeted the secretaries. They explained that Julian was in the meeting room addressing his direct reports and other high-level subordinates and that he should walk in and sit down. Jim slipped into the meeting room. Though in mid-sentence, Julian stopped and said, "Good morning, Jim." The others followed suit and Jim took a seat in the rear of the room. Julian, a large fit man, continued, waving his arms and addressing those in the meeting with a booming voice, "Though we've trained over 500 people in communication and the basics of TQM, I'm surprised that it has taken so long for you, the quality council, to get rolling. For two years I've sat here and observed, but you've done nothing. Now, I'm going to leave and Jose is going to take charge. You will remain here until you all agree on what you should do and how you will proceed. I will no longer observe because you've done next to nothing." Jose was the second-in-command, serving in the role of production manager. This was a position the company used to groom future general managers.

With that, he left and gestured to Jim to accompany him. He was somewhat agitated and walked briskly to his office. On his way, he said to the secretary, "Could you please bring us some coffee?" Jim had seen him like this in the past and had felt somewhat intimidated – in the eyes of his 5,500 subordinates, Julian controlled the destiny of the operation. Yet Jim knew he could confront him, as he had done when Julian and the operations VP had been poised to take aggressive action against some former subcontractors who had signed with the competition. At that time, Jim, when he was still the HR manager, had encouraged Julian to avoid reacting emotionally in a way that could provoke a violent response on the part of the gun-slinging inhabitants of the area. Julian was a very savvy politician and his finely honed political sensitivity prevailed over his more primal aggressive nature.

Jim gulped, while averting Julian's gaze, and said, "Does it seem at all ironic to you that you've just ordered them to be more participatory?"

Julian's eyes flashed for a moment but he calmly responded, "Look, you're a good man but sometimes you don't know squat about us." Still standing, he smiled and walked around to the back of Jim, strongly squeezed Jim's shoulder and moved to his desk. "Excuse me for a moment while I make a few calls to the VP and corporate. Stay here or someone else will come in and we'll never get to talk."

Jim sat and sipped his coffee and glanced at some publications on the coffee table. One was the local PR document from the company's plastics and packaging subsidiary. The Tropical Export Company used so much plastic and packaging in its production and packing operations that it had vertically integrated and had purchased a regional producer. Jim had visited the company from time to time during his tenure as the HR manager. It functioned in a largely autonomous fashion even though it was owned by the Tropical Export Company.

Jim reflected on his last visit. The second in command, the manufacturing manager, had explained to Jim about their approach to TQM: "We get together with the general manager only when we're ready to. I lead the committee, but the participants feel free to argue with me. I provide direction yet I'm not the ultimate authority. Then when we have something to suggest, we invite the general manager in, but only at that stage. If we invite him in too soon, he'll take over and people won't argue, because he's the boss."

Julian concluded his brief phone calls and sat down. "So what questions do you want to ask me?"

"I guess I have trouble understanding how participation will flourish in Punta Blanca," Jim began.

Julian responded: "One has little to fear from participation. If you know the business, you can help people problem solve in a manner that enables them to develop. By giving people authority they will come to you and seek your input. This gives me more power than I would have if I simply told an obedient work group what to do. I want people seeking answers. However, if I already know the answer I don't ask them – I tell them what I want done. I guess what I like most is getting a large organization to do what I want it to do. I see TQM as a chance to try something new. It's a tool for me. At the start, I was encouraged by gringo consultants to push my direct reports to take more initiative in the quality council and to be more accepting of cross-functional teams. However, I've refused to rush things. I know I could beat them over the head and, like good soldiers, they'd do what I want. However, I could be transferred at any time and TQM would stop if they didn't assume ownership."

Jim was puzzled by this comment for what he had just observed in the meeting room seemed to reflect pushing. The secretary then knocked and entered, "The plane is waiting for you, Don Jim. It's going to Palo Amarillo and you're on the roster." Don is a term of respect commonly used by Latinos when addressing men to whom they wish to show deference. With that, Jim bid farewell to Julian and rushed to the landing strip. Jim was to interview Robert, the general manager of Palo Amarillo.

Robert

Robert was born in the Caribbean and spent his early years in another Central American production division where his father had worked. His background was clearly rooted in the neocolonial history of the company, so much so that Robert had not become highly fluent in Spanish though he had resided in Latin America for much of his life. Robert had attended boarding school in Europe and was educated as a military officer. He found that the military was not a suitable career for him. His father then arranged for him and his brother to work for the company. Robert had worked in many different locations including Punta Blanca before his promotion to the general manager's slot in Palo Amarillo. Jim had seen that Robert was very effective during crises, perhaps in part due to his military background. His subordinates described Robert admiringly with the English word "pusher," meaning one who gets things done. Given his style of pushing to get results, Robert was eager to implement the different projects he envisioned, some of which could be done through TQM.

Robert was deeply concerned for the welfare of his employees, which was consistent with the paternalistic background of the company. On several occasions Jim had conflicted with Robert over such company services as the commissary. As a reflection of the corporate cost-reduction emphasis, Jim had suggested that the commissary be spun off as a cooperative and weaned away from the company. Robert had vigorously objected stating that the local merchant would begin charging too much if the company store weren't there to hold down prices.

Robert was strongly socialized to the company-town culture found in the production divisions. He spent most of his free time with company employees or contractors. In contrast, Julian attempted to develop social contacts outside the company, Though very capable and intellectually gifted, Robert's insularity made him somewhat resistant to change. He continued to exhibit the strong command-and-control orientation of the traditional general manager of the Tropical Export Company, even though he seemed to understand the basic tenets of TQM.

Palo Amarillo

Jim enjoyed the flight over the mountain range. Since there was only one pilot, he sometimes got a bit worried about the pilot's health and propensity to heart attack. However, he sat up front with the pilot and chatted on the way. The pilot flew close to a dormant volcano so that Jim could get a good view. They also noted that the landscape had changed after the earthquake. In poetic Latino speech the pilot observed, "Look at how the accompanying landslides tore away the green cover and exposed the raw earth. Vegetation and the bleeding earth then partially clogged the river arteries."

Upon arrival Jim entered the company office and greeted the secretary. She said, "Don Robert had to go to the wharf to intervene in a
labor conflict. He said that you should go to the guest house and that
he would see you this evening at the club."

Jim went to the guesthouse, named after the general manager who
had once lived there. He was tired and decided to simply take it easy:
eat lunch, nap, and go for a swim at the pool. Later, after dinner, he
walked to the club.

In years past, Jim had been entertained by stories from people
reminiscing about the neocolonial era. One time, a local Spanish businessman told Jim, "Many years ago I bought the first car owned by a
'civilian' [i.e., non-company resident] in Palo Amarillo. When it was
delivered on the company train, the general manager initially refused
to allow it to be unloaded, saying he hadn't given his authorization."
Those listening all laughed at this story, even though they had heard
it many times. Laughing at such command-and-control behavior of
the managers was a way to deal with the submission subordinates felt
in such a hierarchy. This command-and-control attitude had not
changed over the years though managers had perhaps become less
direct in their assertion of control. In a sense, TQM allowed the same
type of control but with a gentler face.

Another individual listening in added, "You know how I learned
English – my boss said, 'No Spanish'!" Again they guffawed.

Such tales from the past were part of the folklore that made the
company what it was. However, Jim had also seen the more raw side
during his tenure as the HR manager. Jim recalled how, for one department head, hierarchy was more than simple power associated with
a senior position. He had actually asked Jim to do a survey feedback
of his department to find out if his subordinates held a sufficient
degree of fear of him, the department manager.

Finally, Robert arrived. They greeted one another and chatted for
a few hours over a few beers. During the course of the conversation,
they spoke of many things, including business. Perhaps to taunt Jim,
Robert said, "You know the TQM council has become a manager's
council. I chose to limit membership to department heads. I want
people who understand the way things work around here. Besides,
your emphasis on participation might not be appropriate here. You
know that even if I ask a question, they are trying to guess what's on
my mind. The exception was one young supervisor who was challenging me too much, so I rotated him off the council."

Jim and Robert continued speaking, watching the last quarter of a
play-off game on television. Robert left when it ended.

Francisco

Jim remained at the bar. He didn't have to leave until noon the following day and had finished his business. He then noticed the entry of the former TQM coordinator from Punta Blanca, Francisco. "Francisco! How are you? Do you work here now?" exclaimed Jim.

They shook hands vigorously. "Nice to see you, Jim. Yes, I'm here now. Two years in a staff position was enough for me. It was an interesting experience but I'd rather be a boss. I'm now the purchasing manager here."

Jim thought this was an ideal opportunity to continue gathering information about TQM. They ordered coffee and sat down at a nearby table. "While I was in Punta Blanca, Julian forced the quality council members to sit in a room with Jose, the production manager and second-in-command, until they could get it together to participate," said Jim. They both laughed at the irony.

"I can see how that would work though I suspect you are puzzled," responded Francisco.

"Well, yes, I am puzzled," admitted Jim.

"You think about it and give me a call," Francisco countered teasingly.

Jim smiled. "Okay, so you'll enlighten me later. How about telling me about your experiences with TQM."

Francisco responded with a lengthy monologue, filled with the trials of any staff person attempting to facilitate change in a strong command-and-control organizational culture. This seemed a warm-up to his explanation of the success of cross-functional teams. "After encountering initial resistance from the turf-conscious department heads, Julian told me not to push cross-functional problem solving quite so aggressively. Instead he suggested limiting the problem-solving teams to intradepartmental teams until the department heads became more accepting. Later, Julian instructed me to get the department heads to agree on a respected operations manager who would lead the team attacking the quality problem. The team leader was then empowered to choose the members of his or her team, which included people from other departments. The team leader chose people he respected and with whom he had worked and had developed a sense of mutual respect and loyalty. These people met and analyzed the specific problem. Significant improvements in quality outcomes resulted. The market feedback has been very positive. By the way, how did the survey turn out?"

Jim had conducted an attitude survey contrasting TQM participants with non-participants in both Punta Blanca and Palo Amarillo. "It went well," responded Jim. "Thanks for your help. Basically, the TQM participants in Punta Blanca had a more favorable set of attitudes than the non-participants. This was not true in Palo Amarillo in that there were no significant differences between the two groups. But I'm not sure why. What do you think?"

Francisco thought of responding but decided it best to avoid commentary on his superiors' actions.

The time was then very late. Both were tired and decided to call it a night. The next day Jim returned to the capital to catch a flight to the US.

13

Chang Koh Metal Ptd Ltd in China

Thomas Begley

Chang Koh Metal Engineering Ptd Ltd was founded in 1982 by Teo
Kai San, a first generation Straits-born Chinese. The company's operations were in the production of metal stamping precision parts. In
1993, the company expanded its operations by establishing a plant in
Putian, China, which was the area of China from which Teo Kai
San's parents had emigrated. The founder's son, Andrew Teo, was
appointed as general manager. Andrew was 29 years old and had an
engineering degree from the National University of Singapore. Prior
to joining his father's company, Andrew had worked for an American
multinational company in Singapore and had progressed to the rank
of line manager, a position with substantial authority and responsibility. Andrew joined his father's company because he felt that his success in the multinational was a sign of his skills, indicating that he
deserved a senior position in his father's company based on merit
rather than family connections. He also felt that the systems and
practices he learned there would enable him to bring more updated
management practices to Chang Koh Metal.

Since Andrew's father believed it was important to have a person
who was knowledgeable about the local area in a position of authority, he appointed a relative from Putian, Jian Wei, as the plant manager to assist Andrew in the plant's operations. A primary reason for
choosing China as a site for a plant was the belief that Singaporean
Chinese should find it easy to work with the Chinese in China. After
all, the two groups shared a common cultural heritage. The other
advantages were the readily available supply of labor – Singapore was
experiencing full employment and the company found it difficult to
recruit qualified production workers – and the lower operating costs.

Reprinted by permission of the author.

After a year in China, however, Andrew was not sure the plan to venture there was wise. Although the labor costs were much lower than Singapore, productivity was disappointing, and a number of management and labor problems had arisen which he felt were frustrating his efforts to control the plant efficiently.

Staffing Procedure

Andrew had learned from his previous work experience that it was important to hire the right people with the appropriate qualifications and place them in the positions to which they were best suited in order to ensure smooth operations. But his efforts were hindered by Jian Wei's peculiar hiring practices. To fill open positions, Jian Wei would contact city officials and friends and relatives and ask them for recommendations on who to hire. Most of the time the people hired did not have the skills needed to perform the tasks for which they were hired. Andrew vigorously protested against Jian Wei's practices and instituted formalized procedures to follow in recruitment and selection that called for systematic advertising of positions, evaluation of candidates, and hiring based on qualifications. Jian Wei became upset because he argued that his practices were necessary as a way to keep the channels of communication and mutual exchange open with important officials because the company might need their help in future business dealings. This disagreement created tension between the two men.

Productivity and Quality Issues

The plant in China employed about 150 workers. Andrew adopted the same salary system as he had seen used in his former employer and paid these workers a fixed salary based on the number of hours worked. However, their productivity rates were very low and the workers demonstrated very little commitment to meeting the company's goals. After three months, Andrew scrapped the salary system and instead instituted a piece rate system in which the workers were paid a minimum base salary supplemented by an incremental rate for each unit produced above a certain number. In other words, if the workers produced at or below the minimum production standard for the day, they received the minimum wage. If they produced above that rate, they received additional money for each extra piece produced.

For the following two months, Andrew was proud of his innovative management as the results were impressive. Company productivity targets were met, the workers were exerting themselves energetically, and they were even willing to work overtime at the same rate as the usual work day in order to make extra money. However, within a short period of time, he began to receive several complaints from customers about the low quality of the goods they were receiving from the company. Parts that should have been rejected were instead shipped to customers.

In response, Andrew had the quality control and manufacturing specifications printed on large posters and posted around the plant for all to see. He emphasized to the workers the importance of quality in the final product. He set up a quality control department and implemented 100 percent quality checks. However, all of these efforts failed to stop poor-quality products from reaching the customers. As he investigated, he discovered that those in the quality control department were inspecting the parts, but they were passing almost everything that they inspected. He held a training session for the quality control inspectors, pointed out defective parts to them, and had them demonstrate to him that they could distinguish poor quality from good quality. Since it was clear that they could do so, he sent them back to the production floor, convinced that they would now begin to perform as a true quality control unit. Yet within a short period of time it became apparent that the unit was not doing the job any better than before the training session.

Andrew expressed his frustration to Jian Wei and demanded that he take action to improve the situation. Jian Wei protested that the quality control members' actions were completely understandable – they knew that rejected parts would not be added to the total that would count toward the incentive rate compensation and would therefore reduce the wages production workers would receive. They would not take money out of the pockets of the production workers. Andrew felt that the quality control workers should be shown that failure to act would take money out of their own pockets, so he suggested that a system of demerit points be set up for the quality control employees which would lead to deductions from their wages. However, Jian Wei strongly disagreed with the idea, arguing that it was unfair to penalize these employees for doing what they believed was right. Finally, a compromise was reached in which more supervisors were hired for the quality control department to provide closer supervision of the workers. In addition, Andrew arranged to have all final products shipped to Singapore for final inspection before being sent out to customers.

Rules and Regulations

About 15 technicians were responsible for the maintenance of ma-
chinery. At any one time, one machine would be set aside for maintenance work. Ninety percent of the time a machine was designated as
"in maintenance," actually sat unused. To Andrew's dismay, he found
that the technicians regularly used the "in maintenance" machine to
do moonlighting work to make extra income. To Andrew, this practice was a clear violation of company rules and regulations, a fact that
warranted dismissal of the supervisor of the technicians, who had not
only condoned the activity but had actually participated in it. Jian
Wei supported the employees. He argued that the machine would
have been left idle anyway so what was the harm? All activities were
conducted outside normal working hours and the technicians' jobs
were not being neglected. No additional costs were incurred by the
factory, except in the operation of the machine. Jian Wei thought
that, as boss, Andrew needed to show much more understanding and
sensitivity to the issue than he had. It was unfair to single one person
out for punishment, especially when the company had not suffered
any losses. In addition, Jian Wei was dismayed to hear Andrew talk
about dismissing an employee. He said that such practice just was not
done in China – no true Chinese person would think about removing
a person's "iron rice bowl." Reluctantly, Andrew agreed to Jian Wei's
recommendation to resolve the issue by transferring the technicians'
supervisor to another department.

Problems like these made Andrew very doubtful that the operation
in China could ever be turned into a profitable venture. His father
had been willing to grant Andrew some time to get the plant up and
running before he expected results, but now he was starting to ask
questions about why the plant was still losing money and no trend in
the direction of profitability was evident in the financial performance
figures. He had recently asked Andrew to come up with a concrete
plan to turn the situation around. Andrew was wondering what he
could do.

14

Rus Wane Equipment: A Joint Venture in Russia

Stanislav V. Shekshnia and Sheila M. Puffer

"John, yesterday Lev presented me with a candidate for the human resource manager's position. Tomorrow he is going to ask the board to appoint Sasha Neresyan. What do you think?" Ronald Chapman, Wane Machines, Inc.'s country manager for Russia, was querying John Swift, deputy general manager of Rus Wane Equipment, as they discussed Wane's Russian joint venture on the eve of its third anniversary in November 1993.

The question came as quite a surprise to John, who had virtually given up hope that the human resource manager position would be filled and who would never have considered 30 year old Sasha as a candidate for the job. Not that Sasha lacked desirable qualities as an employee. He had joined Rus Wane in June 1992 as a customs clearance officer and had subsequently earned a very good reputation in the company by skillfully negotiating with bureaucratic and often corrupt Russian government officials who could turn importing of crucial goods and components into a nightmare for the joint venture. Before joining Rus Wane, Sasha had retired from the Army with the rank of captain, having worked in the Middle East using his background as a military translator. His excellent communications skills and fluency in English had helped him build good relations with many local and all expatriate Rus Wane employees.

But being a good customs clearance officer, John thought, hardly makes one a qualified human resource professional. As Ron paused, John wondered aloud: "Will Sasha be respected by senior Rus Wane managers, even though he is at least 20 years younger than they are? And what does he know about HR practices?" John did not have the answers to these questions, but he knew that Sasha was a smart and hard-working young man. What really bothered John was the fact that Sasha had been brought to Rus Wane by the general manager, Lev Nosvikov, who had been a long-time patient and friend of Dr Neresyan, Sasha's father. This hiring proposal was the latest episode contributing to the strained relations between the Russian general manager of the joint venture and his American counterpart.

The US Partner, Wane Machines, Inc.

During its 150 years of operation, Wane Machines, Inc. had grown from a one-person, one-invention workshop in New York City into a multibillion dollar multinational corporation with manufacturing, sales, and service operations in dozens of countries. Wane had always remained in one industry, engaging in the manufacture, installation, and maintenance of large-scale heating and cooling equipment for office and apartment buildings. In the late 1890s, Wane began its international expansion by setting up operations in Europe. From the outset, its strategy had been to be recognized as a local company in every market it entered, and to establish long-term relationships with customers by providing a complete package of services, including product maintenance, repair, and upgrading. Following this strategy consistently for nearly 100 years, Wane Machines became a global market leader with a network of more than 50 companies operating in 160 countries.

Wane Machines had four regional divisions: domestic (the United States and Canada), Europe, Latin America, and Asia. In the 1980s domestic operations lost its sales leadership to the European division, as the market for new construction in the United States dropped precipitously during the severe economic recession. After a decade of spectacular growth, the European market also declined sharply in the early 1990s as the United Kingdom, and later France and Germany, entered an economic recession. To attempt future growth, Wane management began to explore the markets that had begun to open in Eastern Europe and the Soviet Union. In 1989 Ronald Chapman was appointed Wane's country managers of the Soviet Union. Ron, who had a Harvard MBA and 20 years' experience with Wane, was charged with studying the Soviet Market and setting up Wane's operations in Moscow and St. Petersburg. Before this assignment, he had managed Wane's joint venture in Taiwan after working in Japan and Hong Kong for ten years. In his new function, Chapman reported to the area vice president for central and eastern Europe who was located in Wane's European division in Brussels.

Entering the USSR Market

The Soviet market was not entirely *terra incognita* for Wane, as the company had been exporting its products to the USSR through its Austrian company since the early 1970s. During that period Wane sold its high-quality heating and cooling equipment for installation in several Soviet government buildings as well as an American-built hotel. However, it could not penetrate the huge domestic market for several reasons. The ruble could not be converted to hard currency to pay for imported goods, few Soviet enterprises had access to hard currency, and until 1988 all purchases of imports were controlled by government foreign trade organizations with whom enterprises were required to negotiate for imported equipment and other supplies.

By the late 1980s the market potential in the USSR for Wane's products was the largest in the world as 85 percent of the country's 290 million people lived in apartment complexes, most of which required upgrading of their large-scale heating and cooling systems. In addition, more housing was planned under President Gorbachev's "Housing 2000" program, announced in 1986 with the goal of providing every Soviet family with a separate apartment by the year 2000. This would be a massive undertaking, as some 25 percent of families lived in communal apartments in which they shared kitchen and bathroom facilities with other families. Because of these conditions, demand for large-scale heating and cooling systems was expected to double through the remainder of the century.

According to the Ministry of Building Equipment Manufacturing, in the late 1980 annual demand for large heating and cooling equipment was approximately 100,000 units, while Soviet enterprises manufactured a total of only 60,000 units. Production planning, resource allocation, and customer selection were all controlled centrally by government bodies such as Gosplan, the state planning ministry, and Gossnab, the government supply organization. The domestic heating and cooling industry was fragmented: manufacturing plants were under the Ministry of Building Equipment Manufacturing, installation units were attached to the State Construction Committee, and maintenance services were operated by local civic authorities. The major cities of Moscow, St. Petersburg, and Kiev had their own manufacturing facilities and installation units.

For more than 20 years, Soviet factories had been manufacturing the same, unimproved heating and cooling products for the domestic market, having little incentive or ability to upgrade them under the system of central planning. Artificially low prices were established by state authorities with little regard to actual costs or customer demand. For their part, customers, who were construction ministries and building management organizations attached to local governments, paid for goods not with their own money, but with funds allocated by the government. They were usually glad to receive the scarce equipment, even though it was of poor quality and low reliability.

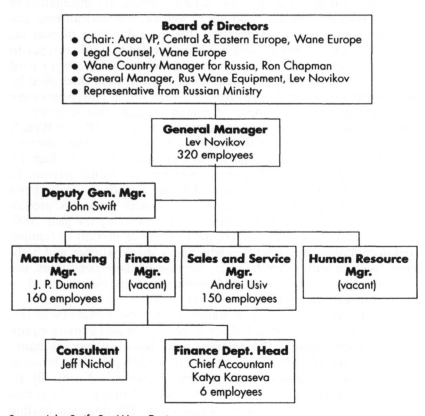

Source: John Swift, Rus Wane Equipment.

Exhibit 14.1   Rus Wane Equipment's organization chart

Formation of the Joint Venture

In 1989 the Soviet Ministry of Foreign Trade put Wane in touch with NLZ, a medium-sized factory located just outside Moscow that manufactured heating and cooling equipment similar to Wane's, but of lower quality. In February 1990, after what appeared to Wane's management as lengthy and sometimes frustrating negotiations, a joint venture called Rus Wane Equipment was formed, with the primary purpose of establishing a new plant to manufacture products virtually identical to Wane's European models. Registered as a Soviet–Belgian joint venture, the new company had initial capital funds of US$11.5 million. Wane contributed $8 million in hard currency and equipment for the new factory to be built with the Soviet partner. The latter contributed use of the facilities in the existing plant to manufacture components, as well as the site for the new factory. Whether NLZ or the government owned the land was unclear, however, because of ambiguous legislation on property. Wane Machines had a 57 percent share of the joint venture, and NLZ, 43 percent. At about the same time, Wane signed a second joint venture with a St. Petersburg partner to install and service Rus Wane's products in western Russia.

Wane's strategy for Russia consisted of three major elements. First, they did not expect to make money for the first three years. Second, they planned to develop export potential for eastern Europe. Third, Wane hoped that the Russian ruble would become a convertible currency in the near future.

The highest governing body of the Rus Wane joint venture was the board of directors. The chairman of the board was Wane Europe's area vice president for central and eastern Europe. The other board members were the legal counsel of Wane Europe; Wane's country manager for the Soviet Union, Ron Chapman; Rus Wane Equipment's general manager, Lev Novikov; and an official from the Soviet ministry of building equipment manufacturing. The board of directors met quarterly to review business plans and the progress made toward achieving them, to approve capital expenditures, and to appoint direct reports. Organization charts depicting the Rus Wane Equipment joint venture and its relationship with Wane Machines are provided in exhibits 14.1 and 14.2.

At the time of Wane's initial negotiations, joint ventures were the primary form of market entry into the Soviet Union. The Joint Venture Law of 1987 had opened the door for foreign investment in the USSR and accorded preferential taxation status and other privileges to foreign joint ventures. Initially, Soviet law restricted foreign owner-

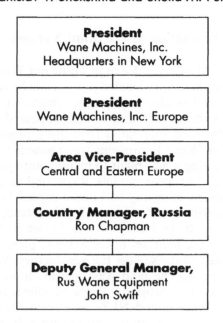

Exhibit 14.2 Wane's Machines, Inc.'s organization chart (abridged)

ship of joint ventures to a maximum of 49 percent, and the head of the operation was required to be a Soviet citizen. In 1988, these provisos were withdrawn by the Russian government, permitting greater foreign ownership and control.

Although Soviet law no longer required a Soviet citizen to hold the most senior position, Wane's policy throughout the world was to put local managers in charge, because they were believed to be the most knowledgeable and capable individuals to run local operations. Therefore, Lev Nodikov, a 58 year old mechanical engineer by training, was appointed general manager of Rus Wane Equipment. He also remained general manager of the Soviet partner, NLZ, a position he had held for 15 of the 25 years he had worked in the industry. His experience, enthusiasm, and strong leadership led Wane's management to view him as the driving force who could manage construction of the new manufacturing facility and see it through to completion under very difficult circumstances.

Construction of the Plant

In October 1990, shortly after the joint venture agreement was signed, Wane's management took the bold step of beginning construction of a plant in the Moscow area to produce heating and cooling equipment for the Russian market. The multimillion dollar investment was one of the first major commitments by a Western firm to manufacture products in Russia, since most companies were unwilling to take such a risk in Russia's highly unstable political and economic environment.

The state-of-the-art plant was built in full compliance with Wane's specifications, making it technologically comparable to Wane's European facilities. The plant was completed in June 1992, an extremely short period of time, especially in the Soviet Union, where such building projects usually took years, and sometimes as long as a decade. Furthermore, the external environment at the time of construction was marked by the breakup of the Soviet Union; severely deteriorating economic conditions in Russia, including monthly inflation exceeding 20 percent; disintegration of the centralized resource allocation system; and confusing and vacillating legislation on corporate taxation, business development, and the status of foreign operations. Inconsistent government policy on foreign direct investment, including taxation and ownership rights, along with erratic domestic policy concerning government subsidies, business law, and ownership of property, contributed to the external problems confronting international firms in Russia.

Rus Wane's Equipment's plant was designed to manufacture Wane's European models of heating and cooling equipment, with minor modifications for the Russian market. Product characteristics, such as length of service and number of callbacks per unit, showed that the quality of Wane's products was more than four times that of Russian competitors', requiring half the energy to operate. Wane maintained a pricing policy not to exceed twice the price of the grossly inferior Russian models. The first product was scheduled to be shipped from the new factory in June 1993, and full capacity of 5,000 units annually was projected for 1995.

In August 1993, only six weeks behind schedule, Rus Wane Equipment celebrated its first shipment with toasts of Moet champagne and Stolichnaya vodka. By September the factory was fully operational, with an available production capacity of 85 units per month. Most of the joint venture's office employees and factory workers came from NLZ, the Russian partner. A select group, they were full of enthusiasm for working on the joint venture and looked forward to excellent working conditions in the new plant as well as democratic and participative Western management methods.

Sales and Service Operations

While the plant was under construction, Rus Wane also set up an organization to sell, install, and maintain Wane's imported and locally produced equipment. Field personnel, who numbered 150, were recruited from various Moscow installation and service agencies. This part of the business was quite successful, offering Western-style maintenance service to numerous foreign organizations and some Russian companies that could afford it.

Early Obstacles

Construction of a state-of-the-art manufacturing facility and establishment of a sales and service network were achievements that few joint ventures had accomplished in Russia up to that time. However, reaching these goals by no means guaranteed Rus Wane's success. Among the obstacles confronting the firm once it became operational were an unexpected downturn in demand, difficulty in securing reliable suppliers, and an unpredictable legal and economic environment.

Despite the Soviet Union's vast market potential, much of Rus Wane's production capacity sat idle in the initial months because of weak customer demand. As a result, only 17 units were manufactured in September, 12 were complete in October, and 15 were planned for November. And Russia and the other countries of the former Soviet Union entered a severe economic crisis, new construction declined dramatically and demand for heating and cooling systems plummeted. No one had exact data, but Rus Wane' s management estimated annual domestic sales in Russia to be 6,000 units, while the total combed capacity of domestic manufacturers was 30,000 to 40,000 units.

Under this tremendous supply pressure, aggravated by the extremely difficult financial position of most of their company's customers, price became a major factor in the purchase decision. Rus Wane's product, sold even at zero profit margin, was still nearly twice as expensive as domestic equipment because of small production runs and costs associated with the sophisticated design. Prospective Russian customers, primarily state- or municipally owned construction and engineering enterprises, were caught in a squeeze. They suffered a cash shortage resulting from sharply reduced government subsidies of their operations, and hyperinflation had eroded their purchasing power. A limited number of price-tolerant and quality-sensitive customers, such as commercial banks, foreign hotels, and joint ventures, appreciated the quality of Rus Wane's products. Even those, however, often preferred to buy competitors' systems manufactured in western Europe, considering the foreign origin to be more prestigious. High inflation of the ruble, along with its devaluation against foreign currencies, eliminated virtually all cost advantages of manufacturing in Russia, and did not allow Rus Wane to sell profitably to customers outside the country as it had planned.

Developing relationships with reliable domestic suppliers was an objective that proved challenging to implement. The company carefully sought out enterprises that had produced for the military sector because they had been held to higher quality standards and stricter delivery schedules than other enterprises under the former central planning system. Such enterprises also often had idle capacity and faced layoffs resulting from drastic cuts in government orders, and hence were eager to find customers. However, even these suppliers were not easily able to meet Rus Wane's standards, and they required a considerable amount of Rus Wane's time and energy for training and monitoring.

Like other companies operating in the Russian market, Rus Wane had to struggle with a constantly changing legal framework and unpredictable government policy. For example, in 1992 the Russian government froze the company's bank account for six months. The State bank had run out of cash and arbitrarily withheld payments owed to Russian and foreign enterprises. In another unfortunate financial incident, Rus Wane was forced to pay $1.5 million in taxes on their new factory building when the Russian government introduced a value-added tax, even though the building had been completed well before the introduction of the tax.

In spite of such problems, the company was growing and its management systems were being developed. With significant cash flows from its sales and service field operations compensating for the losses in manufacturing, Rus Wane was a profitable organization overall, with 320 employees and monthly revenues of $600,000.

Staffing Key Managerial Positions

According to the joint venture agreement, Wane Machines was responsible for sending three experienced executives to serve as Rus Wane's deputy general manager, manufacturing manager, and financial manager for the first two to three years. Russian national would take over the positions at the end of this initial period. The major objectives of this policy were to provide "assistance in technology and management skills transfer, management systems and processes development, and local personnel coaching." Two other senior management positions, sales and service manger and human resources manager, were to be filled by local nationals from the beginning because they involved regular contact with Russian customers or workers at various levels, thus requiring a thorough knowledge of local culture and employment practices.

An experienced local manager had been found to fill the sales and service manager's position, but the remaining key managerial positions had been harder to fill. Wane fell behind schedule in sending its expatriates to Russia, and Lev Novikov, the general manager, delayed hiring a local for the human resources position, preferring to administer that function himself.

John Swift, a 35 year old American, was appointed as Rus Wane's deputy general manager in late 1991. For nearly ten months, while seeking suitable accommodations for his family, he commuted frequently from European headquarters in Brussels; he finally settled in Moscow in September 1992. John had joined Wane in 1989 after graduating from business school. He then completed the corporate management development program and worked for two years in Western Europe as a filed operations manager. Before 1991 John had never been to Russia nor, he said, had he ever had any intention of going there. He was, however, ambitious, and readily accepted the job offer, seeing it as a valuable career move. As deputy general manager, he reported to Lev Novikov, the joint venture's general manager, and was responsible for supervising technology transfer, sales, pricing, and personnel. He also served as the liaison between the joint venture and Wane's European headquarters, and reported to Ron Chapman, Wane's country manager for Russia.

Jean-Pierre Dumont, Rus Wane's manufacturing manager, had 15 years of engineering experience with Wane Machines in his native France, but the Russian appointment was his first management position. Like John Swift, he had little prior knowledge of Russia, yet he was equally eager to take the job. He explained: "It's very rare these days that an engineer gets a chance to work in a factory created from scratch. I am lucky to get this chance and I'm not going to miss it."

Convincing an experienced financial manager to relocate to Russia was not an easy task. After an intensive and lengthy search, Jeff Nichol, a 27 year old Englishman who had been working at Wane for two years as a corporate auditor, was selected in October 1991. Because of Jeff's limited experience, Ron Chapman sent him for training in Brussels for six months before going to Russia. In the meantime, Lev appointed Katya Karaseva, NLZ's chief accountant, to head Rus Wane's finance department. Katya had worked in the industry for 24 years, 17 of them with Lev.

Wane's Russia country manager, Ron Chapman, worked out of Wane's European headquarters in Brussels, but flew to Russia at least once a month to visit Wane's St. Petersburg joint venture as well as Rus Wane Equipment in Moscow, where he would review the joint venture's situation with the general manager, Lev Novikov, and his deputy, John Swift.

Tensions in the Finance Department

When Jeff Nichol arrived at Rus Wane in the spring of 1992, Lev suggested that he be a consultant for a while rather than immediately assuming the duties of financial manager, citing his young age, his need to adjust to the local culture, and his lack of Russian language abilities. Ron accepted the arrangement because he wanted Jeff to spend some of his time at the St. Petersburg joint venture. For a while, Jeff travelled between Moscow and St. Petersburg, spending most of his time learning the Russian language, becoming acquainted with Russian accounting systems, and developing financial procedures for both joint ventures.

Early in 1993, when a financial manager had been recruited for the St. Petersburg operation, Jeff decided it was the right time for him to become financial manager at Rus Wane. John Swift fully supported him. By that time Rus Wane had eight employees in the finance department: Jeff, Katya, and six accountants, most of whom came from NLZ. Unfortunately, this small group was unable to work smoothly together. As John Explained to Ron: "We've got total confusion in the finance department: people don't know who's the boss. Katya does what she wants, and Jeff is running out of patience. His contract expires in March and I don't think he's looking forward to staying any longer. Ron, we can't allow this situation to continue – the company needs a financial manager."

To compound the problem, the accountants expressed their disappointment to John that Western management practices that they had hoped would give them greater participation in decision making had not been implemented. They also complained about not being rewarded on merit, and the fact that the Westerners, whom they considered to be doing comparable work, were receiving substantially higher compensation.

From the beginning, communication between Jeff and Katya had not been easy. The language barrier – he did not speak Russian and she did not speak English – was not the only problem. Several times Jeff had organized training sessions for Rus Wane's finance personnel, yet each time Katya had found excuses not to participate. When, after a year at the joint venture, Jeff had become conversational in Russian, communication between him and Katya failed to improve in any meaningful way. Even though they worked virtually side by side, with Katya in a private office and Jeff in an adjacent common area, they communicated only through interoffice mail.

Jeff made a number of appeals to Lev to try to get his point across. He wrote several memos, with copies to the vice president of finance for Wane Europe, in which he described Katya's mistakes, but the general manager never replied and continued to show his full support for Katya. In addition, the finance staff had been expanding, yet Jeff had never been involved in the selection process. When he raised the issue with Lev, the latter responded that hiring was his problem, not Jeff's.

Discord over the General Manager

In February 1993, John Swift sent a memo to Lev suggesting that he propose Jeff's appointment as acting financial manager to Rus Wane's board of directors for approval, as required by company policy. Lev did not respond. A month later John raised the issue again and received the categorical reply: "He cannot be a financial manager." Without challenging that conclusion, John forwarded his suggestion to Ron Chapman who had shown full understanding of John's viewpoint. The subject of the financial manager's appointment was put on the agenda for the next board meeting. However, the day before the meeting, the item was withdrawn from the agenda. Ron later explained to John that Lev had convinced him not to be in a hurry to appoint Jeff to the position.

Meanwhile, tensions in the finance department continued to escalate. The joint venture experienced some delays in consolidating its first business plan, as well as difficulties in cash management and inventory control. On several occasions Jeff openly expressed his low opinion of his Russian colleagues' professional qualifications. These problems deeply concerned the deputy general manager, but the country manager did not take the matter seriously. Nor did Ron seem to be concerned about other signs of poor morale. For example, the first

Russian hired as a salesperson, who had been trained in the United States and western Europe and was highly respected in the company, left to work for a Russian trading venture. In addition, turnover in the factory was 5 percent a month.

In a discussion the two had about the finance department, Ron assessed the situation quite differently from John: "I think you're dramatizing the situation, John. Rus Wane has an excellent cost accounting system, our corporate financial software has been successfully introduced, and the skills of the finance people have improved tremendously."

"Yes, but Jeff has done it all himself," John replied.

"That's because he doesn't know how to delegate. He needs to work at improving his management style. I am beginning to understand why Lev can't see him as a financial manager. Jeff doesn't know how to manage people and he is becoming paranoid about Katya. I'm afraid that if on Saturday night his girlfriend doesn't show up for a date, he'll find a way to blame it on Katya. By the way, John, Lev is looking for a financial manager from the outside. It could be a good solution."

John was unpleasantly surprised to hear about the proposal. Lev had mentioned nothing about it to him. "You know, Ron, it's always very difficult to communicate with Lev. First, he doesn't like to share any information with me and he prefers to make all the decisions himself. And second, he is simply never here. The last time I saw him was ten days ago."

Although Lev had officially become a full-time employee of Rus Wane Equipment in January 1993, he had never resigned from his position as general manager of NLZ, which was still manufacturing its old product next door to the joint venture's new plant. Some people at Rus Wane were concerned about the situation; their perception was that their general manager was also their competitor's general manager. There had been rumours about the old plant being in a difficult financial situation, but no one had reliable information. Yet it was well known that NLZ had been going through the process of privatization, as mandated by the government, and Lev had been leading it. A major task would be to determine what percentage of shares would be owned by various managers and other employees.

John thought that there was a clear conflict of interest between Lev's role at the old factory and his position in the joint venture. He tried to raise the issue with Ron during one of his monthly visits: "Lev is preoccupied with his own interests, not Rus Wane's. When you are not here, he spends all his time at the old factory trying to turn it into his private property."

Ron angrily interrupted: "Let's drop the subject. This is not your responsibility, John."

Hiring a Human Resource Manager

John suppressed his instinctive response, feeling his anger growing. On several previous occasions he had tried to raise the subject of Lev Novokov's management style with Ron, but the latter never wanted to discuss it. Now, totally frustrated with personnel management issues at the joint venture, John shifted to another sore point: "As you know, Ron, we still don't have a human resource manager here at Rus Wane. I believe Lev hasn't filled the position on purpose. He wants to continue to do things the old Soviet way – to run the company like a tsar."

Ron looked up sharply: "That's a pretty strong statement, John. You've got to have facts to prove it."

John was sure he had the facts. A human resource manager was supposed to have been hired three years ago – just as soon as the joint venture was official – in order to organize the selection process for other positions. However, Lev had decided to manage this function himself. As a result, all of the joint venture's senior managers other than the expatriates, and most of the lower-level managers, had come from NLZ. John considered this move a dangerous mistake. What was worse, he believed, was that quite a few senior managers' relatives had also been hired. The most notable, Lev's son, had already built an astonishing career within 12 months, starting as an assistant, becoming purchasing manager, and then joint to western Europe for 18 months' practical training. John had strongly opposed the decision to send Novikov junior abroad, arguing that there had been better candidates and that Rus Wane's reputation among its employees for fairness and democracy would suffer. Ron had ignored these concerns, and just as he had anticipated, John began to detect silent but strong disapproval and disappointment from employees.

Unhappy with Lev's hiring practices, John championed the introduction of selection and hiring procedures that had been developed for Russian operations by Wane's European headquarters (see Exhibit 14). The procedures for implementing Wane's standard corporate practices – preparing job requisitions, advertising vacant positions, evaluating candidates' résumés, and having human resource and line managers conduct interviews – had been approved by Ron Chapman and were supposed to be mandatory at Rus Wane. However, the Russian managers ignored the procedures. For instance, a week before John's meeting with Ron, an angry Jean-Pierre Dumont told John that a new machine operator had been hired for the factory without his knowledge. It took John some time to find out that the 18 year old new employee was the son of a local customs officer who often cleared shipments for Rus Wane. The young man had no manufacturing skills and was eligible for the army draft the following spring.

When John described the incident to Ron, he got a rather philosophical reply: "Well, you've got to remember the specifics of the country you are operating in. Russia has an Asian culture and European faces should not mislead you. American standards do not always work here. If hiring people you have known for a long time, and therefore trust, is a local custom, you can't change it overnight. And you probably don't need to change it."

John didn't challenge his boss, but he saw no reason to change his mind about hiring practices. He strongly believed that hiring friends and relatives was equally bad whether one was in the United States, China, or Russia. Now Ron was telling him that Lev was going to appoint his doctor's son as human resource manager. John had always regarded a human resource manager as one of the primary business officers responsible for enforcing high ethical standards in the company. Would Sasha be able to fulfill such an important responsibility? How much credibility would he have? And how independent would he be from his boss and likely mentor? There were some of the questions for which John did not have a ready answer.

Prospects for the Future

This latest hiring decision only added to John Swift's growing frustration over the management of the joint venture. He had been appointed to provide expertise in Western management systems and to coach local personnel. Yet his attempts had been foiled at virtually every turn. He didn't know who was more to blame – Lev, for sticking to his former Soviet practices, or Ron, for letting Lev get away with such seemingly counterproductive behavior.

All of these issues contributed to John's worries about the future of Rus Wane Equipment. With the prospect of privatization turning NLZ into more of a competitor than a partner, and the advantages of joint ventures declining as a result of changing government legislation, John wondered whether Rus Wane had the right organizational structure and management systems in place to be a viable player in Russia's rapidly changing business environment. And not the least of his worries was whether there would be a place for him at Rus Wane that would allow him to be taken seriously.

Exhibit 14.3 Wane Machines, Inc.'s human resources policies for Rus Wane Equipment

---

Recruitment and Selection Process
The following recruitment and selection principles have been established in order to assist company management in hiring the best qualified employees. It is the responsibility of the human resources department to manage and facilitate recruitment and selection in collaboration with line management, with the final decision on selecting and hiring candidates made by line management. It is also the responsibility of company management to ensure that these principles are followed and to maintain their effectiveness.

1. Identification of job openings The number of positions to be staffed in the company is primarily determined by the workforce forecast established every year as part of the business plan. Input is then provided by line management throughout the year with necessary adjustments to the plan made in order for the HR department to take action in recruitment and selection. Any vacancy or opening due to resignation, termination or other reasons will be filled according to line management's request. A final list of job openings is then established and updated as necessary. A job requisition form must be signed by line management and the general manager before every recruiting action.

2. Determination of job requirements In close collaboration with line management, each position to be staffed is documented as follows:

- A list of professional and technical requirements as well as a list of personal traits required to do the job (strengths, personality, background experience, etc.).
- A written job description outlining the basic responsibilities of the position, and the main tasks to fulfill position responsibilities and deliver the expected results.

These two documents will be established jointly with the HR department and approved by line management.

3. Attracting applicants A list of possible human resources outsourcing options is presented below. One or several sources listed may be used with consideration given to availability, costs, and likelihood of success.

- Spontaneous, unsolicited candidacies are examined and acknowledged. A curriculum vitae and letter of intention are necessary documentation.
- Advertisements for jobs may be inserted in local or national newspapers: they advertise not only the content of the job through a short description, but also the required profile of the candidate. A description of the company is also recommended.
- State employment agencies: Contracts to conduct employee searches can be used with recognized agencies. Company needs are specified in a job requirements position description.

- Educational institutions: The company should develop and maintain regular and frequent contacts with local or national technical and non-technical institutions considered as potential sources of job candidates. Background on the company should be presented to students. Job postings may be sent to these schools.
- Private employee search firms: Restricted to managerial positions, private employee search firms may be used for candidate searches and screening interviews. The search must be cost effective, with conditions of the services rendered clearly stated in a contract.

The use of one of these options should result in a list of candidates for consideration, as well as detailed information about the candidates recorded on forms.

4. *Prescreening*   The human resources manager establishes a final list of candidates by eliminating applicants whose profile does not meet requirements. At this stage, the human resources department informs candidates who are not selected for interviews that they are no longer under consideration.

5. *Screening interviews*   The human resources manager contacts the eligible candidates for interviews to assess:

- Their knowledge of the company (product, service, and culture, as appropriate). Additional information may be given to answer candidates' questions.
- Their background (education and experience) to determine whether it is consistent with their application. This step helps answer the question, "Can the individual perform the job?"
- The motivation of the applicant to perform the job in the company and to develop within the company's culture. This step helps answer the question, "Will he/she do the job?"

6. *Level of approval for recruitment for senior positions*   The general manager will be involved in any recruitment for a position reporting directly to him/her, and will make the final decision. The general manager will also interview candidates for positions reporting to his/her direct reports. Approval by the general manager will be necessary before filling such positions.

7. *Preselection*   The interviews will be reported tin a written evaluation of the candidate by the HR manager using the appropriate forms. These forms are reviewed with the line manager involved in the recruitment process, and a list of candidates to be interviewed is then established jointly.

8. *Interviews with line management*   The preselected candidates are called for interviews with the line manager. The purpose of the interview is to determine again whether professional aptitude based on experience and skills (technical and nontechnical) will enable the applicant to perform the work. Also, the interviewer assesses the candidate's motivation to work for the company and to meet the company's overall requirements (personal fit with the culture, etc.). At the end of these interviews, evaluation forms are filled out by the interviewer.

9. Evaluation of candidates and hiring decision   A joint evaluation of the candidates by the line manager and the human resources manager is conducted using evaluation forms, and a ranking of the candidates is completed.

10. Hiring decision   The line manager makes the final decision to hire one of the candidates interviewed based on an assessment of their capabilities and potential for development in the company. At that stage, the HR manager informs the unsuccessful candidates by letter of the company's decision. The selected candidate is also informed by the HR manager.

11. Offer to the candidate   A formal offer is prepared by the HR manager in cooperation with the line manager. The offer (including the contract and conditions of employment, etc.) is extended to the selected candidate. At the same time, administrative documents are given to the future employee to begin the employment registration process.

12. Integration in the company   The human resources manager assists the line manager in facilitating the newcomer's integration into the company.

A welcome guide is given to the new employee upon his/her arrival in addition to all necessary documents, identification badges, punch cards, safety brochures, internal regulations, etc.

Mandatory company training (e.g., safety) and any special training are coordinated by the HR manager in the new employee's first few days.

13. New-employee feedback meeting   Six weeks after the starting date of employment, the human resources manager invites the new employee for a feedback meeting to determine how well he/she is adapting to the workplace. Any obstacles are addressed in accordance with company policies.

The HR manager provides feedback to the new employee's supervisor and follows up on any decisions made to ease the newcomer's integration into the company.

Epilogue

John resisted Sasha's appointment as human resources manager, but to no avail. Sasha turned out to be very enthusiastic about his job, and was willing to learn and introduce new things. To John's surprise, Sasha was very independent in his actions and did not seem to be afraid to challenge Lev Novikov. He made sure that everyone in the company followed the hiring procedure developed by Wane, and worked quite well with John.

John was subsequently transferred to the United States, and was not replaced. Jeff Nichol was appointed by the board of directors as Rus Wane's financial manager. However, his relations with Lev and Katya did not improve, and he asked for a transfer four months after assuming the position. Wane Machines sent a new financial manager, a 59-year-old Indian national whom Lev Novikov had interviewed and approved of.

Rus Wane Equipment continued to struggle with low demand and poor collections, but no major top management changes were made. Ron Chapman remained country manager for Russia. The company converted from joint venture status to a joint stock company in 1994, since joint ventures no longer enjoyed special tax or other benefits from the Russian government. A joint stock company was similar to a conventional Western limited liability company.

NLZ was privatized into an employee-owned company, with the state owning no shares. Some employees later sold their stock to Lev for cash. How much stock Lev personally owned was unknown, but he was rumored to have more than 50 percent ownership of NLZ.

In early 1995, Lev left Rus Wane Equipment and returned to work exclusively for NLZ. No Rus Wane employees followed him. Ron Chapman moved to Moscow and became acting general manager of Rus Wane, while retaining his job as country manager for Russia. Wane Machines planned to merge Rus Wane Equipment with Wane's newly created service enterprise in Moscow.

APPENDIX: Note on Russia's History and Recent Business Environment

Beginnings of the Russian State

The beginnings of the Russian state date back to the thirteenth century, when inhabitants of the Kiev kingdom, exhausted by continuous invasions of Mongol-Tartars and other nomads, started to move northward, seeking refuge in the wild forests of the Oka and Upper Vologa rivers in northeastern Russia. The severe natural conditions there, with a climate of long, cold winters followed by short, unpredictable summers, as well as dense woods and swamps inhabited by numerous wild animals, had a strong impact on the Russian character.

The famous nineteenth-century Russian historian Vasilii Kliuchevskii wrote: "No European people can work as hard for a short period of time as Russians can. However, nowhere else in Europe could we find another people so unused to smooth, moderate and continuous work as Russians. The inability to calculate in advance, to prepare before taking actions and to go straight to the established goal had strongly influenced the Russian minds and the way Russians think . . .

made them discuss what they had already done rather than look forward."[1]

Tsarist Times

In the fourteenth century various kings began uniting lands populated by Russian people under their rule, and Moscow became the center of Muskovy, the new Russian state. By the end of the sixteenth century, Muskovy was a strong monocultural, centralized state, which dominated eastern Europe and rapidly expanded its territory. Since the country was fighting almost continuous wars with its eastern, western, and southern neighbors, its leaders organized it as a military state. The tsar was the head of state and commander-in-chief of the armed forces and exercised absolute power over all citizens.

Every Russian male was required to serve in the army or perform other military duties. The type of military service depended on the individual's social status. For instance, landowners were required to provide personal military or civil service to the tsar, while people renting others' land or earning their living by selling personal labor were required to pay state taxes.

In Muskovy society consisted of two classes: servicemen (*sluzhilye liudi*), who ensured that taxes were collected for the tsar, and taxpayers (*tiaglye liudi*). Each class had a number of distinct subclasses such as the nobility from old families (*boiare*) and the new nobility (*dvoriane*), who received land from the tsar in exchange for service. Each subclass performed specific types of state obligations, the old nobility holding top military and civil positions and the new nobility forming the backbone of the army officers' corps.

By the mid-eighteenth century, the distinction between old nobility and new had almost disappeared as the two became a relatively homogeneous class of landowners (*pomeshikl*). Peasants who worked the land had lost their right to move from one landowner to another and had become serfs. Landowners had to make sure that their serfs paid state taxes, provided recruits for the army, and reproduced themselves. If serfs could not pay their taxes, the landlord was required to pay the taxes: if they ran out of food, he was expected to feed them. To simplify management of serfs and systematically collect taxes from them, landowners organized their serfs into communes (mir), in which a group of elders made decisions for the members and collected taxes. Just as landowners. Although serfdom was abolished in 1861, landowners retained the rights to their lands and maintained a high degree

---

[1] Klinchevski, V.O., *Collected Works* (Moscow: Mvsl, 1987) vol. 1, p. 36.

of control over peasants. In early 1917, the growing discontent of the Russian people, exacerbated by war, forced Tsar Nicolas II's abdication. In October, the provisional republican government led by Aleksandr Kerensky was overthrown by revolutionary socialist forces under the leadership of V. I. Lenin, who later became the architect of Russia's Communist state.

The Centralized Economy Under the Communists

At the time of the Bolshevik revolution, Russia was the largest country in terms of land mass in the world and had the fifth largest economy. With a population of some 170 million, 80 per cent lived in rural areas and nearly two thirds were illiterate.

The communists outlawed private property and made centralized government control of the Russian economy at every level a cornerstone of their regime. A nationwide vertical chain of command was created, with the Politburo at the top and individual workers at the bottom. The Central Planning Committee, Gosplan, was the Politburo's economic arm. Gosplan prepared annual and five year plans for the entire economy, determining what products should be produced in what quantities, and by what enterprises. Industrial ministries oversaw the execution of Gosplan's directives.

Virtually every command from an upper level was law for the reporting level, with a specific individual at each level being responsible for carrying out orders. During Stalin's reign of terror from the 1930s to the early 1950s, failure to carry out a command from above, or even an attempt to question it, often resulted in exile, imprisonment in labor camps, or execution. Later, under presidents Khrushchev, Brezhnev, and Gorbachev, dismissal was the typical form of punishment for the most serious violations, and various administrative sanctions were imposed for other infractions.

Enterprise managers were personally responsible for meeting production plans at monthly, quarterly, annual, and five year intervals. Gosplan allocated material resources for output that was delivered to state-designated customers at prices set by state authorities. These arbitrarily set prices had no real relation to true market value, and were often insufficient to cover costs. Costs themselves were not measured or related to performance within enterprises, and concepts of profit and efficiency were defined by central planning authorities without regard to market forces. Managers were expected to meet production plans and a variety of quality, efficiency, and other targets, and provide employment for the people. The Communist party wielded unlimited power over the labor force, using party loyalty as a major criterion for promotion to higher managerial positions. Labor–management relations resembled those between serfs and landowners rather than employees and employers, with trade unions having little real power. Managers expected their subordinates to execute orders, without question, in exchange for housing, day care, recreational facilities, and other fringe benefits.

The guiding principles of the centrally planned economy remained virtually unchanged from the late 1920s until the mid-1980s. By that time, the shortcomings of the system had become painfully obvious even to Soviet leaders as productivity reached historically low levels, creating shortages and a deterioration in living standards.

The Perestroika Years: 1985–1991

In March 1985, Mikhail Gorbachev became General Secretary of the Communist Party of the Soviet Union (CPSU) and, later, President of the country. One of his major objectives was to breathe new life into the Soviet economy with his policy of *perestroika*, or restructuring. He began by allowing enterprises to produce goods in addition to planned quotas, sell them at free prices to customers of their choosing, and use the revenues to compensate employees. Later, he allowed groups of people to set up private companies, called cooperatives, within the centrally planned economic system. The results of this new economic policy were disastrous for the central planning system with enterprises preferring to sell their output at higher free-market prices than produce for the State. By the end of 1991, the old economic system had virtually collapsed as many companies traded directly among themselves, bypassing state ministries and ignoring their orders.

Along with economic reforms, President Gorbachev brought about changes in political and social life with his *glasnost*, or "openness" policies, which included freedom of the press, multicandidate elections, and removal of most travel restrictions for foreign visitors. For the first time, ordinary Soviet citizens had the opportunity to learn about Western economies and lifestyles first hand, rather than through communist ideologues. There was a great deal of enthusiasm about Western countries and a strong desire to learn from them, particularly in the area of economic development.

In 1987 the Soviet parliament established a legal framework for foreign direct investment by passing a law allowing foreign companies to form joint ventures with Soviet partners. Since the USSR desperately needed financial resources and modern technologies, the law granted joint ventures tax free status for the first three years of operation. Initially, the process of establishing joint ventures was slow. Foreign investors cautiously evaluated which "opportunities" might be available in an economy having a non-convertible currency, thousands of outmoded plants, a centralized resource allocation system, and countless layers of bureaucracy. However, within a year or two, the investment pace accelerated, and by the end of 1993 more than 4,000 joint ventures had been created by companies from around the world.

In August 1991 President Gorbachev survived a coup mounted by old-guard Communists who rejected his economic and social reforms. However, he was unsuccessful in containing the secessionist tendencies of the leaders of various Soviet republics and, in December, was forced to resign. On Christmas Eve 1991, the Soviet Union ceased to exist and each of the republics that had belonged to the USSR was declared an independent country. The Communist party was no longer in power, and Boris Yeltsin became the first democratically elected president of the Russian Federation.

Moving toward a Market Economy

In January 1992, President Yeltsin's Prime Minister, Yegor Gaidar, launched large-scale reforms designed to develop Russia into a market-oriented economy. The new policies had three major thrusts: price liberalization, reduction of the state budget deficit and privatization of enterprises. By the end of 1992, Gaidar had freed virtually all prices in Russia, allowing them to be determined by what the market would bear. Hyperinflation and consumer shock were the immediate results, but elimination of shortages and greater availability of consumer goods followed (see exhibit 14.4 for inflation data).

In an attempt to reduce the state budget deficit, Gaidar introduced, also in 1992, additional taxes, including a value-added tax (VAT) and a payroll tax, and sharply reduced government subsidies and low-interest credits to enterprises. As a result many companies cut production, became unable to pay salaries on time, and laid off many workers.

During 1992, Russia's GNP contracted by almost 40 percent from 1991, and official unemployment grew from virtually zero to 3 percent. The government sector suffered the most as enterprises' investments from central funding agencies contracted sharply. Gaidar's policy of allowing the ruble to float freely against foreign currencies led to a precipitous devaluation of Russia's. In 1993, although the value of the ruble continued to fluctuate widely, it became convertible with foreign hard currencies (see exhibit 14.4), giving greater financial

Exhibit 14.4   Inflation and foreign exchange rate dynamics in Russia in 1993

	Consumer price index (CPI)[a] (%)	Ruble/US$[b]	Foreign exchange index[c] (%)
January	134	572	100
February	165	593	104
March	188	684	120
April	216	823	144
May	251	994	174
June	316	1060	185
July	374	989	173
August	447	985	172
September	541	1201	210
October	634	1181	207
November	752	1214	212
December	842	1247	218

[a] Base for CPI: December 1992 = 100%.
[b] Ruble/US$ rates reflect last day of the month.
[c] Foreign exchange index = ruble/US$ monthly rate as a percentage of January 1993.
Source: Monthly unpublished reports compiled by MosGorStat, Moscow City Statistical Committee.

flexibility to domestic and foreign companies for international transactions.

The most visible achievement of the economic reform was rapid privatization of enterprises. By the end of 1993, the private sector represented more than 30 percent of the Russian economy and was expanding by 50 percent a year. The first phase of the privatization program was successfully completed in June 1994, transferring much of the ownership of many former state-owned enterprises into private hands, predominantly managers and workers. The second phase of privatization was planned to immediately follow the first phase on July 1, 1994, with the goal of attracting new capital into state-owned and newly privatized enterprises. However, by the end of 1994, little progress had been made. Internal struggles for ownership and control of many enterprises, as well as the country's unstable political and economic climate, continued to deter many Western investors from making major commitments of capital.

15
The Donor Services Department

Joyce S. Osland

Joanna Reed was walking home through fallen tree blossoms in Guatemala City. Today, however, her mind was more on her work than the natural beauty surrounding her. She unlocked the gate to her colonial home and sat down on the porch, surrounded by riotous toddlers, pets, and plants, to ponder the recommendations she would make to Sam Wilson. The key decisions she needed to make about his donor services department concerned who should run the department and how the work should be structured.

Joanna had worked for a sponsorship agency engaged in international development work with poor people for six years. She and her husband moved from country to country setting up new agencies. In each country, they had to design how the work should be done, given the local labor market and work conditions.

After a year in Guatemala, happily pregnant with her third child, Joanna had finished setting up the donor services department for her current agency and was working only part-time on a research project. A friend who ran a "competing" development agency approached her to do a consulting project for him. Sam Wilson, an American, was the national representative of a US-based agency that had offices all over the world. Sam wanted Joanna to analyze his donor services department, because he'd received complaints from headquarters about its efficiency. Since he'd been told that his office needed to double in size in the coming year, he wanted to get all the bugs worked out beforehand. Joanna agreed to spend a month gathering information and compiling a report on this department.

Reprinted by permission of the author.

What is A Donor Services Department in a Sponsorship Agency?

Sponsorship agencies, with multimillion dollar budgets, are funded by individuals and groups in developed countries who contribute to development programs in less-developed countries (LDCs). Donors contribute approximately $20.00 per month plus optional special gifts. The agencies use this money to fund education, health, community development, and income-producing projects for poor people affiliated with their agency in various communities. In the eyes of most donors, the specific benefit provided by sponsorship agencies is the personal relationship between a donor and a child and his or her family in the LDC. The donors and children write back and forth, and the agency sends photos of the child and family to the donors. Some donors never write the family they sponsor; others write weekly and visit the family on their vacations. The efficiency of a donor services department and the quality of their translations are key ingredients to keeping donors and attracting new ones. Good departments also never lose sight of the fact that sponsorship agencies serve a dual constituency – the local people they are trying to help develop and the sponsors who make that help possible through their donations.

The work of a donor services department consists of more than translating letters, preparing annual progress reports on the families, and answering donor questions directed to the agency. It also handles the extensive, seemingly endless paperwork associated with enrolling new families and assigning them to donors, reassignments when either the donor or the family stops participating, and the special gifts of money sent (and thank you notes for them). Having accurate enrollment figures is crucial because the money the agency receives from headquarters is based upon these figures and affects planning.

The Cast of Characters in the Department

The Department Head

Joanna tackled the challenge of analyzing the department by speaking first with the department head (see the organizational chart in exhibit 15.1). José Barriga, a charismatic, dynamic man in his forties, was head of both donor services and community services. In reality, he spent virtually no time in the donor services department and was not bilingual. "My biggest pleasure is working with the community lead-

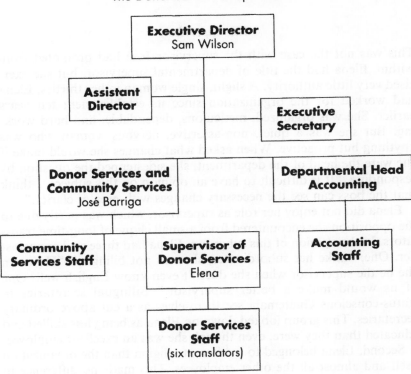

Exhibit 15.1 Agency's national organization chart

ers and coming up with programs that will be successful. I much prefer being in the field, driving from village to village, and talking with people, to supervising paperwork. I'm not sure exactly what goes on in donor services, but Elena, the supervisor, is very responsible. I make it a point to walk through the department once a week and say hello to everyone, and I check their daily production figures."

Like José, Sam was also more interested in working with the communities on projects than in immersing himself in the details of the more administrative departments. In part, Sam had contracted Joanna because he rightfully worried that donor services did not receive the attention it deserved from José, who was very articulate and personable but seldom had time to look at anything beyond case histories. He also never involved himself in the internal affairs of the department. Even though he was not considered much of a resource to them, he was well liked and respected by the staff of donor services, and they never complained about him.

The Supervisor

This was not the case with the supervisor José had promoted from within. Elena had the title of departmental supervisor, but she exercised very little authority. A slight, single woman in her thirties, Elena had worked for the organization since its establishment ten years earlier. She was organized, meticulous, dependable, and hard working. But she was a quiet, non-assertive, nervous woman who was anything but proactive. When asked what changes she would make if she were the head of the department, she sidestepped the question by responding, "It is difficult to have an opinion on this subject. I think that the boss can see the necessary changes with greater clarity."

Elena did not enjoy her role as supervisor, which was partly due to the opposition she encountered from a small clique of long-time translators. In the opinion of this subgroup, Elena had three strikes against her. One, unlike her subordinates, she was not bilingual. "How can she be the supervisor when she doesn't even know English well? One of us would make a better supervisor." Bilingual secretaries in status-conscious Guatemala see themselves as a cut above ordinary secretaries. This group looked down on Elena as being less skilled and educated than they were, even though she was an excellent employee.

Second, Elena belonged to a different religion than the organization itself and almost all the other employees. This made no difference to Sam and José but seemed important to the clique who could be heard making occasional derogatory comments about Elena's religion.

The third strike against Elena was her lack of authority. No one had ever clarified how much authority she really possessed, and she herself made no effort to assume control of the department. "My instructions are to inform Don José Barriga of infractions in my daily production memo. I'm not supposed to confront people directly when infractions occur, although it might be easier to correct things if I did." ("Don" is a Latin American honorific used before the first name to denote respect.)

This subgroup showed their disdain and lack of respect for Elena by treating her with varying degrees of rudeness and ignoring her, requests. They saw her as a watchdog, an attitude furthered by José, who sometimes announced: "We [senior management] are not going to be here tomorrow, so be good because Elena will be watching you." When Sam and José left the office, the clique often stopped working to socialize. They'd watch Elena smolder out of the corners of their eyes, knowing she would not reprimand them. "I liked my job better before I became supervisor," said Elena. "Ever since, some of the girls have resented me and I'm not comfortable trying to keep them in line. Why don't they just do their work without needing me to be the policeman? The only thing that keeps me from quitting is the loyalty I feel for the agency and Don José."

The Workers

In addition to the clique already mentioned, there were three other female translators in the department. All the translators but one had the same profile: in their twenties, of working-class backgrounds, and graduates of bilingual secretarial schools, possessing average English skills. (As stated earlier, in Latin America, being a bilingual secretary is a fairly prestigious occupation for a woman.) The exception in this group was the best translator, Magdalena, a college-educated recent hire in her late thirties who came from an upper-class family. She worked, not because she needed the money, but because she believed in the mission of the agency. "This job lets me live out my religious beliefs and help people who have less advantages than I do." Magdalena was more professional and mature than the other translators. Although all the employees were proud of the agency and its religious mission, the clique members spent too much time socializing or in skirmishes with other employees within and without the department.

The three translators who were not working at full capacity were very close friends. The leader of this group, Juana, was a spunky, bright woman with good oral English skills and a hearty sense of humor. A long-time friend of José's, Juana translated for English-speaking visitors who came to visit the program sites throughout the country. The other translators, tied to their desks, saw this as a huge perk. Juana was the ringleader in the occasional mutinies against Elena and in feuds with people from other departments. Elena was reluctant to complain about Juana to José, given their friendship. Perhaps she feared Juana would make her life even more miserable.

Juana's two buddies (*compañeras*) in the department also had many years with the agency. They'd gotten into the habit of helping each other on the infrequent occasions when they had excessive amounts of work. When they were idle or simply wanted to relieve the boredom of their jobs, they socialized and gossiped. Juana in particular was noted for lethal sarcasm and pointed jokes about people she didn't like. This clique was not very welcoming to the newer members of the department. Magdalena simply smiled at them but kept her distance, and the two younger translators kept a low profile to avoid incurring their disfavor. As one of the them remarked, "It doesn't pay to get on Juana's bad side."

The Organization of the Department

Like many small offices in Latin America, the agency was located in a spacious former private home. The donor services department was housed in the 40 × 30 foot living room area. The women's desks were set up in two rows, with Elena's desk in the back corner. Since Sam and José's offices were in former back bedrooms, everyone who visited them had to walk through the department. Inevitably they stopped to greet and chat with the long-time employees (Elena, Juana and her two friends). Elena's numerous visitors also spent a good deal of time working their way through the department to reach her desk, further contributing to the amount of socializing going on in the department.

Elena was the only department member who had "official" visitors since she was the liaison person who dealt with program representatives and kept track of enrollments. The translators each were assigned one work process. For example, Marisol prepared case histories on new children and their families for prospective donors while Juana processed gifts. One of the newer translators prepared files for newly enrolled children and did all the filing for the entire department (a daunting task). Most of the jobs were primarily clerical and required little or no English. The letter translations were out-sourced to external translators on a piece-work basis and supervised by Magdalena. Hers was the only job that involved extensive translation; for the most part, however, she translated simple messages (such as greeting cards) that were far below her level of language proficiency. The trickier translations, such as queries from donors in other countries, were still handled by Sam's executive secretary.

Several translators complained: "We don't have enough opportunity to use our English skills on the job. Not only are we not getting any better in English, we are probably losing fluency because most of our work is just clerical. We do the same simple, boring tasks over and over, day in and day out. Why did they hire bilingual secretaries for these jobs anyway?"

Another obvious problem was the uneven distribution of work in the office. The desks of Magdalena and the new translators were literally overflowing with several months' backlog of work while Juana and her two friends had time to kill. Nobody, including Elena, made any efforts to even out the work assignments or help out those who were buried. The subject had never been broached.

The agency was growing at a rapid pace, and there were piles of paperwork sitting around waiting to be processed. Joanna spent three weeks having each department member explain her job (in mind-numbing detail), drawing up flow charts of how each type of paperwork was handled, and poking around in their files. She found many unnecessary steps that resulted in slow turnaround times for various processes. There were daily output reports submitted to José, but no statistics kept on the length of time it took to respond to requests for information or process paperwork. No data was shared with the translators, so they had no idea how the department was faring and little sense of urgency about their work. The only goal was to meet the monthly quota of case histories, which only affected Marisol. Trying to keep up with what came across their desks summed up the entire focus of the employees.

Joanna found many instances of errors and poor quality, not so much from carelessness as lack of training and supervision. Both José and Sam reviewed the case histories, but Joanna was amazed to discover that no one ever looked at any other work done by the department. The employees were very accommodating when asked to explain their jobs and very conscientious about their work (if not the hours devoted to it). However, they were seldom able to explain why things were done in a certain way, because they had received little training for their jobs and only understood their small part of the department. Morale was obviously low, and all the employees seemed frustrated with the situation in the department. Nevertheless, with the exception of Magdalena, who had experience in other offices, none of them could offer Joanna any ideas about how the department could be improved.

16
Nissan Italia, SPA

Ayako Asakura and Susan C. Schneider

One afternoon in late November 1988, Mr Sasaki, director of Europe Group of Nissan Motor Co., was busy signing Christmas and New Year cards in his office at the headquarters in Tokyo. He felt the pile of cards was much higher than in the previous year. "This should be because of our recent development in Europe. Now we have Nissan Motor Iberia in Barcelona and Nissan Italy in Rome. And a factory in the UK has just started operation. It looks as if these two years have flown away, keeping us very busy with working for those projects."

Speaking to himself with a satisfied smile, Mr Sasaki started to look back at Nissan's European operations. Though satisfied, he was worried about the future development of, and some fundamental problems in, Italy. He wondered what lessons could be learned for other overseas operations and what were the implications for future globalization.

The Company

Nissan Motor Co., Ltd was established in 1933. The company has always been strongly overseas-oriented and set up its first plant outside Japan in Mexico as early as 1966. Even today it is the only Japanese automobile company that has its own manufacturing base in Europe. This is not only because the company always has been

This case was prepared by Ayako Asakura and Susan C. Schneider as a basis for class discussion rather than to illustrate either effective or ineffective handling of an administrative situation.

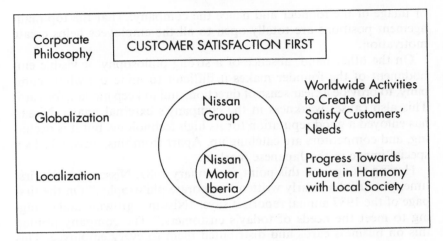

Corporate
Philosophy   CUSTOMER SATISFACTION FIRST

Globalization   Nissan   Worldwide Activities
                     Group   to Create and
                                   Satisfy Customers'
                                   Needs

Localization   Nissan   Progress Towards
                     Motor   Future in Harmony
                     Iberia   with Local Society

Exhibit 16.1 Profile of Nissan

second to Toyota in the domestic market. It recognized the necessity to be close to the market in order to better satisfy customer needs, to get integrated in and to contribute to the local economy. Therefore, Nissan aims at a whole process localization – to be an "insider" through all operations from R&D to sales.

Nissan has dramatically increased its presence in Europe during the last few years. Several international economic and market environments have promoted this trend: yen appreciation, trade friction, increasing competition, and European common market integration. Reacting to those changes, Nissan has clearly positioned its strategy for internationalization and further globalization. The company intends to go beyond export and partly overseas manufacturing, to exploit cost advantage, to establish various activities abroad and to integrate them horizontally.

Corporate Culture

Nissan does not have a strong corporate culture. Since it was established through mergers of some companies between 1910 and the 1930s, Nissan has no clear founder. This is an obvious difference from the other Japanese overseas-oriented companies like Sony, Honda, or Matsushita, whose corporate cultures are directed or affected by the strong characteristics of the founders. This gives freedom to the organization. People are not bound by a certain philosophy, policy, or image of the founder and hence the company. That the top management positions are totally open to all the employees helps create motivation.

On the other hand, absence of a strong philosophy or visible embodiment of the founder makes it difficult to unite the whole company, to provide a clear sense of direction, and to keep moving forward. This also causes weakness in the company's external image. Nissan has enjoyed a good reputation for its high technology, but it is declining, and competitors are catching up. Apart from this, Nissan lacks a special image in the Japanese market.

Having recognized this point, in January 1987, Nissan, for the first time, produced a clearly written "corporate philosophy." On the first page of the 1987 annual report, it says: "Nissan – growing and changing to meet the needs of today's customers." The company printed this on business cards and distributed them to every employee. This statement is translated into the languages of each country where Nissan has plants, offices, or subsidiaries (exhibit 16.1). The translation is not a literal one. It is aimed to express the core policy and objectives and rewritten so that the idea would be best implemented in each situation and cultural environment.

Policy Toward Overseas Operations

Nissan's policy toward overseas operations is not rigid. Taking many different situations into consideration, the company has a "clear end and loose means" policy. There is no standardized way. As far as it is in line with the realization of Nissan's objectives, it allows a certain amount of autonomy to each plant or subsidiary and lets each seek the best way, depending on the situation. For example, while the Mexico plant is run in a typical Japanese style, the American one in Smyrna, Tennessee, is run in an American way with American top management. The British plant in Sunderland is run in a half-British, half-Japanese style. This variety depends on many factors, such as the location, form (greenfield investment or joint venture), history, technological level, product, human resource availability, target market, and so on.

With its long history of overseas business and operations, Nissan points out two issues as keys to success. One is to be an insider in the markets in which the company is present. Another is to promote globalization of the headquarters in Japan. In order to understand the development and the situation of overseas operations of Nissan, there is a good example in Europe: Nissan Italia.

Nissan Italia, SPA

Nissan Italia is a distribution and after-sales service (repair and part sales) company. Sixty-four percent of the share holding is owned by Nissan Motor Co. and the rest by Nissan Motor Iberia.

History

The company, originally named EBRO, was founded as a joint venture of an Italian company and Motor Iberia in February 1978 for commercial vehicle sales and after-sales services. In January 1988 Nissan Motor Co. purchased 49 percent of local shares (the rest was owned by Nissan Motor Iberia) and changed its name to Nissan Italia SPA. In March this share was increased to 64 percent. Therefore, Nissan Motor is now fully in control of Nissan Italia. The mission given to Nissan Italia in the Nissan group is to cover a very protective Italian market from the sales and service side.

It is not, however, the company's first foray into the Italian market. Already, in 1980, Nissan had started a joint venture with Alfa Romeo. But it turned out to be very difficult to control the company because Nissan had only 50 percent of the shares and the personnel decisions were made by Italian managers and the company in Italy. Therefore, Nissan could not take the initiative of the business, and annulled the joint venture in 1987. So it was after this experience that Nissan set up Nissan Italia as a new base for the Italian market. Now, Nissan Italia sells cars not only imported from Japan but also those produced by Nissan Motor Iberia in Spain and, from November 1988, also those from the new factory in Sunderland, UK.

As for parts supply, in 1987 there were two routes: 73 percent from Barcelona (the parts manufactured by Nissan Motor Iberia) and the rest from Nissan Motor Parts Center in Amsterdam (the parts imported from Japan).

Localization – Change to Nissan Italia

Based on Nissan's basic policy of clear end and loose means, and because of its evolution, Nissan Italia is a very Italian company. As in Nissan Iberia (see exhibit 16.2), the Japanese in Italy have adjusted to the local way in terms of organization and communication.

Even after March 1988, when Nissan increased its share in the company, there has not been any drastic change. Mr Arai, president of Nissan Italy, says:

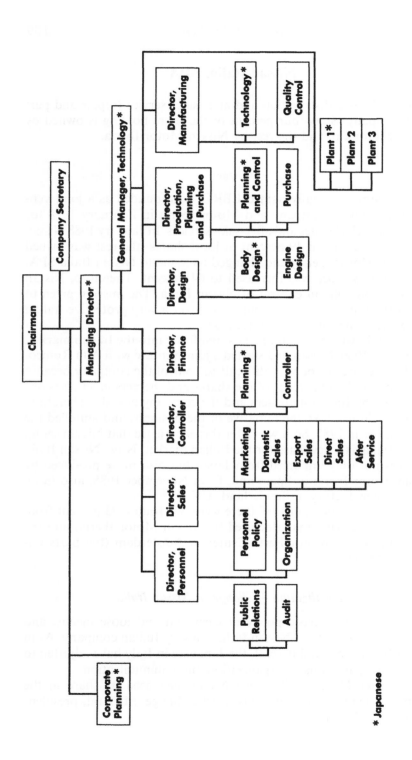

* Japanese

Exhibit 16.2 Nissan Motor Iberia organization chart

"I did not give any speech to address the new president's declaration. This is not a change of that kind. I have been with them a while and nothing would suddenly change. The base of this company is Italy. Furthermore, without any formal words, the people understand Nissan's intention. In the meantime, maybe when we will move to the new office,* I will say a word."

It is obvious, however, that Nissan conveyed a clear message that it was going to be more seriously engaged in a longer-term development in the Italian market through this company. And there were also some other signals to show the company's determination, as seen below. From the viewpoint of the original company, this change was very well accepted because the company was given a chance to jump from a small business status to a medium-sized one.

Present Situation

Organization: The organization remains very local. Although the board consists of three Spanish directors and four Japanese, in practice only the president and his assistant are Japanese and one director and one manager are Spanish (exhibit 16.3). And Mr Oyama, the Japanese assistant, was sent over only in September 1988.

Mr Arai, the president, is a veteran of the campaign in Italy. He has 18 years of experience as a government official in the Japanese Ministry of Foreign Affairs, as a businessman in a big Japanese trading company, and he has been with Nissan since the joint venture with Alfa Romeo.

This shows the organization is not a "Japanese managers with Italian subordinates" structure but is very open to the local people up to the director level. And these people are given full responsibilities: for example, Italian staff fly to Amsterdam or Japan for meetings.

Communication: Italian is always used in the company since the Spanish managers and both Japanese are fluent in Italian. But externally the official language is English. At the moment, the communication between the headquarters and Nissan Italia is mainly done in Japanese, but it will change as English is used more by both sides, that is, headquarters and the Italian staff. In order to improve communication efficiency and to increase the internationality of the company, English lessons for the Italian staff have been started, which will also help promote the open mentality of the organization.

* Nissan Italia planned to have a new head office with warehouse facilities.

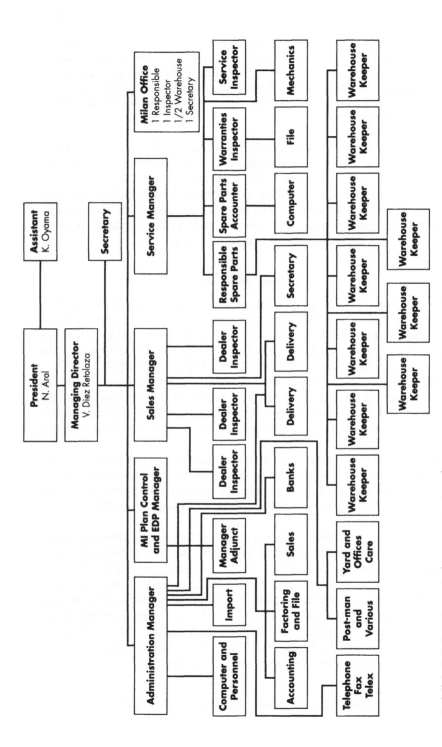

Exhibit 16.3 Nissan Italia organization chart

The company has a very open atmosphere in spite of the individually separated office style. The door of the president's office is almost always kept open and people come in to talk with Mr Arai. He says, "I don't like to use first name terms because it sounds to me too casual. But of course I don't mind other people doing so among themselves." And it is true that this is only a matter of his taste; his relationships with the Italian employees seem very warm.

Japanization: There is no particular effort to Japanize the company. There have, however, naturally been some changes through the history of Nissan's increasing share and hence control in the company. Mr Arai described the change so far as "phase 1."

> "Up to now, Nissan has done everything it can to help this company: invest in the facilities, send the people; finance the capital; and introduce the passenger cars [before the company was dealing only in commercial vehicles]. Phase 1 is the visible change from the top. Now in phase 2 the company should change by itself based on these preparations.
> "What I expect from them is to have the participation mentality and to propose their ideas voluntarily to the company.
> "There are some variances among people's attitude depending on the department. The salespeople are quite participative and give their feedback from the field although they are paid on a salary basis and not on commissions. This is partly because sales results are, being quantitative and obvious, easier to use for control and motivation.
> "Compared to them, people in the office or in the warehouse are relatively passive and do not take the initiative. As their jobs are more difficult to evaluate objectively and quantitatively, this is understandable. But I would like them to change their working mind gradually."

Dealer relationships;   Dealer relationships in the case of sales network business are something equivalent to the supplier relationships in manufacturing. Nissan Italia's dealers are multifranchisers, having contracts with several car manufacturers except Fiat. They sell various kinds of cars and, being independent from Nissan, they are difficult to control. Mr Arai says:

> "They are profit-oriented dealers. But I would like to change our relationships and develop a more long-term one.
> "For this purpose, Nissan Italia makes efforts to improve communication with them, to make them understand Nissan's policy and product superiority, and to ask for dealers' cooperation by, for example, holding meetings, increasing advertisement budgets, and so on. And in the future, we would also like to have our own exclusive dealer network.

Perceived Problems

Working style: Mr Arai says: "Here the manager should give every instruction to get things done. You cannot expect the employees to act positively or manage voluntary activities like QC [quality circles], especially the people in the workshop [repair and after-sales service] who rarely do overtime."

Personnel: Labor mobility is also a big problem to the human resource management. The better a manager is, the greater the tendency for him or her to move to another company, and this makes it difficult to plan in-house training, to keep good people, and to accumulate expertise. "But on the other hand, we enjoy some merits of this mobility, too. That is, we can recruit experienced people from outside whenever necessary," says a Japanese manager with a wry smile.

Expatriate Situation

Until September 1988, Mr Arai was the only Japanese in the company, with Mr Oyama coming to Rome sometimes for long business trips. Both of them do not seem to have any difficulty working and living in Italy thanks to their language ability and personalities. Here are some general comments made by Mr Arai about the expatriates' situation.

Inconvenience of business schedule: The time difference in working hours and differing work patterns cause the expatriates to work very long hours. For example, this requires early morning or late night telephone calls to home, coming into the office on weekends, on local holidays and during summer vacation, which is much longer in Italy than in Japan.

Another thing is that they are expected to act as attendants for visiting Japanese managers or clients. They should play a role of "perfect" attendant: driver, interpreter, tourist guide, and shopping adviser all at the same time from morning to night. This is especially the case in big cities like Paris, London, or Rome.

Japanese circle: In every city with more than a certain number of Japanese, there is a Japanese Association. However, in Rome, compared to Milan where many companies locate, the Japanese population is small, and hence not many activities are going on in the Japanese circle. There is some advantage in this. According to Mr Arai: "If you try to maintain a Japanese lifestyle or to stick together with Japanese, then you might have problems adjusting to the foreign life and people. The more you try to get accustomed to a new environment, the more you can settle down."

There are not many Japanese restaurants in Rome, either. "Rome is a bit different from other cities in terms of the food available. There are not many foreign food restaurants. For example, generally, fancy French restaurants are appreciated as the best cuisine and can be found in any big international city. But it seems that Italians mock French cooking, which they say damages the natural taste of the food with heavy sauce. People are just happy with their own Italian food," says Mr. Oyama, who also loves Italian food.

Children's education: Last but not least, today perhaps the biggest issue for Japanese expatriates is the children's education.

Many foreign cities have a Japanese school with either a full-time or complementary staff depending on the Japanese population. However, since Japanese society is very education-conscious, many parents want their children to enter a good company meaning that they must enter a good university and before that a good high school. Therefore, at the critical age for high school or junior high school, many children (and their mothers) are sent back to Japan.

What is very interesting and shows a particular aspect of Japanese society is that this tendency is stronger for boys; there are many boys going back home to prepare for good universities while there are more girls going to local schools at various levels and staying abroad longer. Since the Japanese working world is still a rather male-dominated society with lifelong employment, it is thought that boys should equip themselves with a higher level of education for their own future happiness.

Back at Headquarters

Looking at the current situation in Nissan Italia, Mr Sasaki is quite pleased with the evolution so far as the first phase. At the same time, however, he has spotted some difficult problems. Most of them are not new; they come up more or less every time Nissan tries to develop business abroad. Therefore, to solve these problems would take a long time.

First, human resource management is of concern. As a whole, Nissan has kept the local identity of each subsidiary and retained almost all personnel. There seems to be no hostility or problem of adjustment. But there is a very fundamental difference among employees' working mentality which has puzzled Japanese managers; namely, local staff are not very participative and communication within the company (especially horizontal communication among functions and operations) is rather poor. Also, high job mobility restrains them from accumulation of expertise and planning for human resource management.

"What can we do to motivate them and make them want to participate? Would the Japanese way of management with regard to motivation and incentive systems work?"

This first question leads to the second question, which is more fundamental. "How far could or should we reinforce Japanization in foreign subsidiaries? Where is the optimal balance?"

"And what is the role of Japanese expatriates and the headquarters?" Mr Saskai knows expatriates' frustration toward headquarters very well and recognizes the necessity of headquarter's globalization. "Expatriate managers are sandwiched between demands from headquarters and the local subsidiary. They need our understanding and support in terms of money, people, technology, and human network and its mental support. But we cannot afford to respond to all of their needs because of shortages in resources, especially at a time of rapidly expanding overseas business. First of all, we should at least be better prepared to use English to facilitate communication between foreign subsidiaries. And more fundamentally, to raise good human resources able to cope with international operations. This will be a real long-term job."

And another question is how to train employees for a globalization strategy? For example, now Nissan sends a few employees to business school, mostly in the United States. "Would we rather send someone to Europe, too, since our presence in Europe has very much increased? Then which school?"

The last question in his mind is about human resource management: "How should we respond to expatriates' problems both in the working situation and in their private lives? How can headquarters support them in their job? How far should the company support them with their children's education or maintenance of houses they leave in Japan?"

But, Mr. Sasaki was brought back to Nissan's policy at the end: clear end and loose means. "Maybe there is no right answer to be generalized, and we should try to think out each context."

17

Creating a Learning Organization Through HRM: A German–Czech Joint Venture

Dianne J. Cyr and Susan C. Schneider

Establishing the Joint Venture

Karnovac Automobilova sprawls across a small industrialized town in the Czech Republic, 60 kilometres from Prague. First opened for business in 1894, Karnovac has built a well-known brand image and over the years has developed and produced a variety of attractive and successful automobiles. Most recently Karnovac had developed three new models (which they were not allowed to produce) and successfully launched a new sports model.

However, during the Communist regime, the quality and competitiveness of Karnovac had deteriorated. Although robots had been selectively introduced in welding and assembly five years earlier, parts of Karnovac were seen to reflect a "20–30 year time lag." In an effort to attract the Western investment required for its survival, the formerly state-owned company was privatized. Ahead of the rest, Karnovac became part of the first major joint venture in the Czech Republic. According to a Czech consultant, "Karnovac has put the Czech Republic on the map for foreign investment. It's been a terrific boost of confidence for the Czechs."

This case was written by Dianne J. Cyr, Adjunct Professor at Simon Fraser University, Canada, and Susan C. Schneider, Associate Professor at INSEAD. It is intended to be used as a basis for class discussion rather than to illustrate either effective or ineffective handling of an administrative situation.

Initially 24 North American, European and Japanese bidders were interested in establishing a joint venture with Karnovac, but by autumn 1990 two contenders remained: Bremen and a French competitor. The strong interest of both potential partners was indicated by a state visit by President Mitterand to lobby for French interests and the delayed retirement of the CEO of the German contender to see the project through. They in turn were ultimately given the most serious consideration for the formation of a partnership. In addition, to learn more about Karnovac and its people, the German personnel visited the plant prior to the partnership decision. The purpose of the visits was to provide advice and to discuss with the people what they wanted from the venture – a concern that was appreciated by the Czechs.

On December 9, 1990, the Czech government chose Bremen as its partner and, following a very detailed study, the joint venture was formalized in April 1991. Bremen had offered to invest two and a half times as much as the French, and promised to maintain social benefits and minimize layoffs within the 20,000 strong workforce. The union voted in favor of Bremen and threatened to strike if the French company was accepted. Furthermore, Bremen pledged to keep the Karnovac name and trademark, adding it to its other brand names. Thus the 100 year old name and trademark of the Czech company could be retained. Bremen, for MD 6.8 billion, obtained management control of Karnovac and gained 31 percent of its assets, a figure expected to rise to 70 percent by 1995.

As the deal went through before the new privatization law was in effect, Bremen avoided getting entangled in the bureaucratic red tape subsequently created by regulation, administration, and lawyers. It also avoided taking on Karnovac's substantial liabilities (reputed to be the heaviest in the Czech Republic) which were placed in a holding company (30 percent of the company) under government control and which could not be included in the privatization program. This ensured that the Czech government would be the only minority shareholder.

The joint venture, according to representatives from Bremen at Karnovac, provided the German manufacturer with an entry point to eastern markets, the successful heritage of the Karnovac trademark, and a well-educated, motivated, and inexpensive workforce. For the Czechs, investment by Bremen in Karnovac would be a landmark in privatization, and would provide not only the sorely needed economic and technological investments, but also the transfer of managerial "know-how."

Management Structure

The joint venture was controlled by a board of directors responsible for the development of strategy as well as daily operations. It consisted of two Czech executives (the chairman and the director of human resources) and three German executives. The chairman, whose appointment was agreed upon by both the Czech government and Bremen, had not worked previously at Karnovac but had experience in the industry as a supplier, and with a joint venture start-up. Production and development, sales and marketing, and finance were all directed by Germans on assignment from Bremen to Karnovac.

The board had two key challenges: to provide leadership and develop the confidence of the local staff in the production of automobiles; and to create a new culture. Each of the five executives was responsible for a functional division which was integrated by a "commission" to promote team work and cross-functional coordination. These commissions addressed issues such as new product planning (which included all members), quality, production planning, investment, and technical needs.

Current Status (February 1993)

Since the joint venture (JV) start-up, production volume, quality, and productivity dramatically increased. Before the JV, 800 cars were produced per day on two production lines. In early 1993, 700 cars were produced daily on one line and, based on estimates, a total of 215,000 cars would be built by the end of the year. When the newly planned plant facility became operational, the rate of current production was expected to almost double, to 450,000 cars by 1996. Productivity had also increased substantially – 40 percent by some estimates – and absenteeism had been reduced. New markets were being developed in the former USSR, China and South America. As of June 1992. Karnovac had began to return a small profit – much more quickly than had been anticipated. A questionnaire survey conducted at Karnovac indicated that employees felt great optimism about the future, and that Karnovac offered long-term benefits for the community.

Implementing Change – Together

The stated goal at Karnovac was to become more competitive by increasing productivity, implementing a lean production philosophy, modernizing factories and products, improving customer-oriented quality, and providing goal-oriented training. In addition to the transfer of technology, German expatriates on temporary assignment were expected to carry out the transfer of managerial "know-how." Bremen realized that local managers had to be actively involved in this process and that it needed to establish a partnership with Karnovac rather than to impose its own systems. According to one manager from Bremen, "the [local] people are hungry for change; they would like management to give them new methods and to have more participation."

A number of pitfalls, however, were quickly identified when trying to balance short-term success with long-term development, and matching employee expectations with what could realistically be achieved considering the large-scale transformation required at Karnovac. Further, finding the trade-off between adopting Bremen methods and practices and creating new policies to match the unique requirements of the JV required understanding of the local conditions and culture. Finding an appropriate equilibrium was expected to be a challenge. A German manager remarked:

> "It is difficult to synchronize the procedures. The experts come from a very big enterprise – Bremen – and they have certain procedures, rules, and regulations, which are proper for a big enterprise. Now they [Bremen staff] are in Karnovac – which was very small in the automobile business, a very small company – and they transfer their procedures, their regulations, their behaviors and attitudes to this company. In some cases, this causes conflict."

Ideally, these challenges would be met by German and Czech managers working together as partners. In many instances German and Czech managers were paired in order to transfer knowledge and expertise from the German parent while providing coaching and support to local managers. For example, in the human resources department, of the two most senior HR managers, one was German and the other was Czech. Czech managers are given responsibility for HR projects under the direction of three German project managers referred to as "teachers of the know-how transfer." As one senior manager suggested, it was important for German and Czech managers to agree on common goals and that the Czechs should have an active role in deciding which goals were to be accomplished, rather than feeling that the goals were being imposed.

The HR approach, outlined in a document called *Integration vs. Domination*, identified the following requisites:

- Delegation of responsibility and employee ownership of this responsibility
- Expatriates who are "know-how partners" and share expertise with local managers
- Continued staff development
- Bilingual communication
- Intensive management training for all executives
- Continued involvement of the union
- A report-oriented organization structure.

Taking Charge

Delegation and responsibility, however, proved to be easier said than done. Clearly, after more than 40 years of Communist influence and a centrally planned economy, creating change at Karnovac required more than new equipment, new work methods, and an influx of German executives. What was needed was a wholesale change in mindset and attitudes. As one Czech manager surmised:

> "The people must be motivated to believe they can be the best. In the Red regime the best was to be an average employee and this experience is deeply rooted in the minds of people.'

The German perspective was captured in the following comments:

> "In the Communist system . . . the management did not show their leadership qualities: it was the opposite. The power was with the workers, not with the supervisors. The workers nominated supervisors who were politically adequate . . . There were no clear rules and regulations clarifying who was the leader and who really represented the company. That is the weakness that we are faced with on a daily basis. It is essentially improving, but we need time, we need changes, we need a lot of things.
> "The issue is that the people have to adjust themselves to a free and democratic society – they are no longer under strict regulations that . . . they were forced to take as a system of life. And they lived with it and now they are free, and they are looking for new values to replace the old regulations, and this is not so easy.
> "The most difficult task is to train the people to see the extent of their own responsibility, because many of the people claim that there are things going wrong which are beyond their control. But now they [Czechs] need to learn they are all responsible for the work they are doing, and for the job they have, and for certain results. They have to work together. This is another issue – to work together in teams with

colleagues . . . This is very important: people must know their responsibilities and find ways to get common solutions in teams and with their partners."

It seemed, however, that some Czech workers were more comfortable with the previous system as it required less initiative and acceptance of responsibility. A German manager complained, "I have to control here much more than in Bremen as a boss." To counter these ideological remnants of the past, employees needed to be encouraged to take risks, to ask *why* rather than obey, and not to "stop after the first step." Change was considered to be less problematic for people younger than 35, or for workers over 60 who had had previous experience with a market economy.

According to certain managers, the JV would have to create a new climate capable of signaling confidence for the new form of enterprise. Crucial to the success of this process would be a clear definition of responsibilities and objectives, so that employees knew what was expected. Questionnaire results indicated that, overall, employees saw change as positive. Furthermore, employees indicated that they had a clear understanding of the goals for their jobs, what was expected of them, and what they had to do in order to receive rewards. At the same time, however, employees of all ages were very concerned about making mistakes.

Although some German staff wanted to provide Czechs with greater involvement and responsibility, often this was not possible because of insufficient training for Czech staff. One Czech manager agreed that although he currently had responsibility for a new area of operations, he did not know how to manage his new duties.

Other German expatriates, conscious that their performance in the JV would contribute to their future career progression at Bremen, felt there was little time available for mistakes while simultaneously easing local managers into new jobs and duties. For example, one senior German executive pointed out that during periods of major restructuring it was more important to quickly introduce changes and stabilize the JV before initiating a "mixed management system" with input from local managers, particularly in new areas, like human resources or marketing. In these cases, expatriates would continue to be central to the new operation. The rapid creation of new departments was, however, somewhat confusing from the Czech perspective. For example, wages previously controlled by the financial division were later monitored by the human resources department. When a function was already in operation, local managers' expertise was used with support from expatriates.

As the venture progressed, there was more and more evidence that Czech managers were given greater responsibility and decision-making power. For example, regular meetings which had originally been organized by German staff were later organized by a Czech, in the Czech language, and using Czech documentation. Another manager suggested that at the outset of the JV, Czech employees respected the German view more, but that over time this had changed. Gradually, Czech managers were trusted, as workers realized that the foreign partner did not have complete knowledge of Karnovac and the local conditions during the transition to a market economy. Over time, as the Czech management became more confident, the German management became more consultative. Both sides realized that it was important to find "compromises" in order to achieve common goals. Survey results, however, indicated that employees believed foreign managers had primary responsibility at Karnovac, and that local management responsibility remained limited.

Cultural Sensitivity

Despite efforts to the contrary, both Czechs and Germans expressed the view that too many German regulations, attitudes and behaviors had been transferred to Karnovac. Employees generally felt that cultural differences only received moderate respect and that, in some instances, German staff needed to demonstrate great sensitivity to the Czech situation. For example, it was suggested that the German expatriates might inquire more often about what had worked well in the past so that this information could be applied to future operations.

Many of these more subtle issues related to how employees were experiencing the change from a planned to a market system. For example, one Czech manager expressed the opinion that 40 years of isolation had resulted in diminished self-confidence for his people. Another Czech manager agreed, adding that rapid changes in the Czech Republic had created "great psychological pressure," and a desire to "show the Germans that we are as good" by working long hours, often 12 to 14 hours per day, in an effort to accomplish their goals.

The Czech people have a strong sense of pride, and wanted to prove their German colleagues that they could independently initiate changes at Karnovac. As one German executive put it:

"One of the Czech managers said to me before this joint venture started, 'I fired 30 percent of the people.' I said: 'Why? Was it necessary?' He replied: 'My people and my management, we are very proud and we said we don't need the Germans to tell us how you can improve the productivity, and how many people you have to fire. We did it ourselves and therefore we control the process.' That was very interesting."

Cultural similarities between Germans and Czechs were mentioned such as common historical development, the high level of industrialization of the Czech Republic after WWII, greater concern for the technical aspect rather than style (as in Spain), and the attitude towards social policy (in contrast to American firms). Problems were seen to be due more to differences in economic/political systems than national culture.

Differences noted in attitudes between Germans and Czechs were related to work versus family concerns. Asking Czech employees to work more than eight hour days a day and to work abroad, even on a temporary basis, created problems. According to the union leader, a 20 percent increase in the volume of work in the plant had sometimes resulted in employees working 12 hours per day. As 40 percent of the workforce was women, he considered this to be a "tragedy" for the family. Also, the Germans were seen to be more aggressive, organized, precise, and punctual. Czechs were characterized as "linear" rather than as "systems" thinkers when compared with the Germans.

Communication

Communication was considered crucial in facilitating the early phases of the partnership, and for sharing the vision of the future. A senior German executive commented:

"It is not only the vision of the board, and they are in agreement. We have had several meetings with all our managers, and we will have more meetings. We discuss all issues with these people . . . I believe if you don't tell people what you want to do and what you would like to achieve, it makes no sense."

Various forms of written and oral communication existed. Karnovac had a company newspaper and a computer network for linking departments and people. Meetings were held on a regular basis and included, for example: (1) board meetings; (2) departmental management meetings; (3) "skip level" sessions (during which board members provide information to employees (15–20) chosen from various levels in the company); and (4) cross-divisional meetings which were problem-focused. In the future, shop floor meetings were to be added.

However, despite a high priority on communication and many existing channels for communication, surveys indicated that communication could be substantially improved. For example, often employees felt that they did not have enough information to perform their jobs, and that managers neither passed on information, nor listened to their ideas. A German manager commented:

> "In the assembly shop the employees were asked to write proposals on cards on how to optimize the [assembly] process. Only ten cards were chosen out of 174 by management. That was very frustrating for the other people because they thought that they had very good proposals. And in my opinion I would say 100 were good. Not everything was actually worth implementing, but there were good proposals – and that is more important than saying, okay, tomorrow we can implement it."

Survey results indicated that employees desired more information about how to become competitive and on company policies. Language was often identified as the biggest problem, "not only in terms of that you have to spend more time because you need a translator, but it is also a problem to fully understand each other." Although interpreters were used, and many Czech managers spoke some German, many employees felt significant language barriers remained.

Human Resource Management Policy and Practice

The vision for human resources was to make Karnovac the best personnel department in the Bremen group within one to two years. In order to create a "progressive and active" department, a two-day workshop was held in October 1991 with all leaders in the personnel department along with the second and third levels (30 people in total) to develop HRM strategy and policy. Together they identified 25 projects and assigned responsibility to leaders and members for implementation. Some of the following issues were addressed by these teams.

Staffing

Karnovac has 17,000 employees: approximately 11,000 are production staff and 6,000 are white collar workers. There are roughly 1,000 mid-level managers and 240 upper level managers, of which 80 are German expatriates. Expatriates were on a three-year contract, which could be extended to five years if required.

It has always been Bremen's intention to avoid major layoffs and restructuring. Ironically, because the unemployment rate in the local region was very low (0.05 percent) Karnovac had found it difficult to recruit personnel with the necessary technical skills and personal attitudes. The attitudes sought in new recruits included willingness to work and improve oneself, ability to be part of a "cooperative team," and willingness to take risks. Furthermore, many qualified workers preferred employment in smaller, private companies.

One manager characterized 30 percent of Karnovac's employees as ambitious, 30 percent as average, 30 percent as lethargic, and 10 percent as counterproductive (representatives of the "old system," of whom perhaps 5 percent could change their attitudes and behaviors and be saved, and the remainder fired). Subsequently there was little fear of job loss for poor work standards as staff were only fired under "extreme circumstances."

Training

If the future vision for Karnovac was for it to become a "learning company," then HRM managers would have to pursue this through "the development of qualified and motivated employees through educational activities which match Karnovac's identified needs." Training goals were set to enhance: (1) efficiency, (2) creativity, (3) work quality, and (4) productivity. More specifically, these goals were to be realized through effective recruitment at the university level, and implementation of effective training programs (presented both internally and externally).

In 1992, Bremen invested DM 5 million in training for Karnovac employees, demonstrating a strong commitment to this vision. In 1991, 4,956 employees received some form of training. This figure increased to 6,156 employees in 1992, and was projected to reach 6,500 employees in 1993. To support the training initiatives, the training department had grown from eight trainers in 1991 to 60 trainers in 1993. A catalog of training programs was regularly updated and circulated.

Training was broadly divided into three areas: technical, professional, and management education. Technical training was provided both by Karnovac and vendors related to the use of specific equipment. Transfer of technology was also facilitated by visits of Czech staff to Bremen plants, and by German technical specialists working alongside Czech employees at the Karnovac plant. Professional training included principles of a market economy and quality management (e.g., TQM, *kaizen*, quality circles). Management training included: setting priorities; time management; delegation; leadership; team work;

and communication skills. Foreign language training was available to all who required language skills in their job, and had been received by approximately 1,700 staff.

Based on the employee survey, the majority of staff at Karnovac felt they had learned more new skills on the job than in the classroom. Employees felt they had sufficient training to do their jobs well, although more technical training was needed. Results of the survey also confirmed that the greatest perceived need for training by employees was in the are of management skills (48 percent of respondents) and foreign language skills (66 percent). In addition, 32 percent of employees perceived the need for training in problem solving. It was also suggested that German managers could benefit from training in Czech culture and history, although none had been provided to date.

Performance Review

The performance of German managers was reviewed at Bremen headquarters. Reviews were scheduled to occur once per year, although they were often less frequent. Other employees at Karnovac were not reviewed but a new system of performance review was planned for December 1993. Managers would need to be trained to use the system and would be evaluated according to ten principles:

1. Ability to agree on goals
2. Delegation
3. Development
4. Judgment/assessment
5. Information/communication
6. Cooperation
7. Conflict resolution
8. Innovation
9. Strategic and entrepreneurial behavior
10. Integration – working together in groups.

Performance in general would be assessed in terms of quality, knowledge transfer, initiative and problem solving, efficiency, and effective use of work time.

One Czech manager noted that it was important to create an appraisal system specific to the Czech situation, rather than one wholly adopted from Bremen. Despite the absence of a review process, employees indicated that they did receive feedback on their job performance from immediate supervisors.

Reward Systems

The reward structure for the German expatriates and the Czech managers was clearly differentiated. German expatriates remained within the Bremen salary structure, but were considered as Karnovac employees working on contract. They received various bonuses (e.g., for JV performance or working in a foreign country) and benefits (e.g., housing in Prague). Czech managers individually negotiated their contracts, salaries and increments with the board of directors. In addition, an annual bonus was available based on Karnovac profits.

Under the old system, base salaries were generally determined by level of education rather than by job performance or function, but overtime pay and bonuses were also available.

> "In former times a worker in the production area could earn more than a manager, because if he did more hours and he was productive, and was not the manager, he got more money. In Communist situations it works like that . . . We changed the system to a Western system."

Also, under the old system, the bonus system had been "misused," as it appeared to depend more on the employee's relationship with his or her supervisor than on performance levels. In addition, rewards were based on production volume often at the expense of quality.

According to the survey, however, employees were still not satisfied with the reward structure. Few thought that pay was satisfactory or that rewards were based on ability and performance. Many employees felt the neither was there a fair distribution of rewards, nor was there a fair chance for promotion. Czech workers were also aware of the disparity in wages that existed between themselves and their German colleagues. A German manager noted:

> "Czech people accept that we left our home towns and that we have to get some money for this . . . Of course they have a little problem that we earn so much in comparison to them . . . At the beginning I didn't feel that comfortable when we walked around in nice black suits."

Employees indicated that personal connections were still important, as under the old system. There were no recognition programs in place at Karnovac. One manager explained that it was important to provide monetary rather than non-monetary rewards because "people live from one month to another." Thus, long-term incentives were not likely to be effective.

A new salary system was introduced in July 1993 based on job descriptions using the Hay system. The job descriptions were to be more flexible in the Czech Republic than in Germany, as there was less separation between blue and white collar workers. Salaries would be determined by the following factors:

1. Twelve salary scale groups based on job classifications (before there had been 40 salary groups, or wage classes).
2. Performance increments for both blue and white collar workers based on annual assessments and worth up to an additional 20 percent of base wages (with an eventual target of 40 percent). The increments were determined by four criteria (each worth 5 percent): quality, transfer of know-how, initiative and problem solving, and efficiency.
3. A bonus system for blue and white collar workers based on two goals: quality and productivity.
4. A one-month bonus based on the achievement of annual goals set for Karnovac.

Employees were also eligible for a variety of social benefits, including use of subsidized vacation facilities, company apartments, subsidized lunches and medical insurance, and interest-free loans. Work clothes were provided for production employees. A Christmas dinner and other social events were organized for managers. In general, most employees felt the benefit systems at Karnovac had not altered greatly since the joint venture start-up and were adequate. However, there were shortages of available housing and child care facilities.

Past Success and Future Challenges

The potential success of the joint venture depends both on the Karnovac heritage and quality of its workforce, and the commitment of Bremen to the transfer of technical and managerial knowledge through training and development. Most important, perhaps, is the philosophy of a change process that encourages shared responsibility and "partnership." By creating new strategies, structures, and practices together, the joint venture benefits from the strengths of both Karnovac and Bremen in creating a business that can thrive in a global, market-driven economy while remaining sensitive to local constraints and opportunities. Sharing optimism about the future of Karnovac, a German executive commented:

> "With such a project, we demonstrate we are optimistic about the future. We trust in the people. We are convinced that we will be the best

in Europe . . . With this skill of the people, I believe I have no fear about accomplishing this objective . . . Technology is not so important in comparison to the people."

Creating a new corporate culture at Karnovac that integrates both global and local concerns is an ongoing process that requires constant communication and continuous learning. The challenge is to instill a shared set of beliefs, values, and assumptions throughout the workforce, which requires the creation of the appropriate HRM policies and practices to make that happen. As the Czech workforce becomes more competent and confident due to training, coaching, and team work, the German expatriates can hand over the reins, and move on to new horizons having learned to meet the challenges of managing in emerging economies.

For Bremen management it is important to bear in mind the results of the same questionnaire survey which was also conducted in a French–Polish and a Swedish–Hungarian joint venture. Compared with others, Karnovac employees felt positive about the future success of the company, and had the clearest understanding of competitiveness and of the link between performance and rewards. However, they were least satisfied with respect to having sufficient information and training to do their job. What could management do to respond to these concerns and fill the information gap? Compared to the other joint ventures, Karnovac employees also indicated that cultural differences were not respected. What could the JV management do to improve cultural sensitivity and mechanisms for continuous learning?

What further investment was necessary to ensure "Integration not Domination?" As one German manager stated, "Wie man in den wals hineinruft, so schallt es heraus," (the more you put in, the more you get out).

18
Technogrid Group and A/O Navicon

J. Stewart Black and Marat Shinkarev

It was March 21, 1992 and Nicolas G. Reisini, the director of New York-based Technogrid Group, was about to leave his office for Washington, DC. There he was supposed to meet a delegation of 15 top admirals from the Commonwealth of Independent States (the former Soviet Union). The delegation, led by Admiral Igor Machonin who was the CIS's second-ranked naval official, was believed to be the biggest group of Russian Naval leadership ever to visit the United States. The Russian admirals were to discuss a wide range of matters concerning cooperation between the US and CIS Armed Forces. They were to engage in negotiations with high ranked American officials including I. Lewis Libby, Deputy Undersecretary of Defense, Rep. Charles E. Bennett, head of the House Armed Services Committee's Seapower Subcommittee, and Richard Kaufman, General Counsel of Congress's Joint Economic Committee. However, meeting with Mr. Reisini, entrepreneur and international trade consultant, was probably the most important issue on the Soviet delegation's American agenda. The Admirals and Mr Reisini would discuss the prospects for the operation of the Navicon Holding Group joint venture, established in the CIS Navy at the end of 1991 by the Navicon joint stock company and Technogrid Group.

Going to the meeting, Mr Reisini again and again recalled the long and difficult process of negotiating with Navicon and his handling of

This case was prepared by Marat Shinkarev under the direction of Associate Professor J. Stewart Black. We gratefully acknowledge the help of Mr Nicolas G. Reisini, director of Technogrid in the development of this case. This case is not intended to illustrate good or poor administration but to serve as the basis for class discussion. Reprinted by permission of the authors.

the deal. Though a formal agreement had been already reached, some important problems still remained. Particularly disturbing was that the respective stakes of each part in the joint venture were still unclear. Mr Reisini was quite sure that his responses towards the Russians' somewhat strange negotiation tactics on this matter at the last meeting in Moscow had been correct. However, there was some scope for confusion, and in this venture, valued at $5 billion, he preferred to be 100 percent sure that everything was clear with no chance of misunderstandings.

Background

By the mid-1980s the Soviet submarine fleet, the biggest in the world, started to undergo an unusual problem. The problem was the necessity of dismantling obsolete nuclear submarines (see appendix 1). Vessels built in the 1950s and 1960s had become dangerous and unreliable. After several serious accidents in the North and Baltic Seas, the Soviet government started a program of destroying old submarines. However, the funds were insufficient, the technology was inadequate, and the pace of dismantling the subs was very slow. Meanwhile, most of the submarines were anchored at sea – a situation that could lead to corrosion and pipe breaks in the systems that cool the ships' nuclear reactors.

On the other hand, dismantling the hundreds of military vessels and then selling the thousands of tons of scrap metal could boost the otherwise seriously reduced Navy budget. Because the cold War was over and Soviet priorities had shifted toward conversion of the military complex to an industrial complex, the idea of getting much needed hard currency by selling the scrap had become very attractive to the Navy brass. Unfortunately, there was a lack of scrap yards and proper technology in the Soviet Union and, therefore, the Soviet Navy officials needed to involve Western companies. This is why, in 1985, they approached Mr Nicolas Reisini, who at that time was Director of Lygzen Maritime Services (LMS). LMS was a ship brokerage firm with $400 million in annual revenues. Mr Reisini was especially appealing to the Navy officials because he was not only a shipping expert, but also one of the few Western businessmen who specialized in doing business with the USSR. Mr Reisini had himself established strong connections among Soviet officials and usually visited Moscow several times per year. Mr Reisini's father had impressed upon him many times that connections were the most valuable assets when dealing with the Soviets.

Mr Reisini also had experience in dealing with scrapping large ships. In 1987, he helped to establish a joint venture between the Soviet Industry of Fisheries and Texas-based American General Resources Co., a large US scrapping company. Also he planned, conceived, and implemented the first multimillion offshore joint venture with the Soviet Ministry of Merchant Marine and major Italian ship owners. Finally, he had acted as exclusive representative for the Soviet Ministry of Merchant Marine in purchasing $400 million worth of ships on a worldwide basis.

When the Navy officials approached Mr Reisini, he was eager to start working on the deal. However, it soon became clear that this deal was going far beyond the framework of ordinary trade. The dismantling of Soviet naval ships, especially nuclear submarines, for scrap on the world market was a new frontier even for Mr Reisini.

A/O Navicon

A/O Navicon, a Russian stock holding company, was created in 1990 and is a hybrid of a traditional Soviet bureaucracy and a "private" enterprise, whose key players are all high-ranking Navy officials. The goal of Navicon is to manage the various assets of the former Soviet Navy. According to the PR Newswire,[1] the stock holding company is a commercial arm of the Navy and it has the sole right to commercially develop and deploy the Navy's assets. Eight Navicon branches, including a commercial bank, are situated outside Russia, specifically in Ukraine, Azerbaijan, Georgia, the Baltic States, Germany, and the United States. Navicon also has 146 brokers working for it at 26 major stock exchanges. In addition, it runs a pension fund for servicemen, is a founding member of St. Petersburg Trading House, and provides funding for the retraining of retired officers. It's assets include oil terminals at major Russian Navy seaports, auxiliary fleets of the former Soviet Navy, and certain military vessels.

The leadership of A/O Navicon is a group of admirals. These men are decisive, energetic, competent, self-confident, and highly determined to succeed in the new environment. "The Navy can no longer depend on the state for support," said Admiral Igor Machonin, the chief of Navicon. "With that in mind, the Navy is looking to become the leading force in moving toward a free-market economy."

[1] PR Newswire, *Financial News Sector*, Feb. 6, 1992.

Technogrid Group

The Technogrid Group is a venture capital and business development firm based in New York City, with international interests specializing in the former Soviet Union. The group was established in 1991, and it is a consortium of financial services and management companies, including New York City-based Parkview Associates, Inc., Moscow-based AO Ivicon, and London and Geneva-based Technogrid Ltd. The principals of the Technogrid Group have extensive US and USSR experience in the real estate industry, the maritime industry, and in the financial services industry. As Mr Reisini stated to a reporter for *LI Business News*,[2] "Technogrid staff members have worked on a commercial basis in Russia and other territories of the former Soviet Union since 1976."

Current Project

Being approached by the Navicon management, Mr Reisini established a Technogrid team to accomplish a project unique in its scale and complexity. The joint venture of Technogrid and Navicon would be responsible for a commercialization of a broad range of assets formerly owned by the Soviet Navy. The venture includes the following:

- The construction of two ship demolition yards on Russian territory to scrap more than 500 conventional Soviet Military vessels as well as coordinating efforts between the US and CIS governments to dismantle 140 nuclear submarines.
- The building of 30,000 prefabricated apartment units in Russia as well as the transfer of technology to Russia to create a joint venture building industry.
- The privatization of the terminals at major Russian Navy seaports and their conversion to commercial shipping facilities and oil terminals.
- The conversion of a portion of the auxiliary fleet of the Soviet Navy into a commercial fleet.

Aside from the enormous size of the deal there are many technological and political complications. For example, the technological com-

---

[2] *LI Business News*, Feb. 10, 1992.

plexity of dismantling nuclear submarines is a large challenge not only in Russia, but throughout the world. Because Russia was a pioneer in building nuclear submarines, it faced the problem of deactivating its older vessels earlier than the West. To facilitate the proposed dismantling of Soviet subs, both Russian and Western specialists would participate in the project. Particularly, Navicon would work in a partnership with Westinghouse, which was well-known for its advanced technologies and experience with nuclear ships.

Political complications demanded that the process of dismantling the subs be accomplished in a very short period of time. Under an East-West accord, Russia should have destroyed 32 submarines in 1991 and 32 more in 1992. However, technological and other complications have delayed these demolitions. To make matters worse, there were a further 140 submarines that were to be destroyed. With existing Soviet capabilities and technology, the task was almost impossible to achieve. Technical and economic support for the project from the American government would be crucial, and Technogrid's management was working on gaining the support of key US government officials.

Compared with the dismantling of nuclear subs, the housing project might seem like an easier component of the overall deal but its huge scale and the constant disarray in the CIS made it complicated as well. However, Mr Reisini was attracted by the potential profits, size of the market, and the enormous potential of future deals. "Our immediate goal is the completion of the initial phase of the housing project," said one of the Technogrid Directors, Charles Hack, who is also an owner of a New York-based real estate firm, Parkview Associates. "We are well on our way to a achieving that goal," continued Mr Hack. Hard currency from the reuse and sales of the various military assets was expected to provide initial funding for a future multibillion dollar housing project.

Housing units are to be made in the United States, containerized for transportation, and assembled into three- and four-story condominium-like buildings at the Russian Naval port facilities in St. Petersburg, Konigsberg, Murmansk, Sevastopol, and Vladivostok. Each location is expected to get 5,000 to 6,000 housing units. (Note: the distance between Konigsberg or St. Petersburg and Vladivostok is about 11,000 kilometers or 6,830 miles; the climate in Murmansk is polar, with conditions including permafrost, while the climate in Sevastopol is subtropical and similar to that of the Mediterranean.) The initial group of apartments will be assembled in Russia by both American and Russian workers. The American workers will act as instructors and gradually turn over all responsibility to the Russian staff, ultimately creating a domestic housing industry within Russia. Although the space and military industries are advanced, the domestic housing industry is in embryonic condition in Russia.

Generally, the participants of the deal were pleased with the speed of the process and the atmosphere of mutual goodwill and trust at the negotiations. In contrast to the traditionally lengthy and tiresome negotiations of the past (for example, Russian negotiations with Pepsi took more than 17 years), the general agreement between Navicon and Technogrid had been achieved in eight months. (See copy of Memorandum of Agreement, appendix 2.)

The Negotiations

The astonishing events in the Soviet Union in 1991–92 had a great impact on the Navicon–Technologrid negotiations. First of all, prior to 1990 such a joint venture would not have been conceivable at all. For example, prior to 1991 foreigners were prohibited from even visiting most of the proposed housing sites. Also, before 1990, the Soviet authorities would never have permitted even its own military officers without a high level of clearance (let alone foreigners) to come close to their submarines, to say nothing of dismantling them.

Even in 1991, the approval for preliminary negotiations had to come from the Minister of Defense. At first, the Americans and their Soviet counterparts faced the traditional ironclad "nyet" from the Minister of Defense, Marshal Yazov. Fortunately, the failure of the coup in August 1991 eliminated this obstacle. Of course, it was necessary to get approval from Marshal Shaposhnikov, the new Minister of Defense of the CIS, and also from the Minister of Defense of Russia, General Grachov. The new leaders were much more pragmatic and realistic: however, getting over the traditional bureaucratic hurdles was still not easy. It required the presence in Moscow of the leaders of Technogrid, and nearly daily visits to the headquarters of the Ministry of Defense and Navy headquarters in Moscow. Many officials did not see any urgency and of course they did not respond to most of the letters from Technogrid. Fortunately, the old powers were losing their authority and were increasingly just interested in their own survival. At the same time the new forces were not quite prepared to conduct day-to-day business. All of this led to a great level of uncertainty. As stated by Mr Reisini: "In the old days you would expect bureaucracy in Russia, but at least you had a clear understanding of whom you should approach and for what. Currently you sometimes just do not know."

Fortunately, Technogrid's allies from the Navy were maneuvering to gain support from the very top of the new government and Navy officials. They were able to use the so-called "hammer" technique. When facing any serious problem, one of Navicon's Admirals, Machonin, Anikanov, or Zaitsev, picked up the phone and "hammered" middle level bureaucrats (most of whom had served in the military at some point and understood that when a high-ranking official said "jump," you asked "how high?" on the way up) into doing what was needed to facilitate the joint venture.

Finally, the way was clear for beginning the technical phase of the negotiations. Meetings were set for October 1991 in Murmansk, then in Sevastopol, and finally in Moscow. They discussed in great detail the types of equipment that would be used for dismantling the submarines and for renovating the bases. All aspects of technology transfer, from construction of housing units to demolition of nuclear vessels, were covered. Separate meetings, often located very far from each other, were held to discuss feasibility studies of scrap yards being built and of the commercial use of the auxiliary fleet of the Soviet Navy. Russia employed dozens of experts in each aspect of the negotiations and created a separate detailed protocol on each issue. Though exhausting, the negotiations were very productive, in part because of the competence of the experts involved on the Soviet side compared with the faceless bureaucrats from the Foreign Trade Organization, the only Soviet representatives of the past. The logistic and technical part of the negotiations were similar to a successful military operation. (See appendix 3 for some notes on Russian negotiation style.)

Later, however, the hard part began. In December 1991, the parties met to discuss the finances of the deal. At least officials from the Foreign Trade Organization were well trained and skilled in negotiating with foreign corporations and understood Westerners' approach to finances. Technogrid's current counterparts had never made such a deal. Worse, the very notions of "market" or "profit" are hardly possible to translate into Russian. In fact, the Soviet word *pribyl* (meaning "for profits") implies exploitation or that profits are always at someone else's expense. While the English term profit can imply exploitation, it generally implies creativity. Indeed, this difference between the two languages in the meaning of the term profit is a reflection of the more fundamental differences in the two social and commercial systems. When the Technogrid officials used the term "profits," their Navicon counterparts imagined "exploitation," not "creativity." The lack of proper financial and especially accounting systems in Russia also contributed to misunderstandings.

In Russia, a cooperative approach is almost non-existent and negotiations mean bargaining. When Technogrid officials tried to find a middle ground to help resolve differences, they often used the term "compromise." The very word "compromise" is a symbol of weakness to Russians. Given the military background of Navicon's leaders, it was clear that they did not want to appear weak by making compromises.

However, by December 17, 1991, most of the problems looked solved or possible to solve, and all participants gathered in a spacious conference room at Navy Headquarters in Moscow. Dozens of Russian Admirals in uniforms, the Navicon leadership, congratulated Mr Reisini and two of his partners on the agreement. Admiral Machonin made a speech and then the Americans were invited to the next conference room. There they were surprised because the room was full of people, mostly civilians. Admiral Machonin introduced them as Navicon's experts in international law and business. "We need to clarify some nuances," said the Admiral. "We reevaluated the worth of our stake in the deal," he continued, "and think that our Murmansk bunkering base is worth $700 million." The Americans were stunned.

Technogrid was going to invest $100 million in order to proceed on the first phase of the project. If the bunkering bases' worth were reevaluated to $700 million, this would substantially reduce the relative equity of the American interest, and hence their role in the venture's governing board would be minuscule. They had not expected anything like this.

All five of the Navy bunkering facilities potentially had great value. After reconstruction, they would serve as exclusive export points from Russia and would be worth billions of dollars. In particular, the Murmansk base would be valuable. However, currently, the Murmansk base was an empty square mile of land with rusty 40–50 year old worthless equipment scattered across it. Only after the renovation and substantial investment made by Technogrid would the base be suitable for use or have a value approaching the $700 million proposed by the Soviets.

"Is it an expert opinion?" Mr Reisini asked calmly, while his partners turned red with anger and the Russians looked defensive. "Yes, I am an expert," answered the Rear Admiral. "Well, if it is your expert opinion, we could not object to it. Let's sign a contract as such and notarize it," said Reisini. "However, I expect you to make a final visit to the US in March," he continued. In the deep silence the parties signed the document.

On the frosty Moscow street the angry partners started to attack Mr Reisini. "What did you do?" they shouted. "You ruined everything." "The Russians will change their position," replied Reisini.

"It's a deal breaker. They just were not ready for such a fast pace and wanted to slow down the process. They expect us to break the negotiations and later will pretend to 'forgive us.' Then they will be ready to compromise. Believe my experience: I know them well."

At the time, Mr Reisini was absolutely sure that he was right. Now, in March, on his way to meeting the Navicon officials in Washington, he was not so confident as before. He wondered how he should approach the upcoming meeting and negotiations.

APPENDIX 1

Brief Note on the Soviet Submarine Forces

Russia and later the Soviet Union have a long and successful history of submarine building and exploration. Military historians credit Russia for the following achievements in submarine development: the world's first underwater vessel designed for military purposes in 1724–6; the first mechanized submarine using compressed air in 1866; the first submarine mine layer in 1915; and the first of the true Russian submarines, the Delfius, was built as early as 1902. The Soviet military leadership maintained this tradition, and since the late 1930s the Soviet Navy generally has had more undersea craft than any other navy. Further significant achievements by the Soviets include the following: a Zulu-class boar was the platform for the first launch of a ballistic missile from a submarine in September 1955; the Kashin class of 1963 were the world's first all gas turbine destroyers; the underwater launch of a cruise missile from a Charlie-class submarine in 1967 was another first; and 1971 saw the launch of the world's fastest and deepest diving submarine, the Atlas-class, made of a titanium alloy. In the spring of 1980 the first Oscar-class (SSBN) nuclear-powered ballistic missile submarine was launched, followed a few months later by the world's biggest Typhoon-class SSBN. The new Mike- and Sierra-class nuclear-powered submarine (SSNs) emerged in 1983, followed in 1984 by the first Akula class. In the mid- and even the late 1980s, the Soviet submarine building and submarine missiles development continued to advance. According to *Jane's Naval Review*,[3] edited by prominent Navy expert Captain John Moore: "the flood of new designs began to condition Western analysts to expect something new almost every year."

However, global changes and the end of the Cold War had a criti-

---

[3] John Moore (ed.) *Jane's Naval Review* (London: Macdonald and Jane's Ltd, 1988), p. 91.

cal impact on the Soviet Navy. Military spendings were cut, warships and, particularly, military submarine-building was halted. Major ship-yards stopped military production and were scheduled for conversion. The world's most advanced, once secret, *Beloye More Podvodnoye Predpriyatie* (White Sea Submarine Enterprise) for example, still con-tinues to turn out submarines, but now its subsea vessels are built for exploration, inspection and even tourist use.

The collapse of the USSR in 1991 led to the collapse of its military forces, including the Navy. Among the most acute problems were the necessity of finding jobs and housing for hundreds of thousands of jobless and homeless Navy officers and their families, and the urgent need to dismantle the hundreds of obsolete nuclear submarines. The first problem could lead to social unrest and even civil war. The sec-ond one could lead to a global ecological disaster and nuclear con-tamination of the ocean. The leadership of the Navy decided to "kill

Exhibit 18.1   Soviet submarines

Description	No.	Class	Displace-ment (tons)	Length (feet)	Propulsion	Armament
Attack submarine	>100	Whiskey	1,035	246	Diesel	Torpedo
Attack submarine	20	Romeo	1,500	262	Diesel	Torpedo
Attack submarine	60	Foxtrot	2,000	295	Diesel	Torpedo
Attack submarine	NA	Tango	3,000	295	Diesel	Torpedo
Attack submarine	NA	Alfa	3,900	265	Nuclear	Torpedo
Attack submarine	NA	Victor	4,000	311	Nuclear	Torpedo
Attack submarine	NA	Echo	4,500	360	Nuclear	Torpedo
Attack submarine	14	November	4,500	360	Nuclear	Torpedo
Ballistic Missile submarine	20	Golf	2,300	328	Diesel	3 SS-N4 SLBM[a]
Ballistic Missile submarine	8	Hotel	5,000	377	Nuclear	3SS-N5 SLBM
Ballistic missile submarine	NA	Delta	8,000	460	Nuclear	12SS-N8 SLBM
Ballistic missile submarine	NA	Delta II/III	9,000	508	Nuclear	16 SS-N8 SLBM
Cruise missile submarine	16	Juliett	3,000	295	Diesel	ASS-N3 anti-ship
Cruise missile submarine	NA	Charlie	4,000	311	Nuclear	8 SS-N-7 missiles
Cruise missile submarine	29	Echo II	5,000	377	Nuclear	8 SS-N3 missiles

[a] SLBM = submarine launched ballistic missile
NA = not available

two birds with one stone" and to finance problem number one by solving problem number two: in other words, to sell submarines for scrap abroad and to use the profits for housing for the officers (see exhibit 18.1 for a description of the Soviet Submarines). The following classes of submarine are the likeliest candidates for the dismantling: Echo class, Foxtrot class, Golf class, November class, and Hotel class. Also there are about one hundred diesel-electric submarines available.

The value of the submarines scheduled for the scrap yard lay not only in the tons of steel they contained but also the significant amounts of extremely rare and costly metals such as titanium. Consequently, these submarines represented a relatively cheap source of these rare metals.

APPENDIX 2

MEMORANDUM OF AGREEMENT

Moscow   18 December 1991

The "Parties" are as follows:

- A/O NAVICON (NAVICON NORD, NAVICON SUD, NAVICON OST, SANKT NAVICON)
- THE TECHNOGRID GROUP (FINANCIAL & TECHNICAL GROUP INTERNATIONAL LTD, TECHNOGRID   LTD, A/O IVICOM).

Based on results of negotiations between representatives of the Parties held in Moscow, Murmansk, and Sevastopol in October and December, 1991, and the subsequent intensive work by Parties on the area of Navicon's interests, and in furtherance of the Protocol of Negotiations dated October 11, 1991 (the "Protocol") among representatives of the Parties, the Parties have reached the following agreements:

1. THE TECHNOGRID GROUP will work on behalf of the interests of NAVICON toward the purposes and objectives as outlined in the Protocol and as set forth in the Memorandum of Agreement. All agreed commercial operations involving NAVICON assets are to be conducted exclusively through this Stock Holding Company (SHC). All commercial operations carried out by Navicon in the same type of direction set forth in Section Number (4) Four of this Agreement will

be subject to the approval of the SHC. The Agreement precedes the formal registration of the SHC. The Parties will proceed on all commercial enterprises as if the SHC agreement has been finalized and registered accordingly. This agency arrangement and agreement will be in effect through and until a legal SHC between the Parties is duly recorded/registered on the territory of the RSFSR.

2.   At the time of the registration of the above mentioned SHC, the rights and results of this Agreement will be transferred by THE TECHNOGRID GROUP and NAVICON to the SHC. These transfers will be obligations of the Parties respectively.

3.   THE TECHNOGRID GROUP will be responsible for managing and arranging for the financing of the initial amount of capital, being US $100,000,000 in order to proceed on the first phase of the project. As set forth in the Protocol, it is intended that the projects undertaken by the Parties will be self-financing and self-repaying. Therefore, in accordance with the Protocol, NAVICON will make available to THE TECHNOGRID GROUP various assets, and the THE TECHNOGRID GROUP will, as agent for NAVICON, manage, dispose of, lease, operate, refurbish and otherwise deal with such assets and the proceeds thereof with the goal of maximizing the value and cash proceeds from the scrapping, salvaging, upgrading, and/or operation of such assets, for purposes of facilitating THE TECHNOGRID GROUP's responsibility for arranging financing for the activities of the Parties set forth in this Memorandum of Agreement and the Protocol.

4.   The project includes the following:
   a. Construction of buildings on the first stage from materials and components delivered by the American side, delivery of equipment for production, the full range of items necessary for construction of houses from domestic materials, transfer of technology for creation of production lines for these houses and training of local labor;
   b. Transfer of modern technologies of high rise building construction and creation of enterprises for production of construction materials necessary to effectuate these technologies;
   c. Complete renovation technology and equipment transfer for mutual exploitation of bunkering bases;
   d. Investigation of the feasibility of creating scrapyards on the territory of the RSFRSR and other countries, as well as transfer of technologies and equipment for the scrap industry;

e. Creation of joint ship management and brokerage companies;
f. Creation of joint companies trading commodities and commodities made of domestic raw materials;
g. Transfer technology and equipment for other programs to be decided by the Parties;
h. Consider all the various methods relating to the transfer of technology, equipment and training for the demolition of nuclear vessels and the utilization and/or disposal of the nuclear blocs.

5. All particular activities of THE TECHNOGRID GROUP and NAVICON on each program will be elaborated further in subsequent memoranda.

6. NAVICON, upon execution of this Memorandum of Agreement, will: (a) nominate the intended assets for THE TECHNOGRID GROUP to work on an agency basis until the registration of the SHC (the "Initial Assets"); and (b) develop a time schedule of each specific Initial Asset and the date when each Initial Asset will be handed over to the THE TECHNOGRID GROUP.

7. THE TECHNOGRID GROUP is developing a time schedule and financial and business plans as well as schedules for the delivery of good for each individual program and will present them for approval of NAVICON. NAVICON is identifying assets for joint activity and sites for housing and other construction and refurbishment, and is otherwise assisting in the creation and operation of the SHC and the activities of the Parties hereunder.

8. The Parties shall work together in good faith, expeditiously, to finalize the details of the projects to be undertaken, to complete more formal documentation of the joint venture and other programs described in this Memorandum of Agreement and the Protocol, and in otherwise fulfilling the objectives of the Parties as set forth herein and in the Protocol.
   NAVICON shall exclude any conflicting operation with third (3rd) parties outside this SHC which will negatively affect profitable operation of the SHC.

9. Working as agent of NAVICON, THE TECHNOGRID GROUP will open offices or use existing offices in the required business areas which will be used by the specialists of NAVICON. Upon registration of the SHC these offices will be utilized by SHC.

10. This agreement has been issued in both Russian and in English and both having the same juridical validity.

A/O NAVICON:

By: _____ I. Machonin

THE TECHNOGRID GROUP:

By: _____ C. Hack

APPENDIX 3

Russian Negotiating Style

Negotiation Primer

Negotiation approaches can be broken down into two basic categories: distributive and collaborative. Distributive describes the idea most people carry in their minds when they think of negotiating – there is a fixed amount of a good which should be "distributed" among the negotiators. A good example of this is slicing a pie into pieces between two or more separate parties. Unless the pie is cut exactly equally, the more one party gets, the less the others get. In a distributive agreement, how the pie is actually cut depends mainly upon the real and perceived power each party has and the effectiveness of the negotiating tactics each employ. This is the classic "zero-sum" game in which one side's gain can only come at the other side's loss.

The collaborative approach to bargaining, on the other hand, looks beyond the basic negotiating transaction. It focuses on what is driving the negotiators to come together in the first place, and tries to develop a range of options to mutually satisfy the needs of both parties.

Russia Primer

The Russian people have never lived under a democratic, individual-oriented political system. Until the Bolshevik Revolution in 1917, Russia was an absolute monarchy, ruled by tsars. There were three classes of people: the aristocracy, with its court nobles and military commanders; a tiny middle class of shopkeepers and artisans; and a vast population of agricultural serfs. The 1917 Revolution brought a small amount of freedom to the serfs, but Stalin quickly turned Russia into a ruthless, autocratic state where decisions were taken out of the hands of individuals and put into the hands of the *nomenklatura*, the elite circle of Communist party officials. The state determined an individual's future. There was no resistance. Thus, the decision-making system of the tsars was replaced by the Soviet system.

Russian Negotiation

Negotiations with Russians is a long and arduous process. Russians are master chessmen and strategists; they begin negotiations from power positions and give up space only when they are ready. Many American firms become frustrated by the complexity of, and the rituals involved in, Russian negotiations. Less than half of started negotiations end up in completed contracts or agreements.

Russians employ a classic distributive approach. Some of the typical comments used to describe negotiating with the former Soviets are: lengthy, difficult, manipulative, uncompromising, risk-averse, and secretive. Russians have always had a high power distance. It is more difficult for them to accept authority to make decisions in negotiations than their Western counterparts.

Negotiation Structure

The structure of the negotiations is fairly complex: the old Soviet system placed layers of bureaucracy between the producer and the end user. The following are characteristic patterns in Russian negotiations:

Protocol/Setting Perhaps due to a long history of isolation, Russians view relations with foreigners as important and deserving of special treatment. They prefer to deal directly with the principals involved rather than through intermediaries, and the level of the principal within the foreign company is an important indicator to the Russians about the sincerity of the negotiations. Foreign companies that send over senior level executives and/or open a representative office in Russia invariably wind up making a better impression. The settings for negotiations are usually chosen by the Russians, who try to keep a home court advantage.

Process Russian negotiations are two-phased. The first phase involves contacting many vendors and estimating the technical competency of their products. This often requires repeated explanations of the product merits to different parties. During this stage most companies feel compelled to disclose more information about the product than is usual. Once the top candidates are chosen, the second phase – the bidding process – begins. Bidding is typically the most frustrating phase for Western business men because even minute details are debated.

Preparation Russian negotiators come to the table very well briefed about the strengths and weaknesses of their counterparts. Whatever information they lack is requested formally. Ironically, requests by the counterparty to get similar information from the

Russians is typically met with opposition and delays. Russians will usually lay out an overall structure for the negotiations. Detailed agendas are laid out for each meeting, and changes to the proposed agendas tend to disrupt the flow of the negotiations.

Length   Though the Russian negotiation process has historically been a lengthy one, as the Soviet bureaucracy is replaced by enterprise managers eager to do deals, the time-span will shorten. From the Russian perspective, doing business with a foreign company is a serious matter and needs to be considered carefully. Relationships need to be cultivated to determine the best fit for the long term.

Contracts and Penalty Clauses   Contracts are carefully worded, usually to benefit the Russian party. Product specifications and working conditions must be precisely laid out. Contracts must spell out every possible detail and foresee every possible eventuality. Penalty clauses are usually installed as insurance against failure or delays.

Countertrade   Russians often bring up countertrade. Their reasoning is simple – they don't have much hard currency available for foreign trade. Countertrade is a useful alternative for getting their products into export markets. It can also be used as part of the negotiations on price. Suppliers who refuse the request for countertrade will be asked to lower their price in return for wanting an all-cash settlement.

Negotiation Style

Russians are true bargainers. There is little attempt to create a joint solution which increases the negotiation value for both parties. They will start off with maximum positions and attempt to place the burden for compromise on the other side. Russians will accept only the parts of proposals which benefit them and will try to ignore the rest. Concessions are yielded only when necessary: they are usually treated as points on a scoreboard, and Russians focus on keeping the total numbers in balance rather than the relative importance of each concession.

The Russians view negotiation as a competition, and so most tactics are justified in their zeal to "win." Russians have learned to use their counterparts' time constraints and contract loopholes to their own advantage. They also will use information collected during negotiations with rival companies to better their own positions. Lastly, most observers have mentioned peculiar twists, such as last-minute venue, agenda, or negotiator changes, outrageous demands that are later denied, and abrupt cancellations of meetings.

Conclusions

Russians are extremely reliable in honoring their commitments and making payments on time. Their negotiation tactics are used to weed out all but truly committed parties. In this way personal relationships based on mutual respect and trust can be developed and nurtured. Russian business relations thrive on deep personal relations. As the legal structure continues to undergo reform, the emphasis on the interpersonal aspect of business may decrease, but only over the long term.

Printed and bound by CPI Group (UK) Ltd, Croydon, CR0 4YY

23/04/2025

14660955-0005